FIFTY YEARS
ON THE
OLD FRONTIER

as Cowboy, Hunter, Guide,
Scout, and Ranchman

BY JAMES H. COOK

With a Foreword by J. Frank Dobie
and Introduction by Charles King

Foreword to the Paperback Edition
by Joseph C. Porter

UNIVERSITY OF OKLAHOMA PRESS
NORMAN

To
The Loved Ones in My Family Circle
and
The Dear Friends
Whose Aid and Encouragement Have Made it Possible
For Me to Write a Book
This Volume Is Most Affectionately Dedicated

International Standard Book Number: 0-8061-1761-3
Library of Congress Catalog Card Number: 57-5951

5 6 7 8 9 10 11 12 13 14

Contents

Illustrations

Foreword to the Paperback Edition

BY JOSEPH C. PORTER

FIFTY YEARS ON THE OLD FRONTIER is a classic of Western American history. Since its publication in 1923 generations of readers have appreciated the book's vivid, perceptive, firsthand account of Cook's life in the post–Civil War American West. Reading *Fifty Years on the Old Frontier* is like sitting and having a long, relaxed, face-to-face conversation with the witty, erudite, observant James H. Cook (1857–1942).

Publication of *Fifty Years on the Old Frontier* placed Cook in a select group of participant-chroniclers of the Old West whose pens left unvarnished depictions of the trans-Mississippi frontier when Euro-Americans pushed into Indian country of the Great Plains and the Southwest. Like John Gregory Bourke, Charles King, and Britton Davis, among other writers of that era, James H. Cook realized that his life had encompassed a significant historical era, and he put his memories to paper. Like them he did not shrink from detailing the hardship, violence, and sanity-testing tedium of frontier life. Writing with clarity and humor, Cook essayed the hard and tragic aspects of that era while neither romanticizing nor vilifying it.

Cook witnessed the conflict between Indians and those taking Indian lands and trying to force an end to traditional Indian cultures. As a cowboy, hunter, and rancher, Cook was directly involved in the economic endeavors that so changed the face of the Great Plains grasslands once the great buffalo herds, so critical to Plains Indian life, were destroyed and replaced by beef cattle. As a professional hunter of wild game, Cook saw the flora and fauna of the Wyoming and Nebraska plains prior to extensive Euro-American settlement, and he watched as cattle ranches and farms changed that natural environment. As a hunter Cook became a guide to sportsmen and tourists eager to hunt western game, and his memories of those expeditions are a remarkable piece in the history of tourism in the West.

The cattle of the ranchers replaced the buffalo of the Indians, and Cook's life was a microcosm of the range-cattle industry. When he was barely in his teens, Cook became a "brushpopper" for Texas cattleman Ben Slaughter in the Frio-Neces rivers country. Brushpopping was the dangerous job of riding into the chaparral and rounding up wild, longhorn cattle—creatures so fierce that they attacked humans. Cook was also a "drover," making five different trail drives with cattle herds north. *Fifty Years on the Old Frontier* distills the essence of the dangers, demands, hardscrabble skills, and grueling hard work that was the life of these cowboys. From 1882 to 1887, Cook managed a ranch in southwestern New Mexico for its English owners, and in 1887, Cook became a rancher when he purchased a spread in Sioux County, Nebraska. Cook's Agate Springs Ranch on the Niobrara River has become a landmark on the Northern Great Plains, and the significance of the ranch and Cook's life is commemorated by the fact that the Cook ranch site is now the Agate Fossil Beds National Monument of the National Park Service.

Agate Springs Ranch underscored two important aspects of Cook's life, his friendship with the great Oglala Lakota chief, Red Cloud (c. 1822–1909), and his contributions to North American paleontology. Red Cloud had met Cook several years before he acquired Agate Springs Ranch. Once Cook had permanently settled on his ranch, which was in the old tribal domain of the Lakota, Red Cloud and he became close friends. Red Cloud and his family frequently visited Cook's ranch, setting up Lakota-style camps for long periods of time. Some Northern Cheyennes, old allies of the Lakota, also befriended Cook. An open-minded man, Cook learned much of

Cheyenne and Lakota history and culture, and he asked non-Indians to put aside their prejudices and to try to understand the Cheyenne and Lakota views of their own histories.

The relationship between Cook and Red Cloud deserves more than passing notice. A brilliant and controversial leader of his people, Red Cloud was a forceful, skilled politician among his own people, and on behalf of his people, he was a shrewd, hard-nosed negotiator with the U.S. government. Never given to self-doubt, Red Cloud took contentious stands that he regarded as being in his people's best interests, but which frequently earned him criticism from government officials, army officers, and other Lakota chiefs. Cook knew about the criticism and controversy that swirled around Red Cloud, and the two friends spoke often of these matters.

Cook devoted many pages in *Fifty Years on the Old Frontier* to Red Cloud, an indication of how much he valued his friendship with the old chief. He was determined to present Red Cloud's views on the devastating history of the Lakota in the half century between the 1840s when the migrants along the Great Platte River Road profoundly disrupted traditional patterns of Lakota life to the disastrous Wounded Knee Massacre of 1890. Red Cloud was a central Oglala leader during this turbulent half century, and his perspective, given in *Fifty Years on the Old Frontier*, is crucial to any understanding of Lakota history. Even as the chief became quite elderly, it is clear from this book that he retained the tough, resilient determination of his younger years. Cook's book is the closest thing that twentieth-century readers can get to a first-person account from Red Cloud, one of the most important Indian leaders in Western American history.

Cook was self-taught, making himself into a widely read, well-educated man. His love of books and learning permitted him to appreciate his contribution to North American paleontology. His Agate Springs Ranch, among other areas of the

Northern Great Plains, became a rich source of fossil quarries, and he became acquainted with some of the most prominent paleontologists of his day as they came to the fossil quarries on his ranch. Indeed, to this day in Nebraska, Cook and his ranch are nearly synonymous with prehistoric fossils.

In his foreword to the 1957 University of Oklahoma Press edition of *Fifty Years on the Old Frontier*, J. Frank Dobie used one word to describe Cook and to explain why his book is memorable, important, and readable so many years after its initial publication. "Perspective," Dobie wrote, "was Cook's special gift." Many others lived active lives on the frontier, but few realized that they had experienced a period of profound historic change for the peoples of the trans-Mississippi West. Fewer still, in 1923, had the good sense to write about it, and still fewer wrote about it as well as James H. Cook. He was, as Dobie might have said, "a good 'un!"

Captain Cook's Place Among Reminiscencers
of the West

BY J. FRANK DOBIE

THERE MAY BE A FEW exceptions—depending upon definition—but as a rule the most illuminating and, to civilized taste, the most readable personal narratives of the West have been written by men with perspective. This is especially true of narratives dealing with life on cattle range and trail. Writers of the best ones have been aware of life and values far away from their own camps and cows. Granville Stuart, called "the Father of Montana," whose *Forty Years on the Frontier* is primary on both early mining and ranching, had a thousand books in his ranch home and had read them. Edson C. Dayton's *Dakota Days, 1886–1898* (privately printed in 1937 and little known) has the word *intellectual* on page 2 and in describing a man's harmony with his horses quotes:

> *I have some kinship with the bee,*
> *I am boon brother with the tree;*
> *The breathing earth is part of me.*

Drunk on "shoot-'em-up" banalities, collectors have been strangely neglectful of John Culley's *Cattle, Horses and Men;* Culley was an Oxford man who ranched in New Mexico, and when I went to see him after he had retired in California, he showed me a presentation copy of Walter Pater's *Essay on Style*. Montague Stevens, another New Mexico rancher from England, a Cambridge man, put into *Meet Mr. Grizzly* more about the sense of smell in animals than is found in any other book this side of W. H. Hudson's *A Hind in Richmond Park*. While I was writing *The Longhorns* I found more natural history about these cattle in R. B. Townshend's *A Tenderfoot in Colorado* than I found in the reminiscences of various native cowmen who had never been, mentally, away from cows. Nor has any gunman, directly or indirectly, recollected so delightfully of Billy the Kid as R. B. Townshend wrote about him in *The Tenderfoot in New Mexico*. Townshend came west from England to ranch soon after the close of the Civil War; he was a Cambridge man, and after many years of westering he returned to England and translated Tacitus under the spires of Oxford.

Perspective implies knowing what to look for in an object as well as a sense of relative values. Violence, exaggerated in fact and more exaggerated in tradition, has prevented many actors on the western scene from seeing beyond violence itself. The average old-timer of open range days put himself wherever possible, and often where not possible, into Indian fights and stampedes and strained his memory to be an eyewitness to badman exploits. Professional sensationalists early made the labels for everything supposed to be interesting about the Old West; violence, danger, and climactic action composed about everything. Thereafter the great majority of Western men who came to chronicle their life experiences tended to slur over anything for which there was not a label—printed in red and marked E X P L O S I V E. Cattlemen have probably lost a thousand times more cattle to screwworms than to cow thieves, but cow thieves have received more than a thousand times as much attention. You will look in vain through range autobiographies for consideration of screwworms. They are as realistic as Poe's romanticized "Conqueror Worm" or as Hamlet's delineation of the "progress of a king through the guts of a beggar," but screwworms have never been labeled as a proper subject for range-life chronicles.

There is plenty of violence in *Fifty Years on the Old Frontier*, by James H. Cook. He could not have been true to the land and the livers upon it at the time he rode among them without revealing this violence, but he saw beyond it. He was born to the tradition of the sea and as a boy wanted to go down to the sea. In the Michigan of his first sixteen years he learned woodcraft, shop craft, and the Bible, before he came to Texas a cowboy for to be. But the perspective in forming his memoirs seems to have been developed after he left Texas and became a professional hunter and guide in Wyoming and New Mexico. In *Longhorn Cowboy*, which he wrote and Howard R. Driggs doctored up, he says: "I took advantage of associations with men of learning to broaden my knowledge. I met Professors E. D. Cope and O. C. Marsh, two of the world's greatest naturalists, and assisted them in their researches. I was of help also to Professors Hayden and King. . . . Conversations with these scientists aroused a desire to learn more." By the time he came to write the chronicle of his adventures, his ranch at Agate Springs, Nebraska, had been host to paleontologists, anthropologists and other scientists from many universities and museums. He could not write about brush popping as if he had known no other talk than that of oxen.

It is significant that Yale University published his book, in 1923. It has been out of print for years. Among valid reasons for reprinting it is the fact that it was the first book within the realm of range books to deal with the brush country of Texas. As author of the second book (1929), *A Vaquero of the Brush Country*, on this singular part of the cattle world, I was acutely conscious of Captain Cook's validity as well as priority. Since those days of the 1870's when he and his fellow *vaqueros* roped outlaw cattle at night on openings between thickets, the brush, despite modern treedozing, has increased, wild cattle still hide in it, and brush popping still demands techniques far removed from those of the plains cowboys, but no man now can experience the pristine wildness of the *brasada* during Jim Cook's youth. He alone of the brush hands of his time set it down.

"Cow Waddies and Cattle Trails," Part I of his book, has for me a freshness and richness not common in what follows. The abbreviated account of managing the WS Ranch in New Mexico is hardly so good as *Some Recollections of a Western*

Ranchman, by William French, who took over managership
of the WS Ranch in 1887, the year Cook left it. The hunting
episodes lack the natural history content inherent in the best
hunting literature. Yet not many cattlemen who fought Indians
became foremost among the understanders of and friends to
the Indians as Captain Cook became. For him, in memory, an
Indian scrap could not be the high point of narrative. Taking
together everything he wrote pertaining to Indians, one gets a
sense of development towards mature mindedness in the man
and writer.

Sometimes in reading reminiscences one judges that the
writer had done better by keeping a journal and publishing it
instead of looking back through the aura of vanished time. I
do not have this feeling towards *Fifty Years on the Old Frontier*. The matter seems better to me for having been sifted by
time and looked at from the perspective of maturity. On January 27, 1942, in his eighty-fourth year, James H. Cook died
at his ranch home at Agate Springs, or Agate, on the Niobrara
River in Sioux County, Nebraska. His son Harold blends ranching and science in a way that throws light on history.

BIBLIOGRAPHY

Cook, James H. "The Art of Fighting Indians," *The American
Mercury*, June, 1931.
———. *Fifty Years on the Old Frontier*. New Haven, 1923.
———. *Longhorn Cowboy*. Edited by Howard R. Driggs. New
York, 1942.
———. "Six-Gun Days," *New Mexico Magazine*, March, 1936.
———. "The Texas Trail," *Nebraska History Magazine*, Vol.
XVI (1935).
French, The Honorable William. *Some Recollections of a
Western Ranchman: New Mexico, 1883–1899*. London,
1927.

Spence, Karl L., and Margaret C. Cook. "Captain James H. Cook Forsook Career at Sea for Colorful Life of Adventure in the West," a sketch in *Northwest Nebraska News*, Crawford, Nebraska, February 5, 1942.

Author's Preface

MANY STORIES have been written, many scenes depicted by great artists, touching the lives of the pioneers of the West. As many varieties of people were represented among the pioneers, no doubt, as in the various other walks of life. Three classes have been portrayed—the good, the bad, and the indifferent. Type specimens from these three classes have been selected and represented by professional actors, on both stage and screen, until the public has become fairly familiar with their characteristics. Scenes of western life have been drawn to represent phases which had passed on long before the camera was in evidence there, the artist's imagination supplying both detail and action. Realizing that few men are today living who have had experiences similar to mine, and that but few records have ever been left by these few, I have attempted, at the earnest request of my family and friends, to write down some of my experiences.

I desire to record one fact regarding those who made a success as good "cowhands" or plainsmen or mountaineers, and who really aided by their various activities in paving the way for the settlement of the West. Such men had to be men of deeds, men of action. No person, so far as I know, has ever accused Daniel Boone, Kit Carson, "Bigfoot" Wallace, Jim Bridger, or others of their type whose names will remain indelible in the history of the West, of being either loafers, dance-hall artists, or desperadoes. The majority of the cowboys of the West were not a drunken, gambling lot of toughs. It required riders with clear heads, brave hearts, and strong bodies to do the work which was required in handling either the great trail herds or the cattle on the ranges. A drunken man riding about one of those great herds of wild cattle was a sight I never witnessed. One could as well imagine a man being allowed to smoke cigarettes in a powder factory. A large percentage of the men who lived the life of the open chose and followed that life because they loved it.

I trust that those who read these tales will take into consideration the fact that all sorts of people pioneered the West. If what I have written proves of interest or value to the reader, I shall journey on with the pleasant thought that I have been permitted to contribute to the enjoyment of others by taking them with me for a little jaunt into the life of the West of Yesterday.

Words fail me when I attempt to express my appreciation of the kindness shown me by so noted an author as my friend General Charles King, in writing an introduction for this book.

To my friend E. A. Brininstool, another well-known writer, I am also indebted for the generous aid given me in arranging the manuscript and otherwise assisting me to bring order out of chaos in a document upon which I have been writing, in odd moments, during a period of twenty years.

JAMES H. COOK

Introduction

THREE YEARS AGO, on an almost summer-like morning, I had
been motored southeastward from a little faraway railway station close to the Wyoming line. From the crest of a divide,
gazing northward over our left shoulders, we could see in the
dim distance the jagged upheavals of the Black Hills of Dakota
—black because blanketed with a dense growth of pines and
cedar. It was my first peep at them since the great Sioux campaign of the Centennial year. Winding slowly down the sunny
southern slope, we came in sight of a wide expanse of prairie,
stretching east, west, and south to the very horizon—a shallow
depression through which, twisting and turning and almost
doubling upon itself in places, lazily meandered a narrow
stream, its banks so bare of timber, even the ubiquitous cottonwood, that not for long leagues were there signs of the
faintest shade. Afar off to the west occasional buttes and bald-
topped, rounded heights were rolled up against the pallid blue
of the autumn sky. One of these, the boldest and blackest,
towered like a landmark above his fellows, and was hailed with
joyous recognition—old Rawhide. Far off to the southwest,
fourscore miles from the point where for the moment we had
halted, loomed still another, larger by far, grander in propor-
tion, and conspicuous in its isolation—another old friend and
guide of the thrilling days of the Indian wars—Laramie Peak,
proudest of Wyoming's monarchs east of the continental back-
bone, the Rockies. For the first time in over forty years we
were gazing again, and now with dimming eyes, over scenes
that had been vivid, imperishable in memory. Driving on again,
we presently rounded a shoulder of prairie upland and stared
away southward to welcome the sight of the old camping

ground where, time and time again on march from Laramie to Red Cloud Agency, we had unsaddled and pitched our shelter tents close to the banks of the lonely Niobrara. But lo! the world had changed. Where was the pebbly ford where time and time again our wearied chargers had slaked their thirst? Where were the broad levels, barren save for the gray-green bunch grass that bordered either bank? Vanished. And in their stead, uplifted before our eyes, there stood a bowery oasis in the very center of what once had seemed a shadeless desert—a vision of leafy shelter, of flowering shrubs and plants nestling under the foliage of dense groups of graceful trees, with trim hedgerows and trellised vines, bordering here, there, and everywhere sparkling runlets of clear, cool water; and in their midst, glistening white in the morning sunshine, with its columned portico and spreading verandas, green-shuttered windows and peaked roofs, a commodious modern homestead on the very spot where, in bygone days, we had built our little cook fires and boiled our soldier coffee—a homestead flanked to the west and south by stormproof stables and storehouses and broad corrals, a type of the very best of our frontier cattle ranches, and the home of one of the very best of a type of American pioneers now well-nigh extinct, yet well remembered—the keen-eyed, cool-headed, fearless men who, for half a century and more, were the guides and comrades of the cavalry of the Army of the United States in its tireless, almost ceaseless task of clearing the way for and guarding the lives and property of the thousands of explorers, emigrants, and settlers who, little by little, sought out and peopled almost every cultivable valley from the Missouri to the mountains and from the Staked Plains of Texas to the British line—the scouts of the Plains, men famous in song and story, of whom Kit Carson and Jim Bridger in the early days, and "Buffalo Bill" Cody and, later still, "Captain Jim" Cook, were the shining lights.

And it was Captain Jim who had tamed this wilderness, taught it to blossom like the rose, and, after over thirty years of herding, hunting, scouting, and trailing, from Mexico to Montana, had settled in the heart of what had been the Sioux country, in the midst of the county that now bears the name of that famous nation, and built a little world of his own where once there grew not so much as the splinter of a lodgepole.

Early in life Cook had known this land of the Dakotas, had mingled with their young men, and learned something of their language, but he was still a stripling when he took to the saddle and the life of a cowboy, far down in the Comanche country and the borders of the Llano Estacado. In 1870, when Bill Cody was in the heyday of his usefulness and popularity—chief scout of the Fifth United States Cavalry in the Platte country—Cook, seven years his junior, was just learning how to fling the lasso; and for five long years he rode the southern plains, sometimes driving herds far north to the Kansas Pacific. He was far to the southwest when the Sioux made the magnificent fight for their famous Story Land—that incomparable region between the Yellowstone on the north and the Big Horn on the west, and stretching away eastward far beyond the Little Missouri. A bold rider, a fine shot, a square, honest man, Cook served successively three or four big cattlemen, earning small wage but no little commendation. Painfully wounded in one of the many sharp encounters with the Comanches, the scourge of Texas, he finally became manager for wealthy Englishmen—"boss" of the ranch, and able now to spend some of his waking hours in reading and studying. And here it was that Cook turned aside from the array of his fellows, the herdsmen of the wide frontier, and began to lay up a store of information—knowledge of history, and not a little of literature—to the end that when, after fifteen years of almost unbroken intercourse with the hunters, cattlemen, and ranchmen of the West, he felt it his duty to bear a hand in bringing to terms that famous Apache chieftain, Geronimo, and was attached as scout to the Eighth Cavalry, then serving in Arizona and New Mexico, in spite of his modesty and reserve, he surprised the officers of that hard-riding regiment: he had read much more than not a few of their number had ever thought of doing. It was on this campaign that Cook's ability, keen knowledge of Indian methods, and familiarity with the wild country won him the confidence and comradeship of some of the most distinguished officers of our cavalry—notably, Colonel Samuel S. Sumner, now major general, retired; Captain S. W. Fountain, now brigadier general, retired; and the gallant and lamented Lieutenant Gatewood, to whom more than to any other soldier belongs the credit of Geronimo's final surrender and submission.

It is a singular fact that Cook, indefatigable in his endeavor to bring Geronimo to justice, was nevertheless a champion and faithful friend, from first to last, of one of the most implacable enemies of the white man, the most daring and brilliant chieftain the Sioux nation has ever acclaimed—Mahpiya-luta, Red Cloud. It was Red Cloud who had warned the government that beyond the North Platte toward the Big Horn, neither soldier, scout, nor settler would ever be allowed; it was Red Cloud who planned and carried out the fearfully effective annihilation of Colonel Fetterman's command at Fort Phil Kearny, in return for which the government never rested until that famous Chief, late in October, 1876, was dethroned and stripped of all semblance of authority, to live out his days a virtual prisoner, yet bearing his humiliation with such dignity as to command the respect of his harshest enemy. So, too, was Cook a friend and champion of the Northern Cheyennes, the story of whose bitter lot he has told with sympathetic truth. It was well known that, at the time of their last superb but futile rebellion against the Indian Bureau, officers of rank and distinction in the army pleaded in vain for justice to this gallant and suffering tribe, and that there were troop commanders who, when ordered to pursue and punish them, dared to link arms and walk forward toward the stronghold of the hunted band, imploring them not to compel a fight which could only end in extermination—so few by this time were the pursued, so many the pursuers. There were officers and men willing to pledge their lives that no further harm should come to the warriors if they would but return with them. But the Cheyennes had been deceived too often. They would die in their tracks rather than again be imprisoned. Cook tells it all, as officers would have told it long ago but that it might have cost them their commissions. Cook so believed in the Sioux and the Cheyenne leaders and warriors that he finally chose their country for the castle he had determined to build for his family—wherefore this beautiful bowered homestead on the banks of the winding Niobrara.

From that home those children, as had been the father's hope and ambition, were sent to the best schools and the foremost universities, and richly have they repaid his love and devotion. The highest honors of Nebraska in the West and Columbia in the East have been the reward of their diligence, and it must be said, too, that in their case the seed has been sown in most fruitful soil. And so it has resulted in the course of years that among the many visitors welcomed every summer to that now famous ranch have been eminent scientists, especially those eminent in biological research. Welcome as these are, it has long been a matter of remark that the same hospitality is shown to the humblest who may seek that isolated castle, that beautiful oasis in the midst of miles of what to eastern eyes seems utter desolation—the far-spreading, shadeless, shrubless, treeless expanse of prairie. Men and women of many a nationality have inscribed their names on the visitors' book at Agate, but there are others, still eagerly coming, ever sure of welcome, most of whom have never handled pen or pencil—Captain Cook's red brethren of the Pine Ridge Agency far to the east. Men of the Oglala band—Red Cloud's children of the Sioux nation—seem to hold him, their most famous chieftain's most intimate and devoted friend, in the light of an indulgent father. It means a long ride by rail or a four days' jog on pony-back, but time and time again they find means to wheedle the agent into passing them on a visit from which no one of their number returns empty handed. "In my father's house are many mansions" is the text that seems to fit the Indian comprehension of the Captain's home, so many a red brother is there, ever eager to put it to the test. I do not know the Sioux name for the friend and benefactor, but I am sure that they have one; and an evening spent in the Red Cloud room of the homestead, filled as it is with relics and souvenirs of the departed hero of the Sioux, can well account for the confidence with which his people flock to the county that bears their name, where, three years ago, two or three old campaigners united with Cook's children in a final appeal to the veteran scout and plainsman, friend alike of the Indian and the paleface, to prepare his reminiscences for publication. The volume which follows is the result.

CHARLES KING,
Formerly Adjutant, Fifth Cavalry, U.S.A.

PART I
COW WADDIES
AND
CATTLE TRAILS:
TEXAS

A good cow horse in action. Such a horse can outdodge a man on foot, stopping and whirling with marvelous agility.

1

"Pore Little Mite from Michigan"

MY EARLY BOYHOOD DAYS were spent in southern Michigan, where I was born August 26, 1857. My mother having died when I was two years of age, my father, who was a seafaring man, placed me with a family named Titus. This family was one of the oldest and most respected in that country; its members had been raised after the severest models of order, industry, frugality, integrity, and every Christian virtue. Their highest aim in life was to try to prepare themselves, and those in their keeping, for the life to come.

I believe that no young person can ever escape from the impressive and controlling influences exerted on the bent of his future life and the formation of his character by those of superior years to whom he looks up with confidence and admiration. To the loving care and training of this noble family during my childhood days, I feel that I am indebted for whatever strength I have possessed in resisting some of the evils that have beset me as I have journeyed along over rugged trails.

Those were great days for a boy of my inclinations. I think the spirit of a hunter was in me at birth. The Titus family and most of their relatives and friends were pioneers of Michigan. The men took pride in their skill as marksmen. Hunting and trapping were their chief forms of recreation. Sturdy sons of the forest, they could swing the scythe or the grain cradle from sunup to sundown. They were masters of the arts of the woods, being equally skillful with axe and rifle, and at home in a log canoe, spearing fish. (In those days it was considered almost a crime to spear a fish, no matter how fast it might be moving, in any spot but just behind the gills, or to shoot a squirrel anywhere but through the head.) At a very early age I was given

3

instruction in the use of a muzzle-loading rifle. I was also taught a few things about the building and managing of a canoe, and how to trap for fur-bearing animals such as the fox, mink, otter, and muskrat.

At that time the passenger pigeons were very numerous in Michigan. Countless flocks of them would come at nesting time and congregate at what were called "roosts." When these birds were leaving the roosts in the morning for their feeding grounds, or returning in the evening, they would be so numerous as fairly to darken the sky. Vast numbers of them were caught in nets at these roosts by market hunters. The squabs were killed with clubs in countless thousands. Pigeon shooting was good within a radius of many miles of these roosts for anyone who owned or could borrow a "scatter-gun." I was not very expert with the old musket of which I had the use when I wanted to shoot pigeons, for the recoil of that ancient firearm was something of which I could stand but a few doses.

The passenger pigeon has disappeared from view. I saw quite large flocks of them in the timber of the Indian Territory (now Oklahoma) in 1874 and 1875. In 1882, I am quite sure that I saw seven of them on the west side of the continental divide, in Grant County, New Mexico. I should have been able to recognize a bird that had been such a common sight to me as a boy, for I think I was, even at the age of my earliest hunting days, a fairly close observer of every creature with which I came in contact.

To the men who in those days instructed me in marksmanship —my most noted accomplishment as well as one of the most useful assets of my life—I am greatly indebted.

I had other creatures besides pigeons upon which to test my skill in shooting. Black, gray, and fox squirrels were very numerous, and a few wild turkeys still roamed the woods about my neighborhood.

Occasionally someone who had been over the trails to California would return to Michigan with wonderful stories about

the West and Southwest. Their tales filled me with a desire to
see the country of big game and wild Indians. I had a chum
about my own age who was as fond of hunting as myself, and
we had no trouble getting our heads together and planning a
western trip, saving the money which we could earn, or which
was given us. We went to Leavenworth, Kansas. At a hotel
there we met some cattlemen, who told us that the best way
to see the West was to get work with some cow outfit and go
to Texas. The best place to "get broke in," they said, was in
either Sedgwick or Sumner County, Kansas. Going thither, we
secured work as herders with a bunch of beef cattle that were
to be held near old Fort Harker. After working with these cattle
for a couple of months, my chum decided to remain in that
country. But, an opportunity presenting itself, I went to southwestern Texas with some cowboys who had brought a herd
of cattle up from that country to Kansas, and who were then
about to make the return journey. I had purchased a fine Comanche pony at Fort Harker for $15.00 and a good secondhand
Texas saddle for $5.00. I had traded a pistol brought from
Michigan for a Spencer carbine, and was therefore fixed for
the journey.

I saw some of the West before we reached our destination.
We trailed leisurely, and I had a good chance to see wild Indians, buffalo, cowboys, freighters, stage drivers, emigrants,
whiskey peddlers, desperadoes, and about all that moved in the
regions through which we traveled. On this trip I learned, too,
something about the details of roughing it. We had no tents
or bed tarpaulins or sleeping bags, not even a "blow bed," or
pneumatic mattress, such as some people who "rough it" now-
adays use. A "Tucson bed" was quite a common thing on that
trip, and on many a trip thereafter. As some readers may not
know what a "Tucson bed" is, I will explain that it is made by
lying on your stomach and covering that with your back. It
was allowable to put your saddle and saddle blanket over your
head, should you happen to have such articles with you, when

any hailstones larger than hens' eggs came along.

Soon after starting on this long ride, we reached what was called the "Cross Timber" of the Indian Territory. Here we saw a few buffalo, wild turkeys, and deer in abundance. This timber was a sort of scrub oak or blackjack. We saw plenty of Indians all the way through the Indian Territory, or "Nation," as it was also called, but we had no trouble with them. A guard was kept on our horses day and night, for walking never was considered good form by cowpunchers. The journey through Texas, as far south as San Antonio, was interesting to me in many ways, but not exciting.

When we reached San Antonio, I found a city that did both interest and excite me. I had heard of the Alamo, and it was one of the first places I visited. Soon after my arrival in San Antonio, I was fortunate enough to meet one of the most noted frontiersmen of Texas—Captain or, as he was commonly called, "Bigfoot" Wallace. He told me the history of the fight at the Alamo. When he recounted how that little band of fearless men died, fighting against about as long odds as the greatest warriors of earth could desire, the brave old veteran became fired with enthusiasm; and certainly he had me excited to the point of thinking that those heroes of the Alamo were the greatest men who ever lived, except, perhaps, Ethan Allen or Daniel Boone.

Captain Wallace was a giant in stature. He had gone through some thrilling and awful experiences during his earlier years, and was still, at the time I first met him, capable of doing considerable damage to an enemy. We became friends, and about a year later he presented me with one of the best of his three-year-old colts. He was raising some good horses of the kind most needed at that time in Texas.

Meeting John Longworth, one of old Ben Slaughter's caporals or foremen, I secured employment from him. I was to go with him out to the Frio and Nueces rivers country and help catch wild cattle, just as soon as Longworth should go broke playing Spanish monte and drinking whiskey. In the meantime

6

I took in the sights of San Antonio. The old "Green Front" and the Jack Harris Variety theaters and dance halls were running full blast, and every night found them packed with the hard riders from the cattle ranges, as well as with other gentry. Gambling halls, where the ceiling was the limit to the amount one could bet on the turn of a card, were numerous and well patronized. Everyone seemed to have money that he wanted to get rid of. Being a tenderfoot or "shorthorn" kid in that country, I could only look on and enjoy the excitement among the people with whom I had chosen to cast my lot. While waiting for Longworth, I also rode out to San Pedro Springs and down the San Antonio River a few miles, enjoying the beauty of the country—to me, a new and interesting world. There was no railroad in San Antonio at that time, but a line was reaching out toward it.

Before many days Mr. Longworth went broke and was sick enough to want to get out of town. In San Antonio he had hired several riders, all Mexicans except myself. All of us started out together, taking with us some pack ponies loaded with provisions and a few cooking utensils. Longworth could speak Spanish fluently. I did not understand a word of the conversation as we rode along, but I became very familiar with the expression *"San Antonio Querido"* ("dear San Antonio"), for it was repeated many times in a song that seemed to please the rest of the party and was sung quite frequently. Longworth appeared rather surly to me, and I soon found out that he was a vicious, dangerous man, but a good *vaquero*, or brush runner, when it came to catching wild cattle.

In about four days we reached the ranch home of Ben Slaughter, father of Charlie, Billy, and John Slaughter, later the big cattle drovers on the Texas trail to Kansas. We made camp a little distance from the ranch house.

After a while a little old man walked down from the house to our camp. He wore a belt filled with Henry rifle cartridges, and the handle of a big butcher knife was sticking out of one of his boot tops. Thinking that he was some old Mexican, I used about all the Spanish I had learned from Longworth on our way out from San Antonio, trying to say "Good evening" to him. When I was through with my efforts to speak a couple of Spanish words, he looked me over for a moment and said, "Yes, this is a mighty pretty evenin'." He then began to talk to Longworth, using both Spanish and English. I soon discovered that this man was none other than Ben Slaughter himself, who was now my employer. I had a talk with him that evening, and he told me he would pay me $2.00 a month more than the Mexicans he employed. My wages were to be $10.00 a month; he paid the Mexicans $8.00. Board was included; so that all I had to do was to earn my money.

Very early the next morning, while the stars were yet shining, as if to help the fire make our coffee, we were astir. I had no more idea what my work was to be like than a pig has about watch-making, but I did know how to eat my breakfast of broadside pork and corn bread. When this meal was dispatched, Longworth and two or three of the Mexicans rode to a pasture a short distance away and brought in a bunch of about forty or fifty saddle horses. All hands now went to the corral into which the animals had been driven, and Longworth selected one for me to ride. He pointed out three or four others that were also to be mine to use. He also selected each Mexican's mounts. I looked mine over very carefully, so as to know them when I saw them again.

Longworth now threw his lasso on the pony he had first selected for me, and told me to saddle up, as we were to go after a beef which was to be butchered. I saddled my pony. When I tightened the cinch the pony jumped into the air and tried to turn cart wheels. I felt a little lump in my throat about the size of a piece of chalk, but after a time I managed to get into the saddle. He proved to be a good cow horse, but an awful bluffer to a stranger. I certainly was glad when he trotted off without trying to "sun my moccasins." The Mexicans, who were expert riders and ropers, had little trouble with their mounts.

When we were all ready we entered a pasture, rounded up fifty or seventy-five head of cattle, and drove them to camp. These cattle were not what would have been called gentle in any part of the United States save western Texas. They had been separated from the wild herds, and were "gentle" to just the extent of having become accustomed to the sight of a man on horseback, so that they could be controlled to a certain extent by riders. They all belonged to the Spanish longhorn breed. It required but little to frighten them into a rage that knew no bounds when they were brought to bay. Longworth told me that this was to be our decoy herd. What that meant I did not then know.

Longworth now drew a rifle from the scabbard on his saddle and started to look the cattle over for a fat one. In the meantime Mr. Slaughter had mounted a horse and come out where we were herding the cattle. He rode close to me and said, "What's the matter? Can't John find a fat one?"

Just at that moment I observed a fine fat heifer coming along the edge of the herd. I pulled the Spencer carbine which I was carrying, pointed it toward the animal (not intending to shoot unless he told me to), and exclaimed, "There is a good one." Mr. Slaughter started his horse toward me, fairly yelling, "Hold on, young man; don't you see that's a T-Diamond?"

"Yes," I replied. "What brand is that?"

"I reckon that's my brand," was the answer. "We don't kill that kind in this country. Kill an LOW or a WBG"—meaning anyone's brand but his own. "They taste better."

By this time Longworth had selected a beef that suited him. He fired but failed to kill it. He fired another shot or two but only succeeded in further wounding the animal. The herd by this time was milling around, badly frightened. One of the Mexicans threw his rope on the animal as it came near him, and started his horse on a run for the purpose of throwing the

9

wounded beast down. When his horse came to the end of the rope, the strain was too great and it snapped, giving the beef an awful jerk. The animal was now thoroughly infuriated, and as it happened at the moment to be headed toward Mr. Slaughter and myself, it charged us. I had not thought such a thing would occur. Acting on impulse, and being probably somewhat excited, I snatched my carbine from my saddle and, when the steer was within six feet of me, shot it in the center of the forehead, killing it instantly. Mr. Slaughter was trying to spur his old pony out of harm's way, but when he saw the result of my shot he turned, saying, "I reckon you'll do to help fight the Comanches." I was pretty proud of my shot, although it was more good luck than anything else.

After the animal was dressed out and such portions of the meat as were desired had been hung up in the mesquite trees near camp, and after the cattle herd had been returned to the corral, we proceeded to put in the rest of the day making hobbles for our saddle horses. They were manufactured from fresh beef hide. This was new work to me, but it was not many months before I could work up rawhide into saddle rigging, ropes, quirts, and reins, doing all sorts of knot-tying and braiding or plaiting. My Mexican instructors were all very kind to me. It was not long before I had picked up a little of their language, especially such words as pertained to the work in which we were employed. The Mexicans seemed to derive pleasure from trying to teach me.

I learned a few things during that day. One of them was that, on account of the plenitude of cattle, and because the climate was too warm for meat to keep longer than a day or two, only the most desirable parts were used. I have helped kill many cattle just to get their ribs and hides. It was a common thing to kill a beef each day in a cow camp. The meat was generally cooked by thrusting long green pointed sticks through it, sticking one end into the earth, and broiling the meat over a good bed of mesquite or live-oak coals.

I began to realize that I was now on the frontier, sure enough. Everybody went armed to the teeth at all hours. No man removed more than his coat or brush jacket when he lay down to sleep. There was danger on all sides, and from many sources. Light sleeping soon became a habit. Nobody had more than one bed blanket, but such as we did have were generally good, strong, hard-woven ones of Mexican manufacture.

When in San Antonio I had purchased at a pawnshop a very fancy bowie knife of great weight. On its blade was engraved this inscription: "Never draw me without cause, nor sheathe me without honor." I must have been a fit subject to take up the spirit of the times quickly, for as I lay in that camp, waiting for the hour to come when we should start out after wild cattle, I wondered who, or what, would be the first victim of that wondrous blade. I don't think I was at all bloodthirsty, but I felt that, should man or beast attempt to secure my scalp lock, I would do my best to protect it.

I had succeeded in transplanting myself from a state where the people—good citizens who loved God and nature—had accepted and, as a rule, lived up to the Ten Commandments; where, when trouble arose between men, it seldom was carried to a point beyond a fist-fight. But in the section of country which I had now entered, different conditions and codes prevailed. The War of Rebellion, then so recent, had caused numerous men who had survived it, and who had committed all sorts of desperate crimes, to seek refuge in the wilds of the land of chaparral and cactus, where the strong arm of the law seldom entered, and where, when it did, the refugee would be apt to have a little the best of it. A majority of the ranchmen in the country preferred aiding a white refugee to helping bring him to justice. This preference sprang from a motive of self-protection, for the enmity of such characters was a most dangerous thing. As there was in that section but little employment other than working with stock, naturally these men took up the life of the cowboy—when their time was not occupied dodging State Rangers or robbing stages and small settlements. Almost every dispute had to be settled with a gun- or knife-fight or else assassination. Such people, added to thieving bands of Mexicans and Indians, wild beasts of many sorts, and other terrors such as centipedes, tarantulas, and rattlesnakes, were a help in making life interesting for the "pore little mite from Michigan."

Sitting around the fires in those cow camps, I heard many a tale of adventure and the experiences of numerous ex-Confederate soldiers. Among these storytellers were members of the band who had fought with W. C. Quantrill, the noted Confederate guerrilla. One of these men used to tell me how he liked to shoot at the buttons of a Yankee's coat, "just to see him jump." No doubt this man would have enjoyed such sport best when Yankee lead was not coming too near his own buttons.

I did not let anyone know where I hailed from. A "blue-bellied Yankee," even if he were but a boy, was about the most unpopular thing in Texas at that period. With many people, anyone who came from the country lying to the north of the Red River was a Yankee.

Photograph by F. S. Daggett

Photograph of statuette presented by the old Coronel family of California to the Exposition Park Museum of Natural History, Los Angeles. Illustrating the method of "tailing down" wild cattle in the brush country of southwestern Texas in the early 1870's.

Photograph by E. A. Brininstool

A typical specimen of the Texas longhorn.

"Strung out." Point of a herd of cattle being trailed through snow.

"Guard duty." An Angus cow watching over her young calf.

2
Wild Cattle

EARLY IN THE MORNING of the day following my first experience getting beef and making hobbles, Mr. Longworth and his crew, consisting of ten Mexicans and myself, started on a cow hunt. We took our saddle horses with us, together with the bunch of cattle from which we had killed the beef. We used pack mules and ponies for carrying our provisions and cooking utensils. We had no slickers (oilskins). Our provisions consisted of green-berry coffee, salt side of pork, corn meal, saleratus, salt, and pepper berry. Our cooking utensils and dishes consisted of a couple of Dutch ovens, a frying pan, a camp kettle or two, and a coffeepot. We had each a tin cup holding about a pint, together with a tin plate and an iron knife and fork. Sugar was not furnished us. Our pack train generally carried a plentiful supply of black navy plug tobacco and some prepared cornhusks for cigarette wrappers. This was the form of smoking in vogue among Texans at that time. This smoking material had to be purchased either at the home ranch of Mr. Slaughter or from passing Mexican traders who were traveling over the wagon trail from Laredo to San Antonio. Matches were very scarce in that country, and each man carried a flint and steel, together with a piece of punk or prepared cotton tape with which to build fires or "make a smoke."

We went about five miles from the home ranch and camped near an old corral. The corrals in that country were all made about alike. A trench some three feet deep was dug in the ground. Strong posts about ten feet long were then placed on end, closely together, in these trenches, and the ground tramped firmly about them. They were then lashed together about five feet above the ground with long strips of green cowhide. The gateposts were very strong, and so were the bar poles used on them. These bar poles were always lashed to the fence posts with ropes when the corrals contained any wild stock. Strongly built wings were run out from the gate, in order to aid the riders when penning stock. Often these wings were built two hundred yards or more in length. What time we had left after reaching the corral, we put in repairing it, as well as the wings, and getting it ready to hold the cattle we had brought with us and any we might be able to catch.

The following morning about sunrise we left the corral, taking with us the decoy herd, Longworth leading the way through the thick growth of chaparral and mesquite. After traveling a mile or more, he led the herd into a dense clump of brush and motioned us to stop driving it. Then, telling two men to stay with the cattle, he rode off, signaling the other men and myself to follow him. I fell into line behind all the other riders, thinking that the best place to watch the performance. We rode in single file for probably a couple of miles.

Suddenly I heard a crash ahead, and in less than two seconds every rider in advance of me was riding as if the devil were after him. My horse knew the work, and plunged after the riders ahead. I held up for a moment; then the thought struck me that, if I did not keep those ahead of me in sight, I might never get back to camp. I did not know in which direction we had been riding, and one acre of ground looked just like all the rest—everywhere brush, timber, cactus. I gave my horse the reins, trailing the ones ahead by the crashing of limbs and dead brush. I was kept pretty busy dodging the limbs which were large enough to knock me from the saddle and warding the smaller limbs and brush from my face with my arm.

I think I rode all over that pony—first on one side, then on the other; then as he dived under some big live-oak limb, almost under his neck. We crossed several prickly-pear patches where the clumps grew from two to ten feet high and about as close together as they could stand. My pony would jump over, knock down, or run through any of them. He was a cow-catcher by trade. He certainly made me "pull leather," and I clung to his mane as well in order to keep in close touch with him.

I had a very strong desire for this chase to end. At last it did. I was in at the finish. All at once I came in sight of one of my Mexican colaborers. His horse was standing still. The man put up his hand for me to stop, and I did so willingly. He pointed into the brush ahead, and I caught a glimpse of some cattle. A few minutes later I heard voices singing a peculiar melody without words. The sounds of these voices indicated that the singers were scattered in the form of a circle about the cattle. In a few moments some of the cattle came toward me, and I recognized a few of them as belonging to the herd which we had brought from our camp. In a few seconds more I saw that we had some wild ones, too. They whirled back when they saw me, only to find a rider wherever they might turn. The decoy cattle were fairly quiet, simply milling around through the thicket, and the wild ones were soon thoroughly mingled with them.

Every man now began to ride very carefully and slowly, riding in circles around and around them, all except myself singing the melody known as the "Texas Lullaby." For all I know, I may have tackled that singing trick with wild cattle for the first time right there, for I was about as excited as the wild cattle were.

After we had ridden around the cattle for an hour or more, I saw Longworth ride out of sight of the herd, dismount, and tighten the cinch on his saddle. He then returned to the herd, and one by one the other riders followed his example. Our horses, having had a badly needed breathing spell, were now in shape for another run. After a few moments Longworth rode away into the chaparral, singing as he went. The Mexicans closed in on the cattle, starting to drive them after him, pointing the herd in the direction of his voice when the brush was too thick for him to be seen. I brought up the rear of the herd. We all kept quite a little distance from the cattle, and each man tried to make no sudden moves or any sounds that would start a stampede. At last Longworth led the herd into the wings of the corral, and the wild ones followed the decoys in. The heavy bar poles were soon lashed.

We had caught some wild cattle, and I had enjoyed a most thrilling experience. My clothing was pretty well torn off, also a goodly portion of my skin. About nine kinds of thorns were imbedded in my anatomy. I was ready for camp. So were all hands, as well as our horses. Such work was a bit hard on both horses and men, but horseflesh was cheap, and men could be hired who enjoyed the work.

The caporal, in leading a string of riders out to circle into the decoy herd any wild cattle he could find, would not only keep a sharp lookout for a glimpse of cattle, but he must also be listening for the breaking of brush or the sound of running hoofs. He would keep an eye on the ground for fresh tracks of any large bunch of cattle which he thought he could follow up, until the cattle themselves could be seen or heard. To go "away around" one of these bunches of cattle after locating them, and then to circle them into the thicket containing our decoy herd, meant that the rider must not consider his future prospects as very bright. It was a case of trusting in Providence and riding as fast as horseflesh could carry one, regardless of all obstacles. It was a clear case of "go" from the second the cattle saw, heard, or smelled a human being.

Not all cow hunts terminated in the manner of my first one. Many times during my experience hunting cattle by the decoy method, we not only failed to make a catch but also lost the decoys. Some rider, not being able to tell the exact spot where the decoy herd was located, and becoming confused by the many turns the wild cattle had made him take, would dash suddenly right into the decoys at the heels of a bunch of fleeing wild cattle. Then, in less than two seconds, there would be a stampede—which simply meant "The devil take the hindmost."

The only thing that a rider could do in such conditions was to single out an animal and, if possible, catch it with his rope. Failing, because of thick timber or bothersome brush, to get his rope on an animal, he had just one chance left: to spur his horse alongside the fleeing beast, catch it by the tail with his hand, and, taking a turn around the saddle horse, dash suddenly ahead, causing the steer to turn a somersault. The horse then came to a sudden stop, and the rider jumped off and, with one of the short "tie-ropes" which he always carried tucked under his belt, "hog-tied" the bull, cow, or whatever age or sex of cow brute he had thrown. This had to be done quickly, before the animal could recover from the shock of the fall, or trouble would come to the "cow waddie" who had caused it. Flight would not be uppermost in the animal's mind at such a time. The animals did not mind running from a man ten or twenty miles, but when brought to bay by this treatment, their rage would be such that a man would have to take great and sudden care if he valued his life. It would be horns versus pistol should a strong animal regain its feet before its pursuer could tie it down or, failing, be unable to get back into his saddle. Tying down wild cattle caught in this manner was a part of the Texas cowboy's trade, and, like a lot of other work in this world, it required practice, and plenty of it.

When animals were thus tied down, they were left until we could go to the home pasture and get some more "gentle" ones to be used as decoys. We then drove this bunch of cattle to the place where the wild ones were tied down. If they had been left for several hours, their legs would be so benumbed and stiffened that they could not run fast. The tie rope was then loosened and the animal allowed to get up among the decoy cattle. Sometimes when regaining their feet they would charge at the nearest live object and keep right on through the bunch of cattle and line of riders. It would then be necessary to rope and throw them again. An animal from the decoys would next be caught and thrown and the two dragged together and tied to each other, by a short rope around their necks, with knots that would not slip. This was called "necking" animals. Sometimes we brought old work oxen from the ranch, to be used for bringing these tied animals to the corral.

Occasionally, when trying to run the wild cattle into our decoy herd, we stampeded bunches of musk hogs or peccaries. When these animals happened to run, crashing and grunting, pell-mell into our decoy herd, it often caused a stampede that meant the loss of our decoys, with the exception of such as we were able to rope and tie down.

The captured wild ones gave us plenty of trouble when we started in to train them to be controlled by herders. When we had as large a bunch gathered as we dared try to hold with only a few herders, we drove them to one of the large pastures owned by Mr. Slaughter and turned them into it. The fences around these pastures were made high and strong, heavy poles being used in their construction.

The day following my first cow hunt, Longworth and the Mexicans went into the corral and cut out part of our decoy cattle. The rest were left with the wild ones. The corral was divided into two or three pens, and these cattle were driven into one of them. They were left there to become used to corrals and also to get hungry, so that, when taken out to graze, they would care fully as much about food as about regaining their freedom. The first though of the decoys left with the wild ones, when taken from the corral, was for something to eat and drink. This helped considerably in holding the wild ones with them. Some individual members in each bunch of wild cattle would usually make a dash for liberty the moment they were released from the corral. These would have to be caught and tied down for a while to steady their nerves. Then each of them would be "necked" to a gentle one, to be led for a time. This occurred when we turned our first bunch out.

In helping to control these wild brutes, I was at that time about as useless and helpless an individual as ever graced a cow camp. I could only sit around on my horse and follow along. I did keep my eyes open, and I was there to stay if I could only learn the art of cowpunching. After a few weeks I learned to handle a rope a little and to do my part in controlling stock that required one to use brain and eye every moment, as well as to be a "range rider." My first few months in Mr. Slaughter's employ made up an experience such as a great many American boys have never enjoyed.

We caught cattle in other ways than by the decoy system. Sometimes we would ride out into the thickets without decoys, jump a bunch of wild cattle, and then, every man for himself, try to catch and tie them. This was fine training for the bump of location, for not only had one to find one's way back to camp after a catch or a failure, but whoever tied down an animal had to lead a decoy herd or a gentle work ox back to the spot in order to get the captured animal. For a person born without the "coyote sense" which would take him back to the meal sack when hungry, that country was a mighty poor place to live in.

After I had worked a while, my Mexican companions aided me in making a pair of rawhide *chaparajos*, or chaps, as they were called in the northern ranges. One of the smaller Mexicans gave me one of his brush jackets. These were made very short, reaching only to the waist. They were made of some sort of Mexican cloth, so strong that it wore like iron.

There were other methods used in catching wild cattle, when they became scarce in our immediate vicinity or had become so smart or "up to trap" that a decoy herd would not hold them. One method employed was to hunt them on moonlight nights. This was done in the following manner, when the moon was full.

We would remain in camp during the day, until about sundown. Then we would all ride to the edge of some one of the little bits of prairie about us. We would generally go a couple of miles or so from camp. Keeping ourselves and our horses hidden in the thick brush, we would wait for the moon to rise.

Then it would not be long before we heard a cow low, a calf bawl, or a bull bellow. It was their feeding time. Sometimes we heard the breaking of brush as they filed out rapidly into the open. Our horses could both see and hear the cattle farther than we riders, and they were trained for this especial work. I think they enjoyed the excitement of the chase. They would seem to know when the cattle were getting close, and at such times they would grow restless and fairly tremble with excitement. All riders, with saddle girths tightened and ropes in shape for a quick throw, now slipped into their saddles. The moment the caporal thought the cattle were out into the prairie far enough for us to make a quick dash before they could rush back into the dense chaparral, he would give the signal; and, like an arrow from a bow, every rider was off after anything in the shape of a cow brute which he could locate on the prairie.

It was a breakneck game, but, like football, good sport for those who liked it. Sometimes a man made a catch with his rope just as an animal dashed into the timber. It was the custom to tie one end of the rope to the saddle horn. When a rider had the noose end around a big animal's horns, neck, or body, and the animal rushed around one side of a big tree while rider and horse went on the opposite side, each going at full speed, something had to happen. Either the rope snapped or there was a collision about half the rope-length from the tree. Sometimes a horse was gored to death in these mix-ups, and a rider had to scramble for dear life.

When pursuing a single animal, it was the custom for a rider to keep up an incessant imitation of a lowing cow. This was done so that, unless too greatly scattered, we could keep in touch with one another. By this means one of us was occasionally able to aid some other rider, in case he had any spare time after tying, or losing, whatever he had started after.

I well remember one little incident connected with these moonlight cow-chasing expeditions. I had tied down the animal I was after and was sitting on my horse—perhaps thinking what a great thing it was to be a cowboy—while I listened hoping to hear someone "lowing" to whom I could be of service. I had not long to wait. Presently I heard a faint lowing that grew louder each moment, indicating that a rider was coming in my direction. I listened intently and concluded that the rider was coming straight toward me, probably following an old cow trail which passed near the point where I was stationed.

I cleared my rope for action and rode behind a bunch of Spanish bayonet plants close by the trail. I knew that something was ahead of the rider, who was by this time within two hundred yards of me. I soon saw that, if all went well, the beast which was being pursued would pass within a few feet of me. A few seconds later a slick black bull, about three years old, dashed past me. I was ready for him, and as he passed I threw my loop over his head. If there was any extra spring in that bull's body, he used it at that moment, with the result that, when he came to the end of the rope, my saddle girth parted with a loud snap, and I went sailing through space with both feet in the stirrups. My head soon bumped the ground, and by the time the rider had reached me, I was needing sympathy or a drink.

I never heard from that bull, or that saddle, again. If the animal kept going at the speed he had attained when my rope encircled his neck, he was soon somewhere east of Suez. The horse ridden by the bull's pursuer was badly winded, and as the bull was gaining ground, there was nothing the man could do to help me recover my saddle and rope. Fortunately my rifle had been flung from its scabbard about the time I was parting company with the saddle. All I could do, therefore, was to shoulder it and go back to camp with the Mexican. I had a fine large bump on my head to take away as a souvenir of the occasion. I was soon outfitted with another saddle and rope from the home ranch, and was once again ready for more sport with the playful longhorns.

In writing of these wild cattle, I realize that it is a difficult thing to make a large majority even of present-day cattlemen, those who have handled thousands of cattle during the past thirty years, understand what the words "wild cattle" really meant in southern Texas at the time of which I write. Buffalo or deer could be no wilder. These cattle would not graze on open ground in the daytime, but would seek the densest thickets or lie with their heads on the ground like deer, listening and sniffing, on the lookout for danger of any sort, and ready for a mad rush through the jungles to a place of safety.

I had been at work but a short time when a Mexican rode into camp with an almost new Henry rifle on his saddle. He wanted to buy some cartridges for it. We had no Henry rifle shells, but did have some Spencer ammunition, and I succeeded in trading him, for his Henry, my Spencer carbine and what cartridges I had. In a short time I secured some ammunition for it from Mr. Slaughter. This rifle proved to be a most accurate shooting piece, and I had the satisfaction of knowing that nobody in Texas had a better shooting iron than I.

3
Conflict Between Man and Beast

MANY A CONFLICT between man and beast has taken place in those old chaparral thickets, unseen, perhaps, save by the eye of some hovering buzzard or sneaking coyote, which would no doubt take interest in such a scene, knowing that, no matter which side won, there was a chance of some pickings for him.

During the first eighteen months that I spent in the state of Texas, I found times when I could slip out of camp for a little still-hunting. There were numerous beasts and birds about us that to me seemed worth the powder and lead it took to get them. Chief of the wild beasts was the jaguar, a big leopard-like cat which, I think, would sometimes weigh as much as one hundred and fifty pounds. It was a most handsome animal. Then there were pumas, or mountain lions, as they were commonly called. These were generally considered cowardly beasts, but I know of a few instances in which these animals had a poor way of showing their cowardice when cornered or wounded. There were also black bear and the ocelot, or tiger cat. This latter was a pretty creature, the largest of which would, I think, weigh about thirty or forty pounds. They were striped somewhat like a tiger, except that the stripes ran lengthwise of their bodies. No two that I ever saw were marked alike.

Droves of peccaries, or musk hogs, were numerous. It was no uncommon sight to see as many as fifty, or even more, in a drove. They were certainly ferocious little beasts. I imagine that the larger boars would weigh from sixty to seventy pounds. An old Texan explained to me that a javalina (musk hog) when in battle resembled, more than anything else, a "ball of hair with a butcher knife run through it." I know that when enraged they have no fear of man, as I had several tilts with them, both

23

on foot and on horseback, when they were brought to bay by my shooting and wounding one or more of them. When one squealed with pain, its comrades would come promptly to the rescue, every individual a warrior. There were numerous hogs in these jungles besides the javalinas—regular old razorbacks. When a person came suddenly on one of these old boars, he had to run or fight. Even a sow with a litter of pigs was no playmate. We sometimes used to eat these hogs when we could find a good fat one. The musk hog was not bad eating when the musk gland was promptly cut out. This gland was situated on top of the hind quarters.

In my experience with wild beasts, I have found that with all kinds of animals the war bump, or belligerent tendency, is much more developed in some individuals than in others of the same species, the variations being usually pretty much the same as in the human family.

There were wild turkeys by the thousand, also Mexican quail. When the acorn crop was good and the mesquite beans and prickly pears were abundant, horses, cattle, hogs, and turkeys would get very fat. We used to have some great feasts, Mexican modes of dressing and cooking being employed. Mr. Slaughter had not engaged me as a hunter of wild beasts other than cattle, or as a collector of skins, but it was rather trying for me to refrain from shooting when I ran across some fine specimen which I wanted to examine more closely, but could not because I was driving or hunting bunches of wild cattle at the time. Riding quietly along, following our caporal on these cow trails through the jungle in search of wild cattle, perhaps after a very sudden start on first glimpsing or hearing a bunch of them, we would sometimes dash without warning upon one of these big felines, probably taking a quiet nap after a night's work or dissipation. Surprised and rudely awakened by the charge of riders through the brush, it would lose no time in getting up into the nearest treetop that offered shelter, from which vantage point it would make all sorts of kittenish remarks about the way things were moving. A domestic cat, speeding for an apple tree with a belligerent bull terrier in full pursuit, could go no farther or say worse things in cat language than did those big uneducated beasts.

There were many white-tailed deer in that country, also raccoons, opossums, civet cats, and skunks, including the little spotted one whose bite was supposed to produce hydrophobia. There were plenty of tarantulas, centipedes, and scorpions, with rattlesnakes too numerous to mention. It was quite necessary to be cautious when picking up wood for our campfires.

There were many birds also, including some very pretty and cheerful ones. One bird in particular I found most interesting. It was called the chaparral cock or road runner. The Mexican name for it was *piasano*. Its legs were very long and strong. It had wings but seldom used them. It had a long, slender body and a very long tail. Its beak was large and powerful. This bird could run like a sinner, and it was interesting to watch it when after a lizard or snake. Then it would jump like a kangaroo and pounce like a cat.

How the animals could get about among the thorny shrubs and mesquite and the catclaw trees, with their hard, sharp thorns, as well as into the awful cactus, with its millions of sharp spines, without constant torture, was always a mystery to me. Their hides may have been thicker and tougher than those of mankind. The cattle seemed to be very fond of the prickly-pear cactus, and would eat them in spite of thorns. When we killed a beef, we found the tongue simply filled with the thorns of this cactus. Mexican freighters on the old Laredo trail used to cut down the large prickly-pear leaves, put them on green forked sticks, and burn off the thorns; then they would feed them to the work oxen. This was the only feed obtainable for a long distance along this road.

During the period when I was being initiated into cowboy life as followed in southwestern Texas, I occasionally came into contact with detachments of the Ninth United States Cavalry. They were at that time stationed at the military posts along the western border of Texas, the old posts of Ringgold Barracks, Fort McKavett, Fort Griffin, and Fort Bliss being then on the map. The Ninth Cavalry was a colored regiment which had been organized after the close of the Civil War. Among the officers I met at that time was a lieutenant named L. H. Rucker. The acquaintance then formed grew into a friendship which ceased only when my friend, after being retired as a brigadier general, died a short time ago.

On a few occasions I rendered a little service to these officers by showing them the way through sections of country with which I had become familiar. This would happen when scouting parties, striking our camp, wanted to know how they could get to some certain spot in the jungle. The Indians knew all the best crossing places on the rivers and where the water holes along the dry creeks were located. These were things which the army officers desired to learn about. In those days most of the white men who knew anything about the country had little love for the United States officer in charge of colored troops; and the officers usually had to depend upon some Mexican for information regarding such matters, or upon some unprejudiced youngster like myself.

Added to the many objects of interest, danger, and diversion were occasional visits paid us by little parties of Lipan and Comanche Indians. These visits were generally made about the full of the moon, the especial object being to ambush a few white men or Mexicans and secure more guns, pistols, and knives. Ammunition was hard for the Indians to obtain at that time, except in some such manner. They seemed, however, to have no objections to incidentally riding or driving off other people's horses. They also had a habit of slipping up near our camps at night, whenever the opportunity offered, and presenting us with their compliments in the form of a little shower of lead or arrows. This caused us to sleep some distance apart and away from the campfire. Often we would change our bed-ground two or three times in a night, in order not to be too easily located. A snoring man was an abomination in a cow camp—as much so as he is today in a sleeping car, but for a far different reason. If we cared for the life of such a man, we almost felt that we ought to guard him while he slept.

While we were at work with the cattle, the Indians would have the advantage of us. Only their poor marksmanship with rifle or pistol saved the life of many a cow hunter. The only chance we had for our lives when, conducting a bunch of cattle, we were fired upon from ambush was to let the cattle go, spur out of range for a hundred yards, jump off our horses, and lie flat on the ground, ready to shoot any Indian who dared to pursue; or, dismounting, immediately to go still-hunting for Indians. We would thus be on more even terms with them. Occasionally some unfortunate stockrider would stop a bullet or arrow. But that was a part of the business, and the work of gathering wild cattle went merrily on, with but few intermissions because of Indians.

There were two Chisholm brothers, one a freighter and the other a cattleman. The old Chisholm Trail from Texas to Kansas through the Indian Territory had, by the time of which I write, been marked out, and a market for Texas cattle established in southern Kansas. The Chisholm wagon trail, so I was informed, started from what is now Wichita, Kansas, and was laid out from there into the state of Texas. Jesse Chisholm was the builder of this trail. Of Scotch ancestry, he spent his life on the outskirts of civilization, trading with the Plains Indians. His father, Ignatius Chisholm, was the son of John D. Chisholm, the last hereditary chief of the Cherokees.

It had been demonstrated not only that the southern cattle could be fattened on the nutritious grasses of the northern plains, but also that they could withstand the rigors of the northern winters, provided they were in good flesh in the fall. Cattle ranching soon grew to be a lucrative and attractive business over the entire grazing ground of the territory lying north of Texas, and gradually it extended northward as far as the Canadian border. And, later, longhorns were to invade that country. Texas now had a market and an outlet for all the cattle it could supply, and the work of driving hundreds of thousands of them to the northern markets began in earnest. Year after year new trails were marked out, following the old line of march pursued by the buffalo when they migrated to the rich grazing grounds of the North in the spring and returned to their winter pastures in the fall.

The cattle which I helped to gather and put into Slaughter's pastures were to be driven to the Kansas markets. The start of the trail herds from southern Texas would be made about the first of March. The men in charge of the driving and marketing of the cattle would take, not only the cattle bearing their own brands, but also any other cattle they could gather, regardless of brands. A record was supposed to be kept, by those in charge of these herds, of the brands and of the number of cattle belonging to other ranchers. After the expense of marketing the stock was deducted, the proceeds of sales were to be turned over to their respective owners. I have reason to believe that in some cases these proceeds failed to materialize, at least under the conditions which prevailed at the period of the early drives from Texas. Later on, a system of inspection of trail herds at different points on the trails, before the cattle left the state of Texas, put a stop to at least a part of the business of handling other people's property by such loose methods.

When Mr. Slaughter and his sons had secured sufficient cattle in their pastures to start some herds to market, and the time of year had arrived for making a start, all the different camps of cow-catchers in their employ—they had been working, of course, over a large tract of territory—were called in for the purpose of rounding up in the big pastures. We had worked gathering cattle all over the country from the forks of the Nueces and Frio rivers to the heads of these streams, and as

far toward the Rio Grande as the old Cotulla Rancho, a point
about midway between San Antonio and Laredo. The range in
which I hunted cattle covered a tract of country about one
hundred miles square, or perhaps a little more. To round up
the cattle in one of the large pastures was quite an undertaking.
These enclosures would embrace an area equal to two or three
townships. When they were originally built, many wild cattle
were fenced in, and the animals which we later put into them
would soon be about as wild as ever. But with a large outfit
of riders, or "brush poppers," as they were frequently called,
we soon had a herd of about twenty-five hundred thrown together. They were then driven into large corrals and a road
brand put upon them. This would be for the purpose of showing what trail herds they belonged to, in case of a stampede or
mix-up with other herds when on the trail.

I had long wanted to see the great buffalo country lying
between the heads of the Nueces and Frio rivers and Kansas—
for the buffalo never ranged in the "brush country." My opportunity soon arrived.

While working in the country, I had made a trip or two for
supplies to both Laredo and Corpus Christi, and I knew something about what southern Texas was like in both the summer
and winter seasons. I knew what it was to get pretty well
warmed up when chasing or branding cattle under southern
skies, as well as what a norther could do by way of chilling
the marrow. I went to Charlie Slaughter, who was to super-
intend the marketing of this first herd of cattle which I had
helped to gather, and asked him if I might go up the trail with
the herd. He replied, "Why, boy, those Yankees up there would
kill you off. You better stay here and catch mavericks." I told
him that, if he would let me go to Kansas with this herd, I
would return as soon as the cattle were sold and chase mavericks
for him. He then replied, "Well, let's go and see Joe about it."
Thereupon I went with him to one of the camps, where I met
Joe Roberts. He had been selected from among the Slaughter

employees as the man who would have charge of this first, or lead, herd of the drive.

When Roberts was told what I desired, he said: "They tell me that you can catch a cow and shoot a rabbit's eye out every pop. Now, if you can ride for the next four months without a whole night's sleep, and will turn your gun loose on any damned Indian that tries to get our horses, why, git ready. We will roll out tomorrow."

Needless to say, when the morning came I was ready. A few days before, I had locked horns with Longworth—a fact which added to my desire to leave that country, or at any rate his companionship. The trouble originated as follows.

I had unintentionally stampeded a decoy herd by running into it with a bunch of wild cattle before I realized where I was. Fortunately, we managed to hold the cattle, but Longworth was furious. I could hear him saying all sorts of things about my ancestors—and he said them in two languages. I did not blame him much, for such a thing was trying to any man who was interested in making a success of his work, and, feeling very sorry for what I had done, I said nothing. I put my leg up over my horse's neck to remove a thorn that was causing me pain. Suddenly Longworth burst through the brush at full speed, headed straight for me! He had broken a dead limb from one of the mesquite trees and held it in his hand. Passing within three feet of me, he struck at me with the club, using force enough to have crushed my head in. I ducked and caught the force of the blow on my shoulders. Longworth continued running after passing me, probably thinking that I would chase him and that he would then get another chance to bushwhack me. My first thought was to try to kill him. Then I recollected what this would mean to me, and, putting spurs to my horse, I struck out for camp, not knowing what else to do, and thoroughly sick at heart.

Reaching our camp, I found a stranger there, preparing some food and coffee for himself. He seemed to be a pleasant sort of white man, and right then I needed a friend and some advice. I quickly told him what had happened and had him look at my arm and shoulder. As he examined the injury, he remarked, "He sure tried to kill you, son." Afraid Longworth would come after me at any moment, I asked the man what I ought to do if he did.

"Why, son, I'll tell you what *I'd* do. I would shoot the top of his damned head off the minute he came in sight."

I thought the matter all over and then told the stranger that if Longworth were unarmed I could whip him. This seemed to amuse the man very much. After a few moments he said: "I'll tell you what we'll do. I'll put my saddle to one side about forty yards and lie down and go to sleep. When that hyena comes to camp, you kind o' mosey around till he puts his gun down. Then you sidle up to him and baste the soul out of him. If he tries to come any game on you, I'll put a bullet right between his eyes, and we will take a horse or two and hide out."

I remarked to the man that all I desired was a fair show to whip Longworth.

"Well, you'll sure git it," was his response.

I must say that I put in a nervous, unhappy time waiting for the outfit to come in (for they had all remained out to help pen the cattle). Finally they came straggling along, Longworth in the lead, whistling—something I had never known him to do before. He rode into camp, taking no notice of me, jumped down from his horse, pulled his rifle from the saddle, and leaned it against a tree. He then unsaddled his horse and turned it loose. Then, to my surprise, he unbuckled his belt, throwing belt, pistol, and knife down on his saddle. Then, walking over to me, he inquired, "Supper ready?"

"You'll take a licking from me before you ever eat again, you cowardly cur," I exclaimed, accompanying the remark with a good slap on his jaw.

"I don't want any trouble with you, boy," he laughed. "I

was a little rattled when you stampeded the cattle, but I wouldn't hurt you for anything."

I observed Longworth looking out of the corner of his eye toward the spot where the stranger was lying, and I thought I could see why he was not wanting trouble with me just then. As the Mexicans had all seen me slap our caporal, I thought I had done enough; so I remarked, "We will call the matter settled." The stranger now awoke and soon joined us. As soon as it could be done without attracting much attention, Longworth curled up for a rest close to his weapons, and I knew that he had an eye on the stranger. He had seen his saddle horse near camp when riding in, and that, I think, was the cause of his whistling and good humor.

Although there may have been no occasion for it, I was now afraid of Longworth, hence my desire to leave him. I have written of this little incident to illustrate what small value was placed on human life in that neck of the woods. Every man felt that he had the power of jury, judge, and executioner, if he could only "save his own bacon" and liberty.

During the time I worked in camps where the only Americans employed were Longworth and myself, I never had an unpleasant word with the Mexican herders. On the other hand, they showed me every possible favor. One day I rode a "fresh" horse which I distinctly remember. (A "fresh" horse, in that country, meant one that had had a few months' rest and had gained a good amount of flesh and sometimes a very "bad heart" since last ridden.) When I threw my saddle on this animal, he jumped into the air and fell over backward, refusing to rise. When I finally did get him up and climbed into the saddle, I did not remain there long. The horse was an expert bucker, and he threw me three times in about as many minutes. The last time I was hurt pretty badly, but I started to get on him again. One of the Mexicans then came up and took the horse from me, and, although I could not understand his words, I knew that he wanted to ride the animal for me.

I said to Longworth, who was near by, seemingly enjoying the sport, "Please tell him that I will try him once more if he kills me." Then, taking another look at Longworth, who was walking away laughing, I vaulted into the saddle again. The next minute the air seemed full of horses, saddles, and boys— but I stuck to him, although how, I never knew. After he quit bucking I was still on his hurricane deck. He then stampeded with me and ran into some heavy mesquite timber near by. I pulled as hard as I could but was unable to check the animal. The limbs of the trees struck me in the face, and I was nearly knocked from my saddle several times by heavy limbs. Just as I had made up my mind that the pony would kill me, the same Mexican came by me like a cyclone and, grasping the hackamore, took a turn on the horn of his saddle, bringing both his horse and mine to a sudden stop.

The blood was running from my nose and mouth, and my face was badly scratched. Felipe, the Mexican, now jumped from his horse and motioned for me to climb down. I did so, and he quickly changed saddles. He then led me to a little pool of water near by and washed the blood from my face, and we started back to camp, he riding my "bucker." The little horse that had caused me so much trouble started in to have some fun with Felipe but discovered that a master was on his back and soon gave up. Arrived at camp, I again put my saddle on the horse. I had no further serious trouble with him.

4

Trail and Ambush

WHEN MR. ROBERTS informed me that I was to be one of his trail waddies, I immediately moved all my personal belongings over to his camp. I was allowed to take five of the best saddle horses which I had been riding, to be used on the trail. Roberts's trail crew consisted of twelve riders and the cook, besides himself. We were now to be favored by having one man whose duty would be to drive two yoke of oxen on our canvas-covered supply wagon and to cook for the outfit. We were most fortunate in having with us on that trip a man who was one of the best ox drivers or bullwhackers, as well as cooks, that ever popped a bull whip over a cattle trail. The men who usually did this work were veterans on the frontier, who had seen long service with wagon trains drawn by oxen. Too much praise or credit cannot be given to those old-time cooks who were numbered among the *good* ones. A camp cook could do more toward making life pleasant for those about him than any other man in an outfit, especially on those trail trips. A good-natured, hustling cook meant a lot to a trail boss. A cheery voice ringing out about daybreak, shouting, "Roll out there, fellers, and hear the little birdies sing their praises to God!" or "Arise and shine and give God the glory!" would make the most crusty waddie grin as he crawled out to partake of his morning meal—even when he was extremely short of sleep.

On the morning when we were to start up the trail, all was in readiness. Those selected to go with this herd were for the most part white men. The others were well known to be good hands with cattle. About a dozen extra men were to help us for a few days while we were breaking in the herd to accustom them to being held by riders both night and day (for we should have no more corrals). They were also to help us out of the brush country to the open plains. After reaching this open country, the extra men would turn back and help bring up any herd or herds that were to follow.

On the trail we were each allowed to take a pair of red blankets and a sack containing a little extra clothing. No more load than was considered actually necessary was to be allowed on the wagon, for there would be no wagon road over most of the country which we were to traverse, and there was plenty of rough country, with creeks and steep-banked rivers to be crossed. We had no tents or shelter of any sort other than our blankets. Our food and cooking utensils were the same as those used in cow camps of the brush country. No provision was made for the care of men in case of accident. Should anyone become injured, wounded, or sick, he would be strictly "out of luck." A quick recovery and a sudden death were the only desirable alternatives in such cases, for much of the time the outfit would be far from the settlements and from medical or surgical aid.

On the first day, I was told to help drive the saddle horses and to keep them with the wagon. The wagon started, and we followed with the horses, the cattle herd following us in the trail made by the oxen and wagon. Roberts pointed out the course which he desired the outfit to follow, and then rode on ahead to select our first camp ground. After going a few miles, he found a place with water and some fairly open ground upon which to bed the cattle down for the night. Returning to us, he told us where to go and where the wagon was to be located, so that it would not be too close to the herd.

When we reached the designated spot, the work oxen were hobbled and turned loose and a meal prepared of corn bread, broiled meat, and coffee. Along toward night about half the men who had been driving the cattle came in and had supper. They then caught out fresh horses and returned to the herd, allowing their companions to come in. After these men had eaten and caught fresh horses, they helped to hobble the entire horse herd, after which they all returned to the cattle.

Roberts ordered me to catch the most gentle horse in my string and come out and help "bed down" the cattle. Roping out my horse, I rode to the herd, which by this time was not more than a quarter of a mile away. Roberts had selected a patch of ground, about two hundred yards from the wagon, where there was very little brush. There were about ten acres in this little prairie, which was surrounded by heavy brush. About dusk the herd was driven into this little bed-ground by the riders, who closed in on all sides and crowded the cattle together until they were in a compact bunch. The men then commenced riding around the herd, keeping a little distance from it.

I shall long remember that night. The moon was new, and it was not very dark until after ten o'clock. None of the cattle had lain down, but they had stopped walking about and were all very quiet, with the exception of one old black cow which had probably been used as a milch cow by some Mexican family at one period of her existence. This animal insisted upon grazing the entire evening. Every rider had to turn her back into the herd sooner or later, for no sooner would one leave her than she would walk straight away from the herd about fifty yards and begin to graze.

I had heard many uncomplimentary remarks addressed to that cow, in at least two different languages, during the evening. I turned her back into the herd myself several times. At last she walked out from the herd about thirty yards and dropped down for a rest. We allowed her to lie there, changing our course so as to take her within the circle we were riding. She would let me pass within ten feet of her and not move. Every time I came around the herd I would try to see how close to that old black cow I could ride—for, like plenty of other boys, I thought I must always be doing something to work off my surplus energy.

Finally the cow allowed me to ride within two feet of her without stirring. The night had now grown very dark, and I decided to see if she would let me touch her. When I came around the herd next time, I rode in as close as possible and, leaning over on one side, touched her neck with my foot. The cow must have been asleep, for she gave a bound and a snort and plunged into the herd—or rather at the place where the herd had just been, for before she could get among them there came a roar and a crash such as I had never before heard, and the earth seemed fairly to tremble. The herd had stampeded!

Not knowing what else to do, I dashed along in the direction in which the herd had disappeared. Once in a while I could hear the yells of our men coming from the brush. I wandered about for some time and at last blundered onto one of the Mexicans. I asked him what was the matter, and he said, "The herd has stampeded, and we will not have one of them in the morning." I asked him what had stampeded them, and he replied, "*Dios sabe*" (God knows)—and I sincerely hoped that no one else did!

The entire herd did not get away, because fortunately they happened to stick together pretty well, and they ran in the direction of one of the large pasture fences. Some of the men stayed with them, holding them along that fence until daylight, when we all got out after them and brought them to camp. Here the herd was strung out and tallied. The count showed that we were short about five hundred head. No one knew what started those cattle, and unless some of the men who were there are yet alive and read this, probably no one ever will. I kept very mum. One of the men had been hurt rather badly by running into the limb of a tree, and two others were dismounted when their horses stepped into holes or tripped over fallen brush.

Roberts said, "We will take the balance of this herd right out of the brush country and then go back to the ranch and get enough more animals to make up the required number." So we rolled away again. I had had my first lesson. My experiment in trying to find out just how gentle that old black cow was proved a tremendous success, although no doubt it cost a little money. My employer's loss was perhaps my gain, for I never again deliberately tried any more such experiments.

We had no more stampedes for some time. After the first night we divided the night herding into two watches, half of the entire outfit being on guard at a time. When we were out of the brush country, the extra help turned back, and as the cattle were now pretty well broken to being night herded, we divided the watch into three tricks, three men going on guard with the cattle at a time and one man on each watch over the horses. Every night all the horses were hobbled, but they had to be herded just the same, for everything depended upon our holding to our horse herd. Horses stampede at night just the same as cattle and are a great deal harder to hold if not hobbled. In those days there were plenty of Indians who would have been only too happy to relieve us of the care of them.

When the extra help turned back, we lay over for a few days until Allen Harris, another of Slaughter's foremen, came up with a herd and brought a few hundred head for us, a messenger having been sent back to the ranch telling of our loss of cattle. We cut these extra cattle out of his herd and, keeping the herds a few miles apart, we started again up the trail.

We saw Indian signs nearly every day, but nothing of importance happened until after we left the head of Frio River and started for a place called the Painted Rocks. Then one night the Indians attempted to stampede Harris' herd by running into it on their ponies, dragging a buffalo robe at the end of a rope. They succeeded in stampeding both the horse and cattle herds, but the men stayed with the stock and held it. The Indians who were hovering about us were Comanches. They were a pretty venturesome bunch, and they must have had quite a lot of excitement and fun out of the trouble they caused us. Once or twice they slipped up close to the herd at night and shot an animal or two on the outside of the herd, using arrows. When an animal was thus struck, it would bawl with pain and plunge around. This would cause a stampede of more or less magnitude and generally supply the Indians with some meat. We were now on the lookout for Indians all the time, and every one of us expected to get an arrow driven into him while riding about the stock at night. We all experienced a great relief when daylight came, for we felt then that we should have at least half a show for our lives.

One night we were camped on a little creek that ran into the Llano River at its head. Throughout that day we had seen a lot of fresh Indian signs. I was on the first watch with the horses. Roberts had arranged for me to be on guard with the horse herd during the early part of each evening and also just at the break of day, those hours being the Indian's favorite times for deviltry. I was known to be the best shot in that outfit, and I was expected to score straight bull's-eyes and not get "buck fever," no matter how plentiful, hideous, or dangerously close the human targets.

The country was rough and broken, and here and there were large cedar thickets or brakes. I was holding the horses pretty close to the wagon immediately after supper, and everyone noticed that the animals were very restless. In those days, for some unknown reason, a white man's horse was generally afraid of the sight or scent of an Indian, just as Indian ponies were afraid of a white man. When our animals scented Indians, they sniffed the air, snorted, ran together, and showed terror by their looks and actions.

At last Roberts came out where I was holding the horses and told me I had better put them into a little opening in the center of a big cedar brake near the wagon. I replied that I was afraid to go in there to herd: the Indians could then slip up close and kill me with an arrow, for I could not see them. However, Roberts said there would be a great deal less danger in the brakes, as the Indians were likely to run in between the horses and the wagon, if these were on the open prairie, and run the entire herd off as well as kill me. Roberts continued, "They cannot run their horses in that brake." So in we went, he assisting me to drive in the animals. Roberts then returned to camp, cautioning me to keep a sharp lookout.

It required all the nerve I possessed to remain there with those horses. I had to ride hard to keep them in the space: they kept snorting and trying to scatter. I circled around them as fast as I could and kept them herded in as small a space as possible. When riding on the side of the herd nearest camp, I was only about seventy-five yards from the wagon. After what seemed an age, I heard one of the boys from the cattle herd come into camp and arouse the men who were to relieve us. Frank Dennis was the man who relieved me. He was one of the old-school cowboys, and as brave a man as ever lived.

The night was very dark and a little chilly. One of the boys had put a lot of dry wood on the campfire, so that I could see the men there very plainly. It did not take them long to get out after being called, for all hands slept with their clothes on, and every rider kept his night horse close by, all saddled, every hour of the night. I started toward camp when I saw Frank advancing. He had thrown his bed blanket over his head and shoulders, Indian fashion, in place of an overcoat. As I passed him I said, "Frank, you will have to ride hard to hold the horses." He was blinded, he said, from having been so long in the light of the campfire; so I rode back with him and around the horses once or twice. At last he replied, "All right, Jim, I can see now, and I'll set 'em for a while." I started for camp again and, riding up to the campfire, swung down off my horse, with my rifle in my hand—for I had been carrying it, ready to shoot at a moment's notice, all the evening.

Just as my foot touched the ground, I heard a couple of dozen shots in quick succession. I turned my head and could see the flash from the guns. I fired one shot in the direction of the flashes. My horse had also turned his head when the shots

were fired. A bullet struck him in the forehead, and he went
down at my feet. I jumped away from that campfire as quickly
as possible and crawled under a big cedar tree, the branches
of which came very close to the ground. The next moment most
of the horse herd came tearing right through camp. We had
ropes stretched from the wagon wheels to some trees to make
a corral in which to catch horses, and the horses ran against
the ropes, upsetting the wagon.

Every man in camp ran for his life into the thicket. The
horses which were tied about near camp, all saddled, ran on
their ropes and broke them and decamped with the other animals—all save one horse. Some Indian had slipped into camp
before the firing started, cut the picket rope of this horse, and
led him away.

The horses ran into the cattle herd, and away went the cattle
into a big cedar brake containing many old dead trees. There
was a smashing and crashing and about as great an uproar as
any cowboy ever heard. The men with the cattle did not dare
yell at the animals or sing to them, lest Indians locate and slip
an arrow into somebody.

I lay quite still under the tree. After a time I heard Roberts's
voice calling out, "Don't let 'em get away with the horses, boys!
Stay with 'em! Come on, boys, where are you?" I do not know
where Roberts disappeared to when the horses stampeded
through camp, but he certainly went somewhere—for a few
minutes. I don't see, either, how he expected us to hold that
horse herd. One by one I could hear the boys answer him. I
did not like to get out from beneath that tree, but I did not
care to be called a coward, so I joined him, although I thought
it the most foolish thing we could possibly do. It was so dark
that an Indian could slip up within three feet of a man and
not be seen.

Frank Dennis not appearing, I made up my mind that he
had been killed. I said to Roberts, "Let's go and see if we can
find Frank. I know where he was riding, and I saw the shoot-

ing." We went and searched, but could find no trace of the missing cowboy. We then wandered about until daylight.

The men who had been with the cattle then came in, bringing some of the horses, and said that they had held the cattle and that the herd was then about half a mile from camp. I had my saddle, but several of our saddles, of course, were gone. So bareback riding was the order of the day for some of the men. I gave my saddle to Roberts.

About sunrise Frank Dennis came into camp. He was a little pale, but quite cheerful. He said, "Well, fellers, good morning; we had a very pleasant night of it, didn't we?" When he swung down from his horse, I saw that there was blood on his clothes, and that his hand was tied up in his handkerchief, which was soaked with blood. He then told us his story.

After I had left him, he rode around the herd a time or two. It seems that a large bunch of Indians had crawled up to within about fifteen feet of the line where he was riding, and as he passed they blazed away at him. He was so close to them, and looked so big, with a blanket wrapped about him, that I suppose they thought they could not help getting him, and that the firing would stampede the horses to boot. The redskins would then have run to their own horses, tied close at hand, mounted, and followed and secured our stampeded animals.

But their plans did not work very well. They succeeded in shooting a hole through the center of Frank's left hand, as well as in giving him two or three little flesh wounds and shooting about a dozen holes through his blanket and saddle. One shot tore the saddle horn off, and an arrow lodged between his saddle and saddle blanket. The horse herd had scattered in every direction after passing camp. Some ran into the cattle herd, where they were held by the boys with the herd, and one bunch of horses was chased up a cañon by the Indians for some distance. The horses were unable to get out of it because of the perpendicular bluffs, and the Indians were afraid to try to drive them back down the cañon, so they had to let the animals go. As it was, the savages got away with about a fourth of our horses.

Along in the middle of that afternoon, two buffalo hunters came into our camp on foot. They said the Indians had just run off all their horses, consisting of ten head. They wanted to get some horses from us, to follow the Indians and try to regain their captured stock. Roberts did not like to spare the horses, but said, "If any of you boys want to go with these men for a day or two, and see if you can get any of our horses, why, go ahead."

I wanted to go, for one. I was tired of being hunted, and I wanted to do some of the hunting myself. So three of us were allowed to go. We first went to the hunters' camp and took the trail of their horses, for we were sure that they would all be thrown together. Some of their horses were shod and could be trailed better than ours.

The Indians did not seem to think anyone would follow them, for after making off not more than about twenty miles, they went into camp. We located their position the first evening out and crawled up as close to it as possible. Here we waited for daylight. We not only wanted those horses, but we were all wild to get a shot at an Indian.

This band of Indians was doubtless striking for Old Mexico, for the members whom we found in camp were nearly all old women and men—about fourteen in all, as I recollect. Several of the young men and squaws had left these members of their party to take the stock to a safe place, while they took another spin around the country to see what more plunder they could accumulate.

The Indian camp was down by a spring in some willow brush, situated in a small valley that was almost a cañon, surrounded by quite high hills on three sides. During the night we crawled up as close to the camp as possible. Our horses were hidden over in another little valley behind us. Three of us went on the brow of the hill which looked down into the camp on one side of the valley, while the two buffalo hunters went on the other side.

The Indians had some of the horses hobbled and some picketed to willows about the edge of the thicket. Just as it was beginning to get light, we could see a stir in the camp, and presently one old Indian came out of his tepee and started to walk to the top of the hill behind their camp. One of our boys, named Bell, lying about fifty yards from me, could stand the strain no longer. Drawing as fine a bead as he could, he blazed away at the old buck. He struck that Indian in the dead center of his body, and the next minute Indians and squaws were running about in every direction. The hunters now opened fire with their old buffalo guns, and some of the Indians started toward us on foot.

One redskin came charging up the hill on a pony, straight toward the spot where I was lying. He was flattened out on his pony, hitting him at every jump with the end of a rawhide rope, the other end being fastened about his pony's lower jaw. One of the buffalo hunters opened fire on this Indian, and that made me lie low, for the bullets from his rifle were striking nearer to my hiding place than to the Indian. When the redskin came within a short distance of me, he suddenly turned to pass me. Not daring to rise up out of the buffalo wallow wherein I was lying, so as to get into a good shooting position, I took a pot shot at him as he passed me. My bullet broke the pony's back, just behind where the Indian was sitting. The pony went down, but the Indian went over its head, landing on his feet and continuing running. He dashed down into a bunch of willows in a little valley just behind me. I felt very uncomfortable where I was, for he had had a gun in his hand when he passed me, having hung to it when his horse fell.

Those of the Indians who had not been shot were by this time running down the valley. I ran down to their camp, yelling to the fellows not to shoot at me, and cut a lot of the horses loose from the willows. Among them was the night horse which had been stolen from our camp before the Indians fired on Frank Dennis. The saddle was still on its back. The other saddles which the Indians had captured from us had all been cut to pieces in their camp. The other horses were hobbling about in every direction, but I jumped into the saddle of the recaptured animal and soon rounded them up. We all got together and drove the entire bunch, Indian ponies and all, to the spot where our own animals were tied. We took some of the Indian saddles and blankets which had been left in camp, for we knew that squaw-saddles were better than none at all, and it was still quite a distance to any place where cowboy saddles could be purchased.

We had secured about fifteen head of Indian horses. We next went to the little valley where we had left our own animals before attacking the camp, and then lit out for the cattle herd and our own camp. We had secured nearly all of the horses lost by the buffalo hunters, as well as most of our own. The boys in camp were glad to see us, but we all felt that the proper thing to do next was to get out of that country as fast as possible. So we set sail on the long trail once more.

Frank Dennis was about the only man brave enough to laugh at our killing some of those Indians. He used to say nearly every day while dressing his wounded hand, "It will teach those red devils to take a joke." But I thought we had taught that band of Indians a lesson in what white men could and would do if driven to it.

We had no more trouble with Indians on that trip, and there were no more stampedes for some time. We were all glad when we reached Fort Griffin. Here we took on board a fresh lot of provisions, and all hands had a chance to go, a few at a time, to see the fort and procure clothing, tobacco, cartridges, and the much-needed saddles.

One rather amusing incident occurred here. In our outfit was a man named Jack Harris—a large, hungry-looking Texan, about forty years of age, and with a war record, I have no doubt.

This man had been having quite a lot of fun out of me all the way along the trail. He would ride up to me every chance he could get and, when very close, suddenly draw his six-shooter, cock it, and aim it at me, saying, "Are you the sheriff that is looking for me?" He would generally wind up by taking his revolver by the barrel, with his finger in the trigger guard, reaching the handle toward me, and saying, "I am tired of fighting; take my gun." Allowing some imaginary sheriff just about time to reach for it, he would reverse the weapon quick as a flash, cock it, and aim it straight in my face. He was doing this "for practice," he said, and I think he was, for I afterward found out that he could be a "bad man" in some places.

One day, just before we arrived at Fort Griffin, he played his little practice game on me. After he had put up his gun, I said, "Jack, don't practice on me any more."

"Why not?" he inquired.

"Because," was my answer, "it would be dangerous for you. If this sort of thing goes on, it is only a matter of time when you will let your thumb slip, and I will go dead, and you will be sorry; and I much prefer being killed purposely than accidentally. If you ever point your gun at me again, you had better pull it off, for I will surely kill you if I can."

He rode away, and we did not speak again for several days. In the meantime we arrived at Fort Griffin. Jack went up to the fort when his turn came, and when he came away he accidentally left his quirt in the sutler's store. He did not miss it until he had reached camp. He then said he would go and get it in the evening, as he was not on the first watch.

When the time came for him to go, I was on guard with the horses, and I had been warned by Roberts to keep a sharp lookout, as there were a lot of Tonkawa Indians living near Fort Griffin, and he was afraid they might try to steal the horses. Besides, there were several white horse thieves and noted desperadoes loafing about the post, gambling with the soldiers. I was holding the horses near the wagon, and the night was quite dark. Just as Harris was starting, I happened to be near the wagon, and I overheard him say, "Boys, I have a notion when I come back to slip up on Jim and fire a shot right close to him. I can scare him out of ten years' growth." Nobody said anything, and he rode off. But I made up my mind that a red-hot reception would await him if he tried any such trick on me.

After he had been gone a little while, I put the horse herd right between camp and the fort. Then I waited for him. In about an hour he returned, but he seemed to have changed his mind about the scare he was going to give me, for I could hear him whistling and singing as he came along in. The nearer to camp he came, the more noise he made. He suddenly rode into the horse herd before he saw it. When he observed that he was in the herd, he shouted, "Oh, Jim!" I slipped off my horse and kept quiet. Jack would ride a few feet, then stop and shout for me. In this way he kept working his way along until he was through the horses and almost in camp.

When he reached camp, the boys were all laughing at him, for he had awakened everybody. I had followed him, after he passed me, so I could hear what was said. When he picketed his horse, I heard one of the boys say, "What was the matter with you out there, Jack? You seemed to want to see Jim awful bad."

"Yes," was Harris' reply, "that little devil is out there asleep somewhere, and if he was to wake up suddenly and see or hear anyone near him, he is just about fool enough to shoot without saying a thing."

"That's about the size of it," I heard Jim Roberts say. "And any little ideas you may have in the way of Indian scares for Jim, you had better let go of."

In the morning, at breakfast, Jack said to me, "Where were you last night when I came back from the post?"

"I was on guard with the horses, loaded for anything dangerous that might come along," was my reply.

"Well, son," he returned, "I won't bother you any more, and we will be friends."

47

From that time on to the end of the trip, we got along all right.

This first year that I was on the trail, every rider from the Red River to the Arkansas was "big swimming," as the boys termed it. We were fortunate in having no serious accidents, but we lost a number of both cattle and horses by drowning. We had some bad hail- and thunderstorms. Sometimes we went for days at a stretch with scarcely a wink of sleep, because of winds and rain, which made the cattle hard to control. In some places on the trail the country would become very boggy after a long rainy spell, and we had to resort to all sorts of schemes to snatch a little sleep when an opportunity presented itself. When three riders could get away at a time, they would go a little way from the cattle and dismount, each man holding his horse by the bridle rein. Then they would lie down in the form of a triangle, each man using his neighbor's ankles for a pillow. In this manner the sleepers' heads were up out of the mud and water.

Sometimes a rider would go to sleep while jogging around the herd. There was a limit to the endurance of even a rough rider. I have been so close to that limit that on one or two occasions I would get a little piece of chewing tobacco from one of the men and, mixing it with saliva, would rub it on my eyelids. This is great treatment when the thoughts seem to be all bent on having a nap. It could well be called a rouser. One eye, also one ear, had to be kept open when trying to sleep about these great herds. At any moment a rider was likely to have to spring into the saddle and ride hard, should the herd suddenly stampede in his direction; or, if the herd ran in any other direction, he must hear the rumble and clatter of hoofs and horns, and make haste, or he would not locate the herd in time to be of any assistance that night.

I think I can understand how men whose spirits are fired by patriotism in time of war will stand all sorts of privations and hardships, as well as the most intense suffering, such as was en-

dured at Valley Forge, and at times during the war of the rebellion; but what spirit fired and sustained the boys who drove
the trail herds during the times of which I write is more than
I can explain. I remember hardly an instance, and I think there
were actually very few if any, in which men proved themselves
to be quitters. To hold on to the stock seemed to be the first
consideration with all engaged in the work.

There are rough spots in the lives of all who have lived in
the open, whether the life be that of soldier, sailor, or plainsman; but I think that the wild and wooly cow waddie received
about as many rough knocks as anybody living on the sunset
side of the Mississippi. During the storms the cattle and horses
would stampede, and to stay with them we had to ride as fast
as a horse could run. Sometimes it would be so dark that a
rider could not see his horse's head. Then a flash of lightning
would come, and we could see the cattle tearing madly along
and locate their position. The next moment one would again
be blinded by the flash. Many were the hard falls the boys had
to take when a horse went down while running after stampeded
stock on those dark and stormy nights. Many were the poor old
"leather-breeches" who came dragging themselves into camp
the morning after a bad night, either with broken bones or
carrying their saddles on their backs, because their horses had
fallen and broken a neck or a leg. And I know personally a few
of the boys who had to be left by the side of the long trail to
wait for the call of the great trumpeter Gabriel, because of
those terrible runs at night.

When the weather was bad we scarcely got enough to eat,
for when it rained almost a week at a stretch, the only fuel we
had on those great prairies, "buffalo chips," would become so
wet that we could sometimes not get enough dry ones to boil
a little coffee, let alone bake bread. But when the weather was
fine and we had plenty of rest and food, I enjoyed cowboy life
thoroughly, and at such a time I would not have exchanged
places with the Prince of Wales.

All the way along, on this first drive, I had killed plenty of game, which I enjoyed very much. On beautiful warm moonlight nights when I was riding around those immense herds, I would say to myself, "This is the life!" My night horse and I became great friends. I always picked my best horse for a night animal and used him every night when on guard. My horses almost seemed to know what I was thinking about, and they seemed to share my feelings. When I felt in a merry mood, they seemed to feel the same way; on dark, stormy nights when the cattle were likely to jump and make one of their terrible runs at any minute, and everyone was keyed up with excitement, I could feel my horse trembling under me; and occasionally, when standing still, I could hear his heart thumping with excitement.

5

Wild Mustangs

ABOUT THE MIDDLE OF THE SUMMER we arrived at Abilene, Kansas. Here the cattle, and such of the saddle horses as were not needed for the return trip to the land of chaparral, were in a short time sold to northern buyers. "Us boys" were mighty glad to get a chance for a whole night's sleep. After resting the horses a few days, we started on our homeward trip. We rode back over the old Chisholm Trail, and by Fort Worth to San Antonio. After reaching San Antonio, I purchased a good outfit for working in the brush, and we rode out to Charlie Slaughter's ranch on the Ceibolo Creek, in La Salle County. I was soon at work again in the cow camps, gathering wild cattle to be sent up to the northern states and territories. I now felt that I had made a good start toward knowing something about life in the saddle and working with longhorn cattle. I did not come in contact with Longworth again.

Little bands of southern and Mexican Comanche Indians still infested the country, and it was still a refuge for bad white men. Captain McNally of the State Rangers at times came out into the brushland in search of desperadoes or Indians. On several occasions I made little trips with his command, guiding them to some camp or corral in the Frio and Nueces River country, with which I was familiar. I did this when the Rangers had reason to think they would be able to locate the person whom they were after. I picked up a few extra dollars by this work, Mr. Slaughter being willing for me to render any possible aid to state officers. I did not at that time realize that in doing this work I should incur the enmity of numerous white men with whom I was going to be associated. Around the camp-fires I heard of the brave deeds of John Wesley Hardin, King

Fisher, Ben Thompson, and other great gun-fighters who were at that time apparently enjoying their lives. Well-dressed and -equipped strangers who rode into our camps were shown all sorts of favors if they needed them. A man on a good horse, wearing a Mexican sash about his waist, and packing a pair of ivory-handled six-shooters, would have no trouble getting something to eat in anybody's cow camp. He was welcomed without question—and if Rangers were known to be near, he would soon be warned of the fact.

Just after Christmas that year I was on a cow hunt, and we were driving some wild cattle to a corral, the caporal riding ahead as usual. Suddenly shots were fired near him, and back he came right into the herd, yelling, "Indians! Look out, boys!" Numerous bullets and arrows came our way. I turned my horse and dashed for a catclaw thicket near by. A bullet from behind me and a little to one side struck my horse just behind the ear, dropping him instantly under full speed. I was thrown over his head with great force, my head striking the trunk of a large tree. I remember seeing a display of fireworks. Then I heard a voice call out, "Are you hurt, Jim?" I had my gun in my hand, for at the first alarm I had pulled it from the scabbard. Trying to stagger to my feet, I heard someone call out, "Get down and lie low!" I did so. I presently recovered and, looking about me, saw one of the men who had been with the herd. He had run his horse into the thicket and, jumping off, dropped down to fight for his life. He told me that when I struck the tree, close to where he lay, I had rolled over and risen up onto my knees, with my gun clutched in my hand. After crawling on my knees for a few moments, I had risen to my feet. The Indians did not follow us into that thicket, and we neither saw nor heard more of them that day.

We lost our entire herd of cattle on that trip. My back was so badly injured by that fall that it was a long time before I could again ride with comfort. Having no one to go to for sympathy, I could only figure that "the hair of the dog was good for the bite," and keep going. I have proved to my entire satisfaction that sometimes when a person is young and disgustingly robust, he can stand some pretty hard knocks and make quick and seemingly complete recovery. I would not advise that kind of header, however, for I am sure that it would not take many of them to wear a person out.

During that winter I saw a new business spring up in southwestern Texas. There were at that time hundreds of bands of mustangs ranging western Texas and the Plains country as far north, at least, as the heads of the Loup River in Nebraska. (I have never seen them farther north.) These horses were descendants of the animals brought over into Mexico from Spain by the early Spanish conquerors; at least, our greatest scholars have thought that the true mustangs of the Plains originated from the stock of "Moorish barb" horses which Cortez and other Spanish explorers brought to Mexico in the sixteenth century. During the numerous exploring expeditions of the early Spaniards, one of which extended as far north as the region now occupied by Kansas and Nebraska, no doubt some of the horses used by the explorers escaped from time to time. Stampedes might be caused by storms, or by sight of the herds of bison likely to come thundering by. Probably at times tired, thirsty horses strayed away from their owners and became lost in their efforts to find water or grass. In this way horses doubtless were scattered over the plains between three and four hundred years ago, and they multiplied.

At the time of which I write, 1870 to 1880, there were thousands of these inbred, beautiful little horses living on the ranges of the West, in the vast country that lies between the valley of the Mississippi River and the Rocky Mountain region. They were true mustangs, named by the inhabitants of Mexico. Their average weight was about eight hundred pounds, I think. The colors that predominated among them were cream, buckskin, and mouse-color. A few black stripes about the legs above the knees, or hocks, and a black stripe along the middle of the back, extending from the mane to the tail, were common markings. The stallions, although they usually had rather heavy manes, did not have a shaggy appearance. They were clean-limbed, and their hoofs were black and perfect, as a rule. Never having known the taste of grain, and deriving their food entirely from the native grasses and forage plants, they certainly were hardy. They could stand more hard riding with no other food than that which they could rustle when turned loose, than any breed of horses with which I have ever had experience, either on the Plains or in the mountains. As blacksmiths or "hoofshapers" never had tinkered with their feet or forced them to wear iron shoes, their hoofs were strong and would stand wear over the roughest kind of mountain trails.

I have seen many bands of mustangs on the Plains as far north as the head of the Loup River, Nebraska. North of that point I have never seen any; neither have I heard from any of the old white trappers or the Indians who lived in that country that they ever saw any. When the wagon roads were made across the Plains to California and to the various army posts that were established in the West, horses and mules escaped from the wagon trains occasionally and joined the bands of mustangs. Strange as it may seem, the well-broken, gentle horses and mules which joined the bands of mustangs and lived with them for a few months or years became, if such a thing could be, more wild and watchful than the mustangs. I am quite sure that a few old long-headed army mules I have noted ranging with bands of mustangs were about the most wisely wild creatures it has ever been my good fortune to see. Back in Missouri or some other state, or under the gentle care of some expert government mule skinner, they had acquired a knowledge of men and their ways. Their extremely delicate sense of smell enabled them to scent a man at long range, especially one who carried about with him a large halo from an old pipe or "chawing plug."

After one of these mules had lived in the open with the

mustangs for a few months, the slightest scent of a man at any minute, night or day, would cause it to snort in such a wildly terrifying manner that the entire band of mustangs would stampede, running perhaps forty miles at topmost speed, before they could get control enough of their courage to look back to see what had caused the excitement. I have observed that both mustangs and range horses have a keen sense of smell and are able to scent the trail made by horses with which they have been associated, following it rapidly over ground where a man could see no sign that horses had passed.

One thing for which the mustangs had to be on the lookout at all times was the big wolf, or "lobo." This cowardly pest was ever hungry for a taste of horseflesh. Animals weakened or crippled from any cause, or very young colts, were easy prey if the wolf could but sneak up and cut their hamstrings with his sharp teeth before the defenders in the band saw him. For the strong, active mare or stallion a wolf might show some respect: a thoroughly enraged horse, fighting with its teeth, striking lightning-like blows with its forefeet, and playing a double tattoo with its heels, is no plaything for even a pack of wolves to tackle.

Stallions and mares which escaped from emigrant and freighting wagon trains on their way across the Plains, and intermingled with the mustangs, caused the heretofore purebred mustangs to become gradually more and more scarce. By 1880 almost all had disappeared from the Plains, and the few mustangs remaining today are to be found only among the herds of Indian ponies on some reservation where the breeding-up process to get larger horses with which to haul freight or till the soil has not been rigidly enforced. Now and then a pony having the conformation, coloring, and marking of the mustang may yet be obtained from the older Indians, who have long known the good qualities of the mustangs. In a few places so-called "wild horses" may be found, but they are not the original breed of mustangs. They are bands of range-bred horses gone wild or spoiled, usually by someone's bad management—or luck—when trying to corral them. A sudden scare at the entrance to the corral will make horses turn and try to run back onto the range. Should they succeed in one attempt, they will be hard to corral afterward, and if they break back from the corral two or three times, they become a pretty badly spoiled lot of horses. But they must not be confused with mustangs.

In the early seventies a number of men were making a business of catching bands of mustangs to sell in the states to the east and north. The method employed in the capture was as follows. In some thicket a little back from the edge of the prairie, large circular corrals were built, high and strong, of heavy posts set in the ground and bound together with green rawhide thongs. The entrance led into a chute or passageway, wide at the outer end and narrowing toward the inner, where not more than three horses could pass through abreast. This type of entrance prevented the horses from escaping in a rush for the gateway when they found themselves trapped, before the heavy bar poles could be put up and securely lashed. From the outside of the entrance to the corral, on either side, were built wings extending in the shape of a large **V**. For a short distance out from the corral these wings, which often extended for a quarter of a mile or more, were made very strong and so high that a horse could not jump over. Then both wings and entrance were concealed by green brush.

When the corral and its wings were in readiness, a lot of riders, widely separated and moving in a half-circle, rode out of the timber and chaparral on the side of the prairie where the horses ranged. The horses, of course, fled before them. The riders at the end of the half-circle then made straight for the ends of the wings of the corral, while the rest of the riders kept the mustangs running toward the corral and prevented them from turning back. The riders drew nearer and nearer together as they approached the corral. As soon as the mustangs were well within the wings, their pursuers closed in on them, yelling and firing their pistols; whereupon the leaders among the mustangs, on the lookout for any little opening in the green thicket, rushed through the opening at the narrow end of the chute—only to find themselves hopelessly trapped.

The fright of these horses can be imagined. They rushed frantically around and around the corral. Sometimes they all made for one side, piling up so thickly that those which were farthest back when the rush started could climb up over those trampled down in front. When a hundred or more were down and piled up close to the corral fence, some escaped by jumping from the pile of struggling horses over the top of the corral. By this method of capture many hundreds of horses were maimed and many killed.

When the horses were securely corralled, the riders generally went to camp and let the terror-stricken animals settle down for a few hours. Then they returned to the corral, and the real scare for the horses took place, for the terrible-looking creatures who had driven them into that awful pen now climbed down from the top of the circle of posts into the corral with them. As the mustangs would be somewhat exhausted by their previous attempts to escape, they soon became a panting, foaming, almost breathless mass of horses. Sometimes the old stallions showed fight, in which case they were promptly shot. Lassos were then brought into play. The horses were lassoed by the feet and thrown down, and either strong rawhide hobbles or clogs were placed on their front legs.

Hobbles for horses are in common use at this date in many parts of the West, but I never have heard of clogs for horses being used in any part of the West other than the brush country of southwestern Texas. These clogs were made by taking strong forked sticks about an inch and a half or two inches in diameter and about two feet in length, and lashing them with rawhide thongs on to the front leg of a horse. With these the animal could make little headway when he tried to run. Like a hobbled horse, he soon became very tired of trying to go at speed.

When all the horses which were neither killed nor injured had been hobbled or clogged, they were usually left in the corral until they were pretty hungry and thirsty. Then the bar poles were taken down and the horses allowed to work their way out of the corral through the narrow chute and into the wings. These wings usually took in some little water hole, or the end of a creek, where the horses could drink. Riders frightened them back if they tried to work beyond the mouth of the wings of the corral for the first day or two. Gradually they were allowed to work their way out onto the prairie to graze during the daytime. At night they were driven back into the corral. After a few days of this treatment, the hobbles and clogs were removed from those horses which were most subdued. At the end of a few weeks the entire herd would be freed from hobbles and clogs, having become so accustomed to control by riders as to be driven in any direction desired.

I never took any part in "mustang hunts" of this type, but I watched the performance a few times. It was certainly a pretty cruel business. During the later days when I hunted big game in Colorado and Wyoming Territory, a hunting partner of mine, best known as Wild Horse Charlie, was, I think, the first man to make a business of catching mustangs on a larger scale, on the open plains. He called his method "walking them down." In the spring of 1876, he captured several bands of mustangs on the plains of eastern Colorado, driving them into Nebraska and Iowa, where they were sold as saddle or driving ponies. In his method he took three or four good riders and made a camp on the range of the mustangs, at a time when advantage could be taken of moonlight for the work. From some good observation point, a rider would then locate a band of horses with his field glasses. Bright and early in the morning the work of capturing the horses would begin. Mustangs have a habit of settling on a range. When possible, they confine their feeding and their flights from danger to certain boundary lines. This fact is well known to plainsmen.

Upon discovering a band of mustangs, a rider approaches them from a direction opposite to that in which he desires the horses to run. As the mustangs have wonderful sight and are always on the lookout for danger, they take to their heels as soon as the rider comes into view. This rider does not race after them but follows fast enough to keep them in sight. The other riders, stationed at as good observation points as possible, note the direction in which the mustangs start to circle, in order that each rider in turn may be relieved every few hours during the long chase. At the end of a few hours, the first man to start after the horses is relieved by another rider. He can then go to camp, change his tired saddle horse for a fresh one, and get a little rest. This relay system, continued night and day, never allowing the mustangs to stop for either food or drink, will, at the end of a few days, exhaust them so that the riders can approach and begin to control the turning of the mustangs in any direction desired. Naturally the riders keep them as close to their camp as possible.

The mustangs cover many miles of ground during the first two or three days of the chase—a distance of one hundred miles for each twenty-four hours is not an exaggerated estimate. On about the seventh or eighth day of the chase, or sooner on some occasions, the aged or weaker mustangs, completely exhausted, play out and stop, or some of the aged stallions turn on their pursuers for a fight. Such stallions are shot by the riders, and the exhausted animals lassoed, hobbled, or "sidelined." Sidelining means tying together the front and hind foot on one side of an animal with a pair of hobbles to prevent it from traveling at speed. At the end of the tenth day after the chase begins, the wild horses are under such control that they can be driven to some strong cattle corral in the country.

A third method of capture is by "creasing." This is used to capture individual mustangs considerd especially valuable because of their beauty, color, conformative marking, or because they show unusual speed. This method has been more talked about than successfully carried out.

To crease a horse, a person must first get within close shooting distance of this most animated target. He must then place a rifle bullet in the top of its neck, grazing the cords of the neck just enough to stun the animal and knock it down so that it can be tied down before recovering from the shock. One must be not only a mighty good shot, but extremely lucky, to make a success of this method; it is very easy either to break the neck of the animal, simply give it a bad scare and a slight wound, or score a clean miss.

I tried it once, but I never attempted to crease a second mustang. While engaged in the work of gathering wild cattle, I caught sight, on numerous occasions, of a small band of mustangs led by one of the handsomest stallions I have ever seen. He was cream-colored, with white mane and tail. His mane was parted and hung equally heavy on both sides of his neck. He had a black stripe down the middle of his back, and also one around his legs. I discovered that this band of horses was in the habit of drinking from a little pool so located in a washout of an old creek bed that it could be approached from only one side, three sides of the washout having high perpendicular banks. These creek banks leading to the water hole made wings that were probably about one hundred and fifty feet long. I conceived the idea that if I could hide in the vicinity of this watering place until all the horses, coming to drink, should be in the narrow runway leading to the water, I could dash up to the mouth of the runway and, as the horses rushed past me in making their escape, crease the desired stallion with my six-shooter. At that time I considered myself hard to beat, either mounted or on foot, in the use of the six-shooter.

After weeks of waiting, an opportunity to try out my scheme at last arrived. While out hunting for some saddle horses which had strayed from our camp, I saw this band trailing toward the water hole. Keeping out of sight, I beat them to the place. I concealed myself and my horse in a dense chaparral thicket about one hundred yards from the mouth of the runway through which the horses would go to get a drink. The horses must have felt that there was no danger, for they rushed in a bunch down the runway and into the water, where they made such a noise splashing and pawing about that they did not hear me approach. They certainly got up some action in getting past me when I rode into the runway. As the stallion came rushing madly by, passing within ten feet of me, I made an attempt to crease him. The result was that I broke his neck. At first I thought I had been successful, but when I saw what I had done I could have cried. Perhaps I did; I certainly felt very sorry to have taken the life of that beautiful creature. I realized then that had I thought to use my lasso instead of my six-shooter, he would either have escaped or been mine. Seldom would one find a band of mustangs in such a natural trap with an opportunity to use either lasso or pistol at such short range. I never made another attempt to crease a mustang.

Some writers have told us of certain tribes of Mexican Indians who were possessed of such speed that, starting out on foot, they could run down and capture the mustang. I have been told about both white men and Indians who, on foot, had run down, killing or capturing, many wild animals, including antelope, deer, and mustangs. I can understand how a man trained to the work of trailing or tracking game could follow an animal for an indefinite length of time, provided the course followed by the animal led over such ground as to make tracking practicable. Unless a man did depend largely upon his tracking ability, he would have to lope along at a lively clip for the first forty-eight hours of his chase after a mustang, or else he would lose sight of his game. At least, he would if the mustang acted in the manner of those pursued by horsemen.

One morning while riding in search of our saddle horses, I found among the animals a young mustang stallion. He was standing with his head down, fast asleep. He had evidently been run out of some band by older stallions, for he was all bitten up. I rode within twenty feet of him, and as he did not awaken, I could see a chance of securing him easily. I took my rope down quietly from the horn of my saddle and threw a loop over his head. When the rope struck him he certainly woke up and wanted to leave me! But no, his wild horse days were over. He was a beauty. I had to choke him down before I could get to him; then I hastily put a "war bridle" on him, made of rope, and in a short time had him broken to lead. I took him to camp, broke him to a picket rope, and soon broke him to ride. He became a great pet and proved to be one of the best horses I ever owned.

A typical mustang, descended from the old Moorish Barb horses.

*Cow horses in action. A determined steer is trying to
break back into the bunch.*

Right to left: Doc Middleton, notorious outlaw of the Black Hills region; Chippy Lampson, ranch owner, traveler, and hunter; and the roundup cook. Note the Dutch ovens in the foreground and part of an old stagecoach in the background. Taken at Agate, Nebraska, about 1900.

6

Tornado on the Trail

THAT WINTER the Indians seemed to be more active than usual, and, not long after the incident in which my horse was killed under me, we were again waylaid. This time I did not fare quite so luckily. I happened to get pretty close to one Indian, and, as I whirled my horse around at the first sound of shooting, he drove a dogwood arrow into the calf of my leg. I did not wait for any more but took that one to camp as soon as possible. As I had several miles to ride through cactus and brush and did not know at what moment I might run into more Indians, I put in rather an unhappy time during that ride. When I did reach camp, some of the stampeded riders were there. They soon helped me from the saddle and, holding me, extracted the arrow by main force. It had been driven through my heavy chaps and boot top into the muscles and cords of my leg. To cut away the leggin and boot top about the arrow was a minor operation, but the rest of it was far different. I think I must have been sorry I ran off with that Indian's arrow, for I remember that I cried when my Mexican friends took the shaft from my leg, and I had a chill or two which I can also still remember. I was afraid the arrow might be poisoned, for I had heard many tales about how the Lipan Indians poisoned their war arrows. The Mexicans split some cactus leaves, burned the thorns off, heated them thoroughly, and bound them on my leg. They also took pepper berries and inserted them in the wound.

I was so nervous with worrying about poison that I struck out for San Antonio that night, following the old Laredo trail, a distance of about a hundred and thirty miles. Shock, worry, and pain all aided, I think, in making me dizzy and sick during that long ride. I got two changes of horses at ranches on the way. When I reached San Antonio, I went to Dr. Herf, or Hurf, who was considered the best surgeon there by the people whom I knew. He gave me kind treatment and care and soon had me braced up. I remember his saying to me, "Why, boy, when anyone has lived the life you do and has no bad habits, you can't kill him with an axe." In a couple of weeks he told me I would be safe in going back to camp, provided I followed his directions in regard to dressing the wound. I returned to camp with a lighter heart and was soon crashing my way through the mesquite after cattle again.

When the first of March came along, I was ready to go up the trail again, and did so. We had no trouble with Indians on that trip, but it was an interesting one just the same. It rained and poured, and then rained some more, seemingly from the very start, until we reached the Kansas line. We had to swim nearly every stream and make a raft out of the wagon box (and anything else we could get hold of that would float) in order to get our provisions over.

When we reached the Canadian River in the Indian Territory, we had an experience with a tornado which I should not care to repeat. We were camped on the south side of the river, waiting for it to subside a bit before attempting to cross. About noon one day we could see that we were in for a bad storm. I had never seen such queer-looking clouds before. They seemed to be all rushing toward the center of the heavens, and we could hear a steady, sullen roar which seemed to come from every direction. We hastily staked the wagon to the ground as tightly as possible and lashed the wagon sheet down with extra ropes.

I was on herd with the horses. Everybody but the cook and myself went to the cattle herd. I was herding the horses a short distance from the wagon. We were as nearly ready as possible when a few hailstones began to strike about us. A few minutes later we were struck by a truly awful blast of wind, hailstones, and water. The horse herd was not hobbled. They stampeded, and I raced ahead of them, trying to check them. The air was now so thick with hail and water that I could not see ten feet ahead. The hail was hammering my head so fiercely that I seemed to see fire. I put one arm over my head until my hand and arm had been pelted as much as they could stand, and then changed to the other.

Suddenly we came to a gulch about fifteen feet deep. The banks were not quite perpendicular, but they were steep enough. I could neither stop nor turn my horse. One hundred badly stampeded horses were at my heels. Over we went! My horse struck on his feet but slipped and fell into the middle of the gulch. The horse herd all came over, tumbling about me. I managed to hold my horse until the herd had all passed. The hail was striking me in the face and on my hands, and raising blood blisters. I could not hold my horse longer, and he jerked away from me and went with the storm, but he did not overtake the other horses.

By this time the water was coming down the little gulch in which I was lying, and I had to get out of the way quickly or be drowned, for, in a very few minutes, the water was seven or eight feet deep. When I crawled to the top of the bank, I drifted with the storm, walking about a quarter of a mile out to a very level country. I was now in water and ice nearly to my knees. My head, face, and hands were one solid bruise, and I was played out. I made up my mind that my time had come, and that probably all the rest of the boys had been killed. The roar of the storm was awful. Every minute I expected some large hailstone to knock me senseless, and I knew that I should drown if knocked down. All I could do was to stand there, waiting for the end, praying one minute for the Lord to save me and wondering the next if my body would ever be found.

Suddenly the storm passed by, and I found myself standing in ice water about two feet in depth. I could not see land in any direction. I was shaking with the cold and could scarcely stand.

Finally I began to walk—or rather to wade—about, trying to warm myself a little. The water went down rapidly, and I soon found places where I could get out of it. When the storm had cleared away so that I could see a mile or two, I observed a high hill and struck out for it, hoping to be able to see something from its top, for I had no idea in which direction the camp lay. From the top of this hill I could see the timber along the Canadian River, and then I knew about where the wagon was. I started for the river, but could not see either a hoof of cattle or a horse in any direction. I walked along slowly, wondering if everybody else had been killed and what I should do. Going over a little hill, I saw some object lying on the prairie about half a mile from me. I could not make out what it was at first, but I kept watch as I walked toward it, and finally I saw it move.

I soon saw that it was a man. And, you may believe, I was glad to see him. He saw me and came to meet me. It proved to be one of my companions, and it was a happy meeting.

He had been with the cattle when the storm burst, and was riding an outlaw (spoiled horse), giving one of his better mounts a rest. He knew that the first hailstones which struck that horse would start the animal bucking, and that he could do nothing toward helping to hold the herd. When the first hailstones began to fall, he dismounted, unsaddled the horse, and tried to hold him, but the animal soon jerked away. The cowboy at once put the saddle over his head and shoulders for protection and squatted down on the prairie to wait for better weather. He happened to dismount in a little valley—rather a poor place to wait for the clouds to roll by, for in a very few minutes after he had fixed himself comfortably under his saddle and saddle blankets, about six feet of water came down the valley! Therefore, he had to keep backing up the hill against the storm, trying to shelter his head with the saddle, but not succeeding very well. He was badly hammered by the hail, but not so much as I.

We went on to camp and found the cook safe, but with an

experience of his own to relate. We went down to the timber, dragged some wood to camp, built a fire, made a big pot of coffee, and dried our clothing. After a while one of the boys from the cattle herd came into camp and said the cattle were all right and that none of the boys had been killed. The cattle had stampeded and run several miles, passing right through a big camp of Cheyenne Indians, adding, no doubt, to the terrors of their situation. The storm circled, the cattle at last got out of it, and the stampede was stopped. The rider who gave us the information had been sent in to see what had become of the wagon and horses.

Being by this time ready to report for duty, I took the saddle horse ridden by this man and rode to a high hill near by to see if I could discover any of our horses. I could discern a large band of horses, but, as they were in a nearly opposite direction from that taken by our stampeding animals, I felt sure that they could not be ours. However, I thought I might be able to drive these animals into our camp, thus getting mounts with which we could hunt our own. But when I reached these animals, I saw that they were indeed our horses. The storm had driven them in almost a complete circle.

I had found out what a tornado could do and how it felt to be caught in the edge of one. In the center of its pathway, which was not over a quarter of a mile from our wagon and where the timber grew along the Canadian River, great trees had been torn out by the roots and piled into tangled masses, some of them being carried several hundred feet. Many little willows growing on the river bottom were still rooted to the ground, but the bark was twisted and stripped from them. Had the center of that tornado struck our outfit, I think there would have been a badly scrambled lot of horses, cattle, and cowboys, with a small amount of trail cook and camp wagon thrown in for good measure, lying about somewhere in the Indian Territory. The strip of country covered by the destructive portion of this tornado was, I believe, about half a mile in width. The hail lay in drifts three feet deep in the low places. Thousands of prairie dogs and little prairie-dog owls, as well as rabbits and rattlesnakes, had been drowned out of their holes and chilled or beaten to death by the hail. Even the grass was smashed off at the roots and washed away in the drifts of hailstones. Luck, or Divine Providence, was with us on that occasion, for material substance, even such as saltpeter, would, I fear, have been of but little assistance.

When we reached Kansas we found the cow towns ready to receive us. Branch trails led to Newton, Abilene, Ellsworth, and Great Bend. These towns were lively places, at least during the trail-cattle season. Quite a large percentage of their population consisted of gamblers and tough women during the busy season. Buffalo hunters and freighters, sometimes emigrants and soldiers, aided by the arrival of a few hundred cowboys, would soon make almost any town nothing less than lively, to say the least. Everybody—except the clergy—either packed a gun or two or else kept them within mighty close reach. All disputes of any importance just had to be settled by a gun- or knife-fight. "A man or two for breakfast" was not considered a very uncommon event. The dance halls and gambling resorts were the breeding places of most of the troubles that led to manslaughter, aided by the firewater dispensed over the numerous bars.

After the cattle which we had driven up the trail that season were disposed of, I returned to southern Texas and again worked for the Slaughter boys for a time. I then secured a more lucrative position with an old cattleman named Bishop. I went from San Antonio with Mr. Bishop and received a bunch of cattle which he had purchased not far from Indianola. I held them until his trail foreman, a man named Burton, came down from Erath County with a crowd of cowboys, and then I turned the cattle over to him. Mr. Bishop wanted me to stay and help Burton get the cattle branded and drive them out of the brush country. I did so, and I shall never forget that bunch of cattle. They proved to be the very worst animals to stampede that I ever dealt with.

After we had them all branded, we started to drive them out of the brush. The very first night they stampeded, and I was about the only man with the cattle when daylight came, for Burton's cowboys, and even Burton himself, had never run wild cattle in the timber, cactus, and chaparral, and they were afraid to let their horses run. Burton's horse fell and got away from him. The cattle happened to stick together that night, or I could not have stayed with them all. The next day I persuaded Burton to hire some Mexicans who were used to working with stock in the brush, but in spite of all we could do, we lost about six hundred head before we got the herd to a prairie country where there was a big corral into which we could drive them nights. Mr. Bishop came to us here and wanted Burton and me to go back into the brush and see if we could locate any of the lost cattle. Leaving the cattle herd in charge of one of the cowboys, we hired some Mexicans and started, Mr. Bishop telling me that if I would gather those cattle he would give me charge of one of the pastures into which he and a partner were putting cattle. We took a couple of pack horses with us, and for about three weeks we had a regular picnic in that brush.

The cattle had got away from us when we were camped at the forks of a river, and we went there and established a camp. Fortunately we had bobbed the hair off the tail ends of these cattle when branding them, and by this mark we could distinguish them at some little distance from the other wild cattle running in the brush. We caught quite a number of the animals the first week. By that time all the others were mixed with the wild cattle, and we had to rope nearly all which were caught. We found most of the cattle, but we nearly wore our horses out doing it.

Several times when I had been riding after the cattle, I had noticed a band of saddle horses. They had gone wild and could not be driven into a corral. I had observed that nearly every day this particular bunch of animals would stand under the shade of a mesquite tree that stood by itself out in the middle of a little prairie. These horses were all very fat, and I thought how nice it would be if I could catch one of them to ride, so as to give my horse a chance to rest. One morning I took my rope and walked out to this little prairie, which was only about half a mile from camp. I climbed into the tree and, after making a loop in one end of my rope and tying the other end to a big limb, I waited for the horses to come, so that I might try to snare one of them. I waited and waited for hours. At last, just as I was about ready to give up the scheme, I saw the horses come in sight. They ambled over to the tree where I was waiting, after they had walked over every other spot on that little prairie about ten times. I did not dare move, for fear of frightening them, and I was so badly cramped when they did come that I could scarcely move. The horses did not have the slightest idea of danger from such a source.

When they were directly under me I looked them all over and picked out what I considered the best-looking animal in the bunch. I waited until his head was under me. Then I tipped up the edge of the loop slightly and let it drop. The rope was about forty feet long. I had to laugh to see how that horse jumped when the rope struck him. I had dropped the loop over his head, and the moment it touched him he gave a tremendous jump and snort and away he went. I did not laugh long: I was standing on the limb to which the rope was tied, and when the horse came to the end of it, away went the limb, broken off right at the trunk of the tree. I was not thinking about that part of my little snare trick; I was so tickled to note the surprise of the horses that I did not think of anything else. I went to the ground like a rock. It was my turn to be surprised, and I received a pretty hard fall. I was very glad that no one saw me. The horse which I had roped ran into the heavy timber near by, and I followed the trail of the limb he was dragging. He soon wound himself up, and I walked up to him. After working with him a few minutes, I put a noose over his nose and lower jaw and led him to camp. When I arrived I put one of the Mexicans on him, for I had had fun enough for one day. The horse bucked a little, but soon gave up, and he proved to be a good cow horse. I rode him until we left that country, and then turned him loose to run wild again.

When we had secured all of the Bishop cattle which it would pay to bother with, we took them to the main herd. Mr. Bishop was waiting for us, and he took me to the Dell DeWeese pasture at Esperansas Lakes and gave me charge of the pasture. I had two men to assist me, and, as we had very little to do, I had plenty of time to hunt. I killed a great many musk hogs, one armadillo, several deer, and a great many wild turkeys.

I made two trips to San Antonio, and on one of them I took a run over to Galveston for a few days. About the middle of February, Mr. Bishop came out to the pasture. He told me that Mac Stewart was to take one of the herds north for him, and that I might go with him if I so desired. I was very glad of the chance to go, and to be again with my old caporal. Stewart came to the pasture in a few days, and we went to another place called the Indian Bend pasture, on the Nueces River, where we gathered a herd and rolled out. After starting, about two hundred of those cattle with which Burton and I had had such a time were put into our herd, and they spoiled all the others. They would sometimes stampede several times in a single night, and they kept this up all the way up the trail. By the time we had driven to the Indian Territory, we were all about played out. It had been raining a great deal, and we had lost a lot of sleep.

One night we had a terrible storm and were up all night. It rained all the next day, and we were with the cattle again all that night. The rain continued the following day, and when night fell every old cowboy in the outfit—that is, those over thirty years of age—quit the herd and went to camp, where they lay down in the mud. They said they could not stand it any

71

more and must have rest. The only ones who stayed with Mac Stewart (for he was with the cattle all the time and would have fallen dead from his saddle before he would ever have let them get away from him) were three very young cowboys named Charley Dyer, Bert Helbert, and Addison Spaugh, and myself. I could scarcely keep myself awake at all and would even go to sleep riding along, in spite of myself. At last I went to the wagon, got a piece of tobacco from the cook, and repeated my old trick of rubbing some of the spittle on my eyelids and into my eyes. By thus torturing myself I kept going. The cattle were so nearly worn out by this time that they could not run, but kept drifting about all night. In the morning the sun came out warm and bright, and the cattle, after grazing a while, all lay down to rest. We had had very little to eat for a good many hours, as we had little fire, the buffalo chips being soaked and useless. One of the men who had been in the camp all night now watched the herd, and the rest of us had a good sleep of four or five hours.

Stewart did not say a word to the men who had left the herd, but I could see very plainly that they would never again go over the trail with him. We had better weather for some time after that, and everything went smoothly.

7

Buffalo, "Katy," and Sioux

WE HAD SEEN quite a number of buffalo on our way north, and I had killed several that came near the herds, but they were fast being exterminated by the hide hunters. At Fort Griffin, when we passed it, I saw a pile of buffalo hides near the sutler's store at least fifty yards square and ten feet high. The buffalo were now being killed by thousands all over the buffalo range.

I had rather an amusing experience with a buffalo on this trip. Just prior to our arrival at the Cimarron River, Mac Stewart, who had been riding a mile or two ahead of the herd, came back. Riding up to me he said: "Jim, there are five or six buffalo coming straight for the herd from the west of us. If you want some fun, go catch your horse and fly at 'em. Get some good fat meat." Riding to the horse herd, I caught out my private animal. He was as good a cow horse as ever breathed, but he did not know it all when it came to buffalo hunting.

A few days before, I had overheard one of the boys in camp remark that shooting a buffalo in the center of the forehead would not kill him. He insisted that no bullet could go through that thick bunch of hair and skull. I told him that, the first chance I had, I would show him that I could kill a buffalo by shooting him in the forehead. The other boys laughed at me, but I told them to wait a few days before they laughed too much. Here was my chance to show them. I jumped on my horse bareback, taking only my Winchester carbine with its magazine filled with cartridges. I wanted to ride as light as possible, for it was a very sandy country.

At Fort Griffin I had tried to buy a pair of pants or overalls that would fit me, but they had no boys' sizes, and in fact only

73

a few pairs of any size at all. What they did have on hand were many sizes too large for me, but I had to take a pair of them, for I was simply "out" of pants. I cut off the legs to make them short enough and stuck them into my boot tops. The waist I could only wrap about me, buckling on my cartridge belt good and tight to hold them up. On this occasion I removed my cartridge belt and pistol to lessen the weight on my horse.

All at once the buffalo appeared in sight, and after them I flew. I kept out of sight until I was close to them, and then rode to them "quite swiftly," as the boys used to say. There was a very large bull in the bunch, and I made for him. I overtook and passed a two-year-old bull, and just as I was passing I took a shot at him and saw him fall. I kept on and was soon close enough to the big bull to give him what was called a "kidney shot." Down he went, as if with a broken back. I left him standing on his forelegs, with his hindquarters dragging on the ground as if paralyzed.

I then started for camp to get some of the boys to come out and see me shoot him in the head and kill him. When I reached the spot where I had shot the young bull, it was gone. I rode up on a little hill near by and, looking around, observed that the young bull was going full speed straight for our wagon. The cook had stopped to get dinner near a little lone tree which was struggling for existence in that barren country. He had stretched a rope from the wagon to the tree, and he had the line covered with meat which he was jerking. There were four men in the camp in addition to the cook, as well as several rifles in the wagon. However, none of them thought of shooting when they saw that bull coming. One man went up the tree and the others dived into the wagon. The bull did not look to right or left but kept straight on the beeline he was making for Alaska. He struck the rope about halfway between the tree and the wagon. I sat on the hill and watched the whole performance. Nobody thought of firing at the buffalo until he was about a quarter of a mile beyond them. It was now my turn to laugh. They all looked at each other as much as to say, "I wonder why we didn't."

"Now, then," I said, "if some of you fellows will go with me I will show you whether a buffalo can be killed by shooting him in the head or not. I don't need a rifle; I will kill him with my pistol."

I left my rifle in camp, not dismounting from my horse. I did not buckle on my belt but stuck my .45 Colt revolver in my boot top. When we came in sight of the buffalo, he began to flounder about and shake his head. Our cow ponies would not go near him, so I said, "If one of you fellows will hold my horse I will walk up and kill him." Handing my reins to one of the boys, I jumped down, pistol in hand, holding up my overalls with the other hand. In this manner I advanced on the wounded bull. When I got within eight or ten paces, the animal was about as furious with pain and rage as a buffalo can be. I did not shoot immediately, because he was tossing his head, making it impossible to shoot him in the forehead. As I stood there holding the pistol pointed at his head, waiting for an opportune moment to nail him, he suddenly made a supreme effort and, rising on all four feet, made a furious lunge at me.

I never thought any more about shooting: I whirled about and started to run, forgetting all about my overalls and letting go of them. Instantly they dropped down around my feet, completely hobbling me. Over I went on my face. I whirled over on my back and looked to see what had become of the buffalo. He was down now for good. His back had not been quite broken by the bullet, but in his wild plunge for me he had finished my work. His head was within six feet of me. I very quickly arose, walked up close, and sent a ball through his brain. I then walked back where the boys were and asked them what they thought of my style of killing a buffalo. One or two of the boys were about as pale as I was about that time, for they had expected to see me gored in one more second. When I asked them if they were convinced that a pistol bullet, when properly directed, would kill a buffalo bull, one of the boys remarked, "Your luck beats all our science."

We then returned to camp, and on the way back I showed the boys where I had knocked down the little bull with my first shot. I had probably "creased" him—that is, shot him through the top of the neck, shocking the spinal cord just sufficiently to stun him for a few minutes. When he got to his feet again, he was probably more or less crazy and just ran in the direction in which he happened to be headed. The boys said that he never looked at the wagon as he passed it, and that his eyes were as red as two balls of fire. When we reached camp, and the story was being told, one of the boys remarked, "The next time Mac sends you buffalo hunting he had better send somebody with you to hold up your pants."

We took the cattle to Dodge City, Kansas, and from there to Ogallala, Nebraska. The herd which I was with was sold to the firm of Ross & Wyatt of Greeley, Colorado.

While we were holding the herd at Ogallala, I had a rather narrow escape from getting my neck broken. I was helping Dick Head, my caporal at that time, cut some cattle out of one of the herds. They had been sold to Major Frank North and W. F. Cody (Buffalo Bill). North and Cody were establishing a cattle ranch on the Dismal River near its head, and Major North was in Ogallala purchasing cattle for that ranch. I was riding a horse which was hard to beat at the work of cutting out cattle from a herd. This animal had a habit, however, of taking the bit and throwing his nose high in the air and then running away with his rider. At such times he would not look where he was running; with his eyes fixed on the sky, he would plunge over or into anything in his path.

On this occasion Major North was sitting on his horse at a little distance from the herd where we were cutting out cattle. I did not know who he was. My horse suddenly took one of his spells, being at the time headed directly for the Major. I did not try to hold the animal in, for I knew it was useless: it would only make him throw his head higher in the air. The only way of stopping him was to quirt and spur him for a quarter of a mile or so. By that time he would be so winded that I could circle him around and stop him.

When the horse started with me I shouted to the Major to get out of the way, but he did not try to do so. Evidently he thought I was fooling and could rein in the animal. The result was I struck his horse amidships and knocked him flat to the ground on top of his rider. My horse fell over them, threw me on top of my head, and then partially rolled over me. I was badly stunned. Some of the boys ran to me, helped me to the river bank close by, and poured water over me. When I could remember what had happened, I asked for my horse, for I wanted to go at once and kill that "idiotic granger" who had let me run into him when he had plenty of room and time to get out of the way. The Major had been hurt somewhat, but not so badly as I. His horse rose at once, and the Major mounted him and went to Dick Head, saying that he "would like to kill that idiotic cowpuncher." He insisted that I had not even tried to stop my horse, but had ridden straight at him, evidently intending to run him down. Dick had a good laugh and then explained to the Major that, taken alone, I was quite harmless, but that horse and I together were a terrific combination. Dick then got on his horse and came to see how I was getting along. I told him that my business was to remove that granger for letting me run into him. Dick explained who the granger was, and I rode in to camp and was then introduced to Major North.

He was a well-known man in Nebraska at that time. He had charge of the Pawnee Indian army scouts for some time, and doubtless had had a few bumps of one kind and another during his earlier years, but the bump I gave him made a pretty lasting impression on his memory. The last time I met him was in 1884 at the World's Fair in New Orleans, and he spoke then of the awful jolt I gave him up on the South Platte River. He said that up to the time of that fall he had not known there were so many stars in the sky as he then saw.

In the fall of 1874, when on my way back to San Antonio in company with some cowboys with whom I had been over the trail on a trip to Kansas with a herd of cattle, I rode into the town of Denison, Texas. It was located a short distance from the line of the Indian Territory, on the M.K.&T. Railroad. Denison, being at that time a new railroad town and the end of a division, was a lively place for certain varieties of business. As usual in such towns, gambling houses could be easily found, and they were run "wide open." The boys whom I was with were all older than I, and they seemed to get a lot of pleasure out of the games and other forms of amusement offered. They told me that it would do our saddle and pack horses a lot of good to let them stand in the corral and eat hay for a week or so. I loafed about the place and waited for them to roll for old San Antonio. Meeting in Denison a man who asked me where I was from and what I was working at—he probably sized me up as a pretty young and verdant lad—I told him that I had been up the trail with cattle and that I was waiting for my companions to get ready to proceed on our journey. The man seemed to take an interest in me, for, after hearing my story, he told me that he was a railroad man. He said he thought I was making a mistake by living the rough, hard life of a cowboy, and that if I went to work as a brakeman on the trains or as a fireman on a locomotive, in a very few years I could probably become a conductor or an engineer, especially as the railroad line in Denison was a new one.

I asked him how I should get a job in case I wanted one. He said, "Come with me, and I will take you down to the railroad office, where you can file an application for a job." I must have been an impulsive youngster, for I started right out with him. On my way down to the railroad office I decided that I would rather be a conductor than an engineer; so when we reached the place I signed an application blank for a job as brakeman. I then returned to the place where my companions were hanging out. The following day, while I was sitting in the gambling house watching the games, someone touched me on the shoulder and said, "Are you the lad who was down to the railroad office yesterday looking for a job as brakeman?"

I was somewhat startled, but replied, "Yes."

"Well," said the man, "one of our brakemen was just hurt while unloading some freight, and we want a man to take his place and go right out on Number 6. Can you come right down there to the office with me?"

I told one of my trail companions what I was going to do; then I went to the office with the railroad man. Arriving there, I was asked a few questions and given a job, also a switch key and a book of rules and instructions. I was then introduced and turned over to a conductor named Wheeler. He was to take out Number 6. Mr. Wheeler introduced me to his rear brakeman. The train was being made up ready to start. This brakeman told me that I was to be the front brakeman and ride on the front end of the train or in the cab of the engine when on the road. The division in which I was to work would be from Denison to Muskogee (in the Indian Territory). This division was shunned by some railroad men at that time, for there were few stations and plenty of Indians all along that run of about a hundred and fifty miles. Whiskey being hard to get in the Territory, the Indians would cross over into Texas, where they had but little trouble getting all the white man's spirit water they wanted. Sometimes large groups of these Indians would climb into the empty cars and ride back and forth on the trips across the state line. Train crews who would try to prevent the Indians from taking these free rides would be in danger of their lives, either through fighting and trying to put them off the train, or through being shot from the top of the car when passing through the Indian country. These Indians were a half-civilized lot who had been moved into the Indian Territory from the southeastern part of the United States. The railroad passed through the country held by the Indian tribes, who were principally Choctaws, Chickasaws, Creeks, Seminoles, Caddos, and Cherokees.

I made my first trip safely, using a stick when having to couple cars, as advised by Mr. Runyon, the engineer of the train. In those days this road was not equipped with patent couplers and air brakes. Many of the cars which were used for hauling baled cotton had no tops—only a running board over the center of the top for brakemen to walk on. As the roadbed was new and pretty rough, a green brakeman would have hard work getting from one car to another when attempting to set a string of brakes. There were no coal chutes on this division. The railroad company had opened some coal mines near a place called Stringtown, a station consisting of a signboard and a sidetrack. A spur of the road was built from Stringtown to the mines. Coal was loaded on flat cars at the mines and left on the siding at Stringtown. A train in need of coal would run its engine close to these flatcars; then the fireman and the head brakeman had to shovel into the tender of the engine what coal was needed.

These were snags which I had not been looking for in my attempt to become a train conductor. I did not enjoy working my way from brake to brake over the top of a swaying train, and when I got back to Denison I had concluded that I would rather be an engineer than a conductor. So I told the railroad officials in the office that if I could get a job as fireman I would tackle it; otherwise my resignation was coming to them. To my surprise an opportunity was given me to shovel coal into the firebox of a greedy old coal consumer run by my new engineer friend, Mr. Runyon.

I made the trip with him to Muskogee, trying hard, when I was "stoking her up," to keep the door of the firebox closed at least part of the time. I can safely say that I shoveled more coal on that one trip than some people have shoveled in their whole lives. The muscles of my back and arms being unaccustomed to such exercise, it seemed to put a hump in my back like that of a cat when eating glue. It must also have given me a bad heart, as the Indians say, for on the return run from Muskogee to Denison, when within twenty miles of the latter place, I stepped over to Mr. Runyon's side of the cab and declared positively that if any more coal were needed by his engine, he would have to shovel it himself—I had quit. Instead of giving me the cussing I expected, he said, "All right, my boy." I know that he did shovel what coal was needed to complete the run. When we reached Denison, I did not go to the roundhouse with the engine but hopped off at the station platform, walked straight up town, and, looking up my cowboy friends, told them that I was going to make a start for San Antonio "right away off quick!" and if they were ready to go, to come on. They had just about used up their summer's wages; so they were ready to accompany me.

I never put in a bill for my services rendered the M.K.&T. Railroad company. And I have never regretted leaving them so suddenly, for I firmly believe I should not have made either a good conductor or a good engineer.

In the year 1876, I helped drive a herd of Texas steers, numbering about twenty-five hundred, from a point on the Nueces River, Texas, a short distance above the town of Corpus Christi, to what was then known as the Whetstone Bottom on the Missouri River, Dakota. These cattle had been purchased by men who had contracted with the United States Interior Department to supply a number of Indian agencies with beef. The herd, being all strong cattle, made good time and led the drive made that season from southern Texas. It was the first great herd of cattle to be driven through western Nebraska into Dakota.

Our experience in getting as far as the North Platte River

in western Nebraska was that common to those who drove
the trail in those days—high water, stormy weather, stampedes
of both cattle and saddle horses, hunger at times, also great
thirst, as well as a few other discomforts, all of which aided
the cowboy in rounding out his full measure of whichever he
might choose to call it, misery or joy.

We crossed the South and North Platte rivers a few miles
east of the town of Ogallala. From there we drove over to
Birchwood Creek, thence to the headwaters of the Dismal and
Loup rivers, and on north through the great chain of shifting
sand hills, now so well known. There were ten men in the outfit, including Mac Stewart and the cook. In addition to our
regular crew we had a guide named Aaron Barker, who had
been employed at North Platte City. This guide knew western
Nebraska probably as well as any man living in those days,
having been associated with the Sioux Indians in that part of
the country for years. He and a few associates had, I was told,
been employed in handling many Sioux ponies at the expense
of their rightful owners.

We passed through the sand-hill country at the season when
the sand cherries were ripe and at their best, as also were the
blossoms on the soapweeds; and as the cattle seemed to have
found something about them that pleased their palates, we were
soon so scattered that it looked to me at one time as if we never
should get together again. This was my first experience with
sand cherries, and it left a pleasant impression on my memory.

Driving on north from the headwaters of the north fork of
the Loup River, our guide escorted us to one of the sand-hill
lakes, then unnamed. The weather was very warm, and we
had a long drive without water before we reached the lake.
The cattle scented the water long before we reached it, the
direction of the wind being favorable, and they strung out for it
at a trot. We tried to hold the leaders back, but when we arrived within half a mile of the water, the herd split into bunches

and, in spite of all our efforts, rushed madly into the water. About a hundred head of them were mired down before we could crowd the others to a spot in the lake where the mud and guano were less deep.

At that time, and probably for centuries before, the lakes in the sand hills of Nebraska were the breeding places of all sorts of wild fowl. Upon our arrival countless flocks of ducks, geese, pelicans, swans, and many other varieties of waterfowl hovered over and flew about us, no doubt greatly surprised at our abrupt intrusion.

The task that confronted us, before we could expect anything in the shape of supper, was to save the cattle which had mired down. This proved to be a considerable task, for our saddle horses would mire down trying to get in close enough to the cattle for us to throw our ropes over their horns and pull them out. As some of the best cattle in the herd were in the mire, we wanted to save them if possible.

Fortunately there was a clump of willow trees growing at one side of the lake. We cut clumps of these, tied them into bunches, and used them to make a sort of corduroy road to those of the cattle which were farthest from shore. On these our horses or work oxen could get a secure footing from which to pull. Every head of cattle which we extricated was ready and willing to fight all mankind the moment they could get to their feet after being dragged out to solid ground. The horse of one of our men was badly gored by taking too many chances. Its rider thought his horse could outstart and outrun any steer.

Something frightened the cattle that night along in the small hours, and our neighbors, the wild fowl, must have wondered at the sounds of thundering hoofs and the clashing of horns, accompanied by lesser noises such as the yells of the herders, as they crowded and swung the point, or leaders, of the stampede back into the rapidly following mass of cattle, or sang strains of the old "Texas Lullaby" to them when we finally gained control over them and had them milling around in a compact bunch or standing, trembling and alert, ready for another wild rush at the slightest unusual scent or sound.

When we started north of the Platte rivers, all of us knew that we were to go into a country much of which was regarded as belonging to the Sioux Indians, by both inheritance and treaty rights. Many of the bands of Sioux and Cheyenne Indians were greatly opposed to the invasion of the Black Hills country by the white gold-seekers. A bridge just being completed across the North Platte River was making possible a great highway for supplies and mail to be carried in to the miners. It also enabled thousands of fortune hunters to enter lands in which, they seemed to think, riches could be had by picking up gold with little labor or expense. Most of our outfit had had experience in trailing herds through a country infested with Indians of many tribes, who had all sorts of notions regarding the rights of white men to travel through or to make trails across their hunting grounds. The dangers which beset the lives of those who opened up the old Texas cattle trails to the north made them perhaps a little careless of the danger of being wiped out by Indians. Everyone went armed with a heavy revolver and a knife. But few carried rifles. One reason for this was that the added weight on one side of a horse, on those long, hard trips, was a great cause of saddle galls—something to be strictly guarded against on an eighteen-hundred-mile drive, for a horse with bad saddlesores cannot thrive, and much hinged on the condition of the saddle horses when handling those immense herds of wild cattle. On this trip it happened that I was the only man who owned a rifle. This was hauled in the wagon, except on occasions when we needed a little game for a change of diet. There were plenty of elk, deer, and antelope in the country at that time. We had seen only a scant handful of Indians, and none of these came near us while we were driving the cattle to their destination, but on our return to the Platte River we found some.

We left the guide and wagon when the cattle were delivered to the contractors, and used pack ponies on the return trip, "flying light," as the boys called it. Arriving at the Niobrara River one day about noon, we camped for dinner on the northern bank of the stream, which, at that point and season of the year, was about fifty yards wide and four feet deep, with a very swift current and plenty of quicksand. Just about the time our coffee and bacon were ready, we observed an Indian ride into full view on top of the bluffs which skirted the river valley lands, about half a mile distant. We saw him signaling with both his horse and blanket, and in a very few minutes the bluffs for half a mile up and down the stream were occupied by mounted Indians.

This was interesting, but it became more so when they swarmed down from these bluffs and charged our camp—a yelling, screeching line of riders, beautifully painted and nearly naked. Some had rifles and pistols, but the greater part were armed with bows and arrows. Most of our little band felt, I think, that our time on earth would soon be ended, but, as the Indians did not shoot, none of us pulled a gun. They were all riding bareback, and they certainly made an impressive picture. Their impetuous rush soon brought them upon us, and they formed a complete circle about us. One old warrior with a badly scarred face dashed up almost to my feet, where he pulled his horse to a sudden stop.

Trying to appear greatly pleased at meeting him, I said in as strong and cheerful a voice as I could command, "How, mita Kola" (How, my friend). He jumped from his horse and looked at me for a few moments. I then said to him in the Lacota tongue, "I look at you. My heart is glad to see my friends." He stepped forward to me and inquired, "What is your Lacota name?" I told him the name given me by the old chiefs of his people—for such men as Red Cloud, American Horse, Little Wound, and Young-Man-Afraid-of-His-Horses were friends of mine at that time.

The old warrior then wanted to know where we came from and where we were going. I told him that we had just driven a herd of cattle to the Indians upon the Missouri River and were now on our way back to the Platte River to take a herd to the Red Cloud Agency on the White River. I then said to him, "My Lacota friends have bad hearts, but they must not kill the cowboys who bring the cattle which the Great Father sends to them, or the soldiers will come in great numbers and with many big guns and wipe out the Sioux nation."

He then said that his people were hungry. I told him that we had but little food, and that we should be hungry before we could get to the Shell River (North Platte).

Our little talk probably did not take up the amount of time which I have occupied in writing this account of it, but it was a most interesting one—to me, at least.

Springing upon his pony, the old warrior called out to his people who I was, what our party were doing in the country, and what I had said to him. Yells of "How! How!" came back to him from every direction. Packing our camp outfit on our ponies, we started in to round up our saddle horses and drive them across the river, the entire band of Indians helping us. Their mood had changed, and there were many "How's!" exchanged as we parted on the south side of the Niobrara.

I have always felt that if ever I had a close call to being used as a pincushion, with arrows in place of the pins, that was the time; and I think there were others around me who, after the ordeal was over, felt as weak as I. Doubtless my efforts to pick up a little knowledge of the Sioux tongue and sign language saved my scalp on that occasion, and possibly the scalps of the entire party; for there must have been fully three hundred Indians in the bunch which swooped down upon us so unceremoniously.

After leaving the Indians who had so kindly helped us across the river, we made tracks toward the Union Pacific Railroad. In connection with this incident of my life, I want to illustrate the fact that in almost all parties of men there are some who have very short memories and forget to be grateful for mercies received. I was riding with one of my companions ahead of our band of saddle horses, leading the way and approaching the top of a steep sand hill that lay in our course, when we came suddenly upon two old Sioux warriors on foot, leading two tired ponies packed with antelope meat. These Indians were taken by surprise at our sudden appearance, but they put on a brave front and made signs of being greatly pleased at meeting us. They wanted to shake hands all around and say "How, how!" as fast as possible to us. One of our party who was troubled with a short memory drew his pistol and remarked, "Let's kill these two old devils, anyway." But he was quickly persuaded by the rest of our party not to do such a rash thing as to take advantage of these Indians who were at our mercy, directly after having, only by the mercy of God, been allowed to escape with our lives from the tribesmen and relatives of these same two old helpless Indians.

Those days are long past. When the last of the old Sioux warriors have come to visit me in my home each year, I have often told them of the awful scare they gave me on the banks of the river upon which I have now made my home for so many years. We can all laugh over it now as a good joke. But at the time it appeared to me to be about as serious a predicament as I was ever in.

8
Virtues of the Cow Waddie

To WRITE A WORD PICTURE which would fully portray the details of a bad stampede of one of the great herds of wild Spanish longhorn cattle which were driven over the trails during the early seventies would be beyond my ability. But, having had numerous opportunities for close-up studies of these stampedes, as a little unit among the boys who were hired to control such affairs, I will here set down some of my impressions of them.

The requirements for getting all possible thrills from a cattle stampede were these: First, you must have a herd of wild cattle numbering about 2,500 or 3,000 head, captured in the land of mesquite, chaparral, and cactus jungles, and ever ready to be stricken with panic. Then, some evening when the shades of night were approaching, you must have this herd bedded down on the best selected bed-ground which could be found, in a section of country which might perhaps be badly cut up on all sides by water- and wind-erosion, with plenty of gulches varying in depth from one to twenty-five feet and as wide as a horse could jump or a hen fly across. The next requirement was a really dark night, when all light from moon or stars had been so obliterated that one could not see the head of the horse upon which one was mounted, or even a hand held before the face. There were plenty of occasions of that sort on the Great Plains, as elsewhere. The stage is now nearly set. Nothing further would be needed save a few deafening crashes of thunder, accompanied by blinding flashes of lightning, with perhaps a liberal allowance of rain, hail, and a gale of wind.

Climb aboard an old cow pony, my dear reader, and ride in spirit with me, under such conditions, to one of those longhorn herds, bedded down for the night at the close of a day's drive. The first guard of the herders will have taken charge of the cattle. The trail foreman is with them, doubtless hoping that the heavy storm clouds which have been gathering in the northwest, and which can be seen rapidly approaching, will disperse before reaching the herd. He knows full well what a bad run of the herd might mean, both in loss of cattle and death or mutilation of riders. He well knows that contending with the forces of nature, coupled with a herd of cattle maddened by fright, is a serious proposition. The boys in camp, who are off guard, are standing or lying near their saddled night horses, holding their bridle reins and ready for a quick mount.

Those who are on guard ride slowly around the herd, perhaps singing the cowboy lullaby. The horses they ride seem, at times, to sense the coming of a bad storm, with its attendant excitement and danger. At such times they are keenly alert, watching every move made by the cattle herd. The majority of the herd may be, at this time, lying down, resting and chewing their cuds, but they, too, show signs of nervousness—none of them are lying flat on their sides with their long legs stretched out, relaxed and content. Now and then some animal will raise its head and sniff the air uneasily, as if scenting danger. Each animal lies with its legs well under its lean, lithe body, ready to spring to its feet in a second and be off in a mad race for safety from threatening dangers.

Perhaps because the air was heavily charged with electricity, which would have some bearing on the nervous condition of the cattle, perhaps for some other cause, it took but little to start a stampede. The stumbling of a horse or the sound of a little whirlwind tearing across the country—even a strange scent borne to them on the wind—might be all that was needed to start trouble. Without a second's warning a stampede would start with a roar and crash, followed by the steady thundering of thousands of hoofs and the smashing and clashing of horns against horns.

They are off! Panic-stricken, wild with fright, away they go, over badlands, prairie-dog towns—any- and everything that comes in their way. All the riders are now in the saddle, racing at top speed through the pitchy blackness of the night, guided only by the sounds made by the fleeing animals, and depending to a great degree on the eyesight of their horses to keep them near the cattle, and to avoid bad gulches into which all might be piled indiscriminately.

There was little use trying to stop a stampede when the herd presented too wide a front. The great mass of the frightened animals in the wake of the leaders would, by their weight alone, force the leaders over any obstacle which they might encounter. Over bluffs and banks they would go, piling up when the fall was great, not without some broken necks, backs, or limbs. After running for perhaps half a mile, the herd would become strung out, the strongest and fleetest having forged to the front, while the less fleet and weaker animals could only follow along as rapidly as their strength would permit, but all trying, as it seemed, to be with their leaders at the finish.

As soon as the herd was sufficiently strung out, the riders would try to get near the lead cattle and if possible swing or turn them, so that they would circle back into the mass of cattle following. This was done by crowding along on one side of the leaders, the cowboys yelling and singing to them. This would force the cattle into a compact bunch again, all running in a circle, or "milling." This milling would be stopped in a short time: the riders would check some of the cattle on the outer edge of the herd and start them traveling in the opposite direction. This, after a short time, would stop the mill.

Sometimes one stampede would follow another, the cattle having hardly time to recover their breath between runs.

After a bad run, the boys generally tried at once to learn if all the riders were still with the herd. Some might be missing. One might have stuck to a bunch of cattle which, for some reason, had split from the main herd. Another might have been missing because his horse had fallen with him, possibly breaking a bone or two. Or he might have ridden over some embankment in the darkness while running at full speed, both horse and rider being killed or maimed. If a horse fell with its rider in front of a big herd of stampeded cattle, the rider's chances of being trampled to death were excellent.

During the summer of 1875 I was engaged for a time, with another young cowboy, herding a bunch of about four hundred big Texas steers which we had cut out of our trail herd and were to deliver in a short time to some cattle buyers, to be fattened for the Kansas City market. We were holding these cattle a few miles north of Ellsworth, Kansas. A few hundred yards from the spot where we bedded them down for the night there was a small stream of water which meandered through a deeply cut channel. Gullies cut into both sides of this channel-bed through a little high uplift of country.

One evening we brought the cattle in to their bed-ground. I remained with them while my companion went in to camp to cook supper and get a change of horses. We could see that a bad storm was approaching, but it struck us sooner than expected. It started with a gust of wind and a little rain, and darkness came on rapidly. Hastily snatching a bite of food and preparing himself for a hailstorm, my companion rode back where I was trying to hold the cattle on the bed-ground. They were trying to drift with the storm, but did not appear to be frightened or excited. We could hear the roar of the approaching storm. I shouted to my pal that I would go back to camp and get an extra blanket to put over my head and shoulders as protection from the hail. I rode rapidly in, got a piece of a saddle blanket or an old gunny sack, and started back toward the herd. Before I could reach the cattle, they were off on a mad stampede. A terrific clap of thunder, which fairly jarred the earth, had started them.

It had now become so dark that it was impossible for me to see the cattle except during the flashes of lightning which came with blinding effect every few seconds. I rode at the top speed of my horse in order to reach the lead cattle and help my pard swing them. Between the flashes of lightning the darkness was so intense that I could not even see the horse I was riding.

The cattle ran in the direction of the rough ground and the creek channel. They happened to head into a sharp bend of the creek, where the cut banks were very high and perpendicular. A sudden flash of lightning lit the surroundings just in time to save my life and picture a scene I can never forget. My companion and his horse seemed poised in mid-air for a moment, far out over the edge of the high bank of the creek! Several head of the lead cattle were following him to what was undoubtedly certain death. My horse needed no tug at the reins to stop his headlong rush: he braced his forefeet into the earth suddenly and firmly enough to bring him to a sudden halt, not more than five or six feet from the edge of the bluff over which my companion had just disappeared. How it happened that the cattle following in my rear did not crash against my horse and send us both over the bank, I shall never know. An instant of blinding light, and then intense and inky darkness reigned again.

In that Egyptian blackness I was helpless, so far as going to the aid of my pard was concerned. I knew that, because of the darkness of the night, I should hardly be able to find a place to get down into the creek bed to go to his aid. How I might help him was uppermost in my mind. I finally decided to ride to Ellsworth and notify the people, there being not a soul nearer. Working my way carefully, I managed to elude the creek bottom and started for Ellsworth at top speed. There I aroused a druggist. He notified the sheriff and the coroner.

At daylight I led them to the spot where the accident had occurred. We soon located the body of my friend. His horse had fallen on top of him, crushing the boy to death. A dozen or more head of cattle were lying about, also killed by the fall.

The coroner, after making an examination, said that my companion had undoubtedly been killed instantly. His body was taken to Ellsworth and there buried by the authorities—for nobody knew where he was from.

I have read of cowboys riding in front of these stampedes trying to stop them by shooting into the ground just in front of the noses of the lead cattle. If such methods were ever employed by those who handled the really wild herds, I never knew it. There was plenty of danger, when trying to stay with a stampeded herd, without having to think that one might at any moment have to stop a bullet fired by some excited cowpuncher. It was a bad time for pistol practice, and bullets have strange habits of doing all sorts of peculiar stunts, even when fired into the ground. The ties of comradeship were strong among those who rode side by side in the struggle to gain control of those stampeded herds; and every man knew, when such occasions arose, that one or more of their number might, as a result, be left by the side of the cattle trail.

The best thing about a cattle stampede happened, like turkey hash a day or so after Thanksgiving, on the morning after, when the sun came out bright and clear, and the cattle and their herders were all accounted for, and the tired and hungry boys came straggling into camp. It was to hear the cook yelling, "All set, fellers! Come and get it!"

Far back in the written records of mankind, we find that cattle were used as beasts of burden and as food. Those who cared for the herds of cattle were called cowherds. Their social rating was not, I fear, very high, and their equipment was certainly primitive. I gather from the little research I have made in this direction that all a cowherd used or needed as equipment was the skin of some beast, which would serve both as clothing and bedding and also as a sling with which to slay, smite, or frighten away the fierce, man-eating beasts from himself and his herd.

The next cowboys of whom I ever heard much were the Gauchos or cattle-herders of South America. Their lives and methods of work with the great herds there were in some respects but little different from those of the cowherds of long ago. But the wild cattle of the pampas country could not be controlled by men on foot—and, therefore, horses, saddles, and that most cruel but useful invention, the bolas, were brought into their daily work.

On the North American continent, the Mexican herder or *vaquero* became a fixture soon after the Spaniards brought horses and cattle from Spain. Cortez, I believe, brought the first branding irons for horses and cattle to the North American continent. These irons were used on the first domestic cattle of which we have any record here in the New World. This brand was made in the form of three Christian crosses—a large one in the center and smaller ones on each side of the upright support of the larger cross. During the centuries that the Mexican *vaqueros* or cowboys worked with the Spanish cattle, they became expert in handling them. When these domestic horses and cattle had multiplied and scattered, they became as wild as the native animals of that time and country.

After Texas had become a part of the United States and the War of the Rebellion was ended, the American cowboy was brought into prominence. The great jungle country of southwestern Texas contained hundreds of thousands of wild Spanish cattle. The Americans who first undertook to handle these cattle for profit found that they had the task, not only of securing a market for them, but of getting Americans who could do a Mexican *vaquero's* work—men who were willing to take the chances and endure the hardships of long drives with the cattle to a country far to the north of the land of the Mexican *vaqueros*, a country inhabited by savage tribes of Indians (of whom, no doubt, many greatly exaggerated stories had been told them). This was the time when the real American cowboy, of whom so much has been said and written, was created.

Their instructors in the art of cowboy work were Mexicans. Soon there was formed a nucleus of cowboys, added to rapidly as the years rolled by.

As it is my lot to have been numbered among the first of the American boys who worked with the wild cattle in the mesquite and chaparral thickets of Texas and on the trails leading from that state, I shall endeavor to relate a few remembered incidents and impressions connected with the cowboys and their lives.

The cowboy was first brought into disreputable prominence by the lawless and rowdy acts of a few of their number. Many of those who committed such acts were ex-soldiers of the War of the Rebellion—men who had seen much violence and bloodshed and seemed to enjoy it, particularly after taking a few drinks of liquor. The percentage among them of men in any way bad was, I think, as low as among any class of men with which it has been my privilege to associate. The first cowboys of Texas certainly may have *looked* bad to those who were not accustomed to such outfits as were worn by the boys when engaged in their work. (One peculiarity about the cowboy, by the way, was that he was always called a "boy," no matter how many years he had lived.) A revolver and a sheath knife were very necessary parts of a cowboy's equipment. Both these weapons had to be carried in the most get-at-able manner, for there was some danger in a cowboy's occupation. Sudden and expert work with both pistol and knife was quite likely to be required at times in the work with the cattle. These cattle were wild creatures which could not only flee from a human being like other wild animals but could fight, and would do so as promptly as any grizzly bear I ever saw. When using a rope, or lasso (as it should be called), in the thickets where the wild cattle ranged, the cowboy usually kept one end of the lasso tied hard and fast to the horn of the saddle. This was done for the reason that if, when a rider was going full speed in pursuit of an animal and swinging his rope, the loop of the lasso should accidentally catch on some object, such as the limb of a tree or some stiff shrub, he would be likely to lose it, and might also find his hands badly burned by the rapid passage of the rope through them.

Often when a rider caught a large animal and brought it to a sudden stop by the lasso, it would turn and charge its captor. If the steer succeeded in goring the horse, perhaps this none too gentle mount would attempt to escape or throw its head down and try to buck its rider into kingdom come; in which case rider, horse, and cow-critter were likely to get into a badly tangled mess. There was just one way out of such a scrape, and that was to cut oneself free from that lasso as quickly as possible. Sometimes a rider found himself in such a predicament that he had to shoot the animal to which he had made fast, in order to save his own life. Constant practice with both knife and pistol made some of the boys very expert with these weapons.

In addition, the Comanche and Lipan Indians inhabited the cattle country of Texas at that time, and they seemed to have a liking for shooting arrows into cowboys. As the country afforded splendid opportunities for ambushing anyone engaged in catching the wild cattle of the jungles, the cowboy had to be prepared to shoot quick and straight.

The Texas cowboy carried his style of dress and equipment (which was partly Mexican) up the cattle trails with him to the northern ranges. Here it was quickly adopted by the boys from the eastern states who came to work with the cattle when the North Middle West became a cow country. The Texas custom of tying a lasso to the horn of the saddle was dropped in the North, because it was not necessary in a plains country. The California style of lasso (which was twice the length of that used in the brush country of Texas) was adopted there. A few round turns taken about his saddle horn would hold a lassoed beast, and if for any reason things went wrong, the turns of the rope could be quickly thrown off. Should an animal get loose from its captor, it could easily be caught again, for it could not well get out of sight in that open country. In the brush country conditions were different. Should a rider there ever lose sight of a cow after it had captured his rope, the chances were good that he would never see either cow or rope again.

Texas cowboys had their own style of saddle and of riding a bucking horse. The cowboys on the cattle ranges of the Middle West used a California saddletree, usually with a double-cinch, or Texas, rigging, which a California *vaquero* would despise. The California rider used a center-fire or broad single-cinch, hung center from the rigging of his saddle. In riding a bucking horse, his saddle would be cinched well forward, the horn being well out on the animal's neck. The saddle would rock somewhat, but it would remain in a more horizontal position on a bucking horse than would a double-cinched saddle. The latter would be placed farther back on a horse, and would have but little rock to it when a cow horse was trying to spill a rider.

The California *vaquero* would lean well forward when riding a bad pitching horse, whereas the Texas rider of the old school would sit with only one leg thrown across the saddle, or else lean back. When lassoing wild stock with a single-rigged California saddle, it would be necessary to have it cinched very tightly to prevent its turning. Double-rigged saddles, or those with both a front and back cinch, did not require this. The comfort of a horse was not greatly considered by many of the old-time Mexican *vaqueros*. I think the Texas cowboy's idea of leniency toward his mount helped many an old cow horse out of the misery of wearing a tight corset.

The cowherds of the olden times left little, if any, record of whatever natures or dispositions they may have possessed. The stories of the gentle shepherd lads of those days have been handed down in song and story. Shepherds of whom we have all read were allowed to follow the Star of Bethlehem to the spot where it poised over the manger. As yet, the cowboy never has been glorified to any such extent.

Few, if any, of the first of the old Texas cowboys were men who had had the benefit of a college education. Not long after the ranges of the North were fairly well stocked with the Texas cattle, the business offered such inducements to men from the East—men who had capital—that soon a fad for starting a cattle ranch in the West was created. Theodore Roosevelt, the Oelrichs brothers, and other well-known men came from as far east as New York City and Boston and established cattle ranches in Wyoming, Montana, and South Dakota; others— among them the Marquis De Mores and Sir Horace Plunkett —actually came from across the Atlantic. These ranches soon brought many young college fellows from the East and abroad, for whom the life on the range and with the roundups, the excellent big-game hunting, and the general excitement offered many attractions. Soon many men could be met on the ranges of the West who were graduates of our greatest educational institutions. To meet such men on a range and find them wearing a cowboy outfit down to the last detail, or decked out à la California *vaquero*, with fancy, expensive silver spurs and bridle bits, became a common experience. Theodore Roosevelt and a few other writers about western life, such as Owen Wister, author of *The Virginian*, put a little halo upon the cowboy's head that exists to this date—enough of a halo, at least, so that cowboys are still in demand for Wild West shows and motion picture camps and studios. The real life of the cowboy on the range has changed greatly all over the West. Lasso, gun, and knife—especially the gun and the sheath knife—are no longer much in evidence. A .45 caliber hammer, a sack of fence-staples, and a wire cutter, splicer, and staple-puller combined are all the tools needed by the modern cowboy.

The simple life led on the range by the old-time boys who lived entirely in the open, away from stuffy bunkhouses and fancy chuck wagons loaded with canned goods, was, I think, far better than that followed later on by those who came under the changed conditions of the business. Life near to nature, devoid of excesses or frills, tends to make men in every sense of the word. A large percentage of the boys I have known— those of the old school, at least—were honest and true as steel to their employers, generous to a fault, if such a thing can be, and always respectful to women and to the aged of either sex.

The cowboy, during the very early stages of his existence, had to endure greater hardships than any other class of men who lived frontier lives. Soldiers, freighters, hunters, and trappers could, on most occasions, protect themselves in some manner, or to some extent at least, from bad storms. But the real cowboy would not desert a herd in order to protect himself from heavy weather. Many have gone to their deaths in blizzards, tornadoes, and bad thunderstorms by staying with the herds. Many a boy I have seen shivering with cold and drenched by rain in some awful hailstorm has shouted at me between chattering teeth, "Nobody out, and nobody going out!"

Great muscular strength and a knowledge of scientific boxing and wrestling were not considered indispensable requirements among those who worked with cattle during the early days on Texas cattle trails. Fist-fights, which were engaged in among soldiers of the regular army, freighting outfits, and men following other vocations, were called "dog fights" by the cowboys. Fighting "dog style" was of such rare occurrence among cowboys that in all the time I followed that life I never saw one instance in which men threw down all weapons and engaged in a slugging match in order to settle any dispute or to demonstrate their strength or nerve. But skill in the use of the weapons then carried, from lasso to butcher knife, was considered an accomplishment. I have mentioned the lasso as a weapon for the reason that, in the early days of *vaquero* life in the jungles of the Southland, duels to the death were fought with lassos. A realistic combat of that kind, engaged in by two expert *vaqueros* mounted on well-trained cow horses, would make an interesting picture on the screen and give a more truthful representation of a combat between the early-day cowboys than the pictures showing a bunch of them engaged in a bar-room set-to, punching the spots off each other.

As nearly as I can remember, the chief themes of conversa-tion about the old campfires in cow camps were of the cut-shoot-and-gamble order. The wonderful exploits of this sort performed by a few well-known characters in Texas put them upon a pedestal for a time and got them admired by many cow-boys and a few other sorts of people. If anyone were to go to the trouble of looking over the list of names of those cowboy ideal fighting men and tracing them to their finish, the facts would show that with very few exceptions their lives were punched out by cold lead. To put a head on a man so that he "could eat hay like a horse," by rapping him over the skull with a six-shooter, was considered high art all over the West at one period. It was not considered a disgrace to engage in a combat of that sort when the crowded conditions of some dance hall or barroom would cause a gun-fighter to shoot several of his friends in order to slay his antagonist with a fire of lead.

The uninitiated are prone to think that the vocation of the cowboy was a continuous experience of excitement, dangers, and lawlessness; that his arrival in the small western towns gave the timid inhabitants much alarm and afforded infinite amuse-ment to some who had no interests at stake, when he proceeded to shoot up the town. In many western towns, the cowboys certainly indulged in some drinking, gambling, shooting, and other vices. Such scenes were common to the life on the fron-tier. But they did not form the principal purposes of the busi-ness life of those engaged in the cattle and other industries, and they were merely incidental to the main process of affairs, which was steadily grinding the rough and savage material of the times and localities into the more symmetrical and refined forms of civilized existence.

The sunshine and winds of the prairie aided, I think, in developing men naturally self-reliant. In all classes of men there were drags—"scrubs"—who managed to ride along by some means on the shoulders of the good ones. Some of the more fancy-looking ones were not of the greatest value to their employers. They were often fair-weather sailors, with no pride when it came to doing unpleasant tasks well, however much they had of another sort of pride which would make them die game in a saloon brawl.

I look with pride upon those of the old cowboys who have always done good work, whether on the range, as governors of states, or in the presidential chair. The movie picture and Wild West Show cowboys may continue to live on for many generations, but the cowboys who are left of the days when there was not a wire fence on the range between Corpus Christi and Assiniboine are now wearing many silver threads in their hair—if perchance they have not been blessed by old Father Time with a marble top to adorn their brain boxes.

I hope that every one of those old boys who may happen to read what I have written about cowboys will feel that I have at least hit some of the high ground of truth.

PART II
HUNTING BIG GAME: WYOMING

*James H. Cook as a hunter of big game in
Wyoming Territory, 1880.*

9
Hunter and Trapper

DURING THE EARLY SEVENTIES and up to 1878, I put in most of my time on the Texas cattle trails or working in the cow country of southwestern Texas. After making the trail drive north into Kansas in 1874, instead of going immediately back to Texas I made a trip with some cowboys and hunters up into Wyoming and northwestern Nebraska. I visited Fort Laramie and the Red Cloud Agency, as well as some of the other old military posts in that part of the country.

At Fort Laramie I camped with Baptiste Garnier for a couple of weeks. He was better known as "Little Bat." He was a hunter and army scout, well known to army people of those days. I went with him on a trip to Red Cloud Agency. There were plenty of deer and antelope in the country just north of Fort Laramie then, and we had an abundance of good venison on that trip. Late that fall I sold my saddle and pack horse in Cheyenne and went back to Texas as far as Houston by train.

After the drive over the cattle trail in 1876, I again went to Fort Laramie, Wyoming. From there I went northward into Montana with some hunters whom I met at the fort. We had planned to look over the country south of the Yellowstone River and along the base of the Big Horn Mountains, with a view to locating some good trapping grounds. Forest or prairie fires would often cause game and fur-bearing animals to change their range from time to time. Too much hunting or trapping would also have the same effect, and hunters and trappers were constantly looking for fresh grounds.

The Sioux Indians were causing the United States government considerable trouble at this period, and we had to keep a good lookout for their war parties. Crazy Horse, Dull Knife, and Sitting Bull were having their temporary innings. The men whom I accompanied on this trip were all old hunters and trappers who knew the Indian country very well. They also knew how to protect themselves as much as possible when in an Indian country, but they all concluded that trapping on any stream north of the North Platte River would be a dangerous proposition during the winter of 1876–77. We had chances to be useful more than once to parties of United States troops who needed information about the country or who needed dispatches carried from one command to another in the field.

We went back to Fort Laramie, and then I went south again, traveling by the old Santa Fé Trail from the Arkansas River to Santa Fé. From there I went to El Paso, Texas, and on south to my old range in southwestern Texas. I wanted to become a hunter and trapper and had at that time no other ambition, but the call of the wild cows of Texas must have had some irresistible influence upon me, for I stuck to the trail work until the summer of 1878. Then I broke the invisible fetters that bound me to the life of a Texas cowboy, and evolved rather suddenly into a sure-enough hunter and guide. Here was a life in which I felt I could make good, for I was not afraid of work, and I felt sure that during my experience in the West I had gained some little knowledge of what such a life called for.

The last herd of cattle which I accompanied on the drive from Texas was sold to Messrs. Ross & Thomas of Greeley, Colorado. Messrs. Bishop & Halff of Texas owned this last of the herds which I helped drive over the long trail. Ross & Thomas had at that time a ranch on Crow Creek, Colorado, at a point about eighteen miles east of Greeley. At this ranch the cattle were delivered to their northern owners, and the cowboys who had accompanied them from Texas were turned loose to rustle their livings as best they could.

I went to Cheyenne, Wyoming, with one of my trail comrades. After being in that town a few hours, I made the discovery that my companion had a pretty strong appetite for firewater. He soon disposed of his few hard-earned dollars, and then, quite naturally, he turned to me for aid. I stayed with him pretty well, but presently it got to be a question merely of how many hours it would take him to bust my bank. I had to choose between arranging to "split the blanket" with him and attempting a little reform work. I decided on the latter course, for I had been interested in this comrade for months. He was different from anything I had ever met in the cowboy genus. He was a very refined-looking man of more than ordinary intelligence, and, I should judge, about forty-five years of age. He had received an education which fitted him for an occupation far above any required in most cow camps. He had been sent out to us from San Antonio just as we were starting on the trail north. He did his work well as a "drag driver," but he rarely spoke to anyone, and when he did it was to the point. Most of the men in the outfit did not like him, but for some reason I felt sympathy for him—perhaps because he appeared so lonely and out of place among those with whom he had been thrown.

Knocking about in Cheyenne, I found a man who owned a team and a camp outfit, whom I could hire to take us up into the mountains of Colorado for a month. I wanted a good rest, and I thought that such a trip might help my comrade get back on his feet again, to a point where, for a time at least, he could control his appetite for liquor. We went up into the mountains and had a good rest-out, besides catching all the trout we could eat and shooting plenty of game. At the end of the month we returned to Cheyenne. By this time I had decided that I must go my own trail. If my comrade should manage to remain sober, he would have no trouble securing work from some ranchman; so I divided with him what money I had left and bade him good-bye. He made good by securing work from, and finally becoming foreman for, Major Frank Wolcott, a cattleman of Wyoming.

After bidding my comrade good-bye, I went over to the

Black Hills Corral & Feed Yards, where I had left my two horses while going on the hunt. Here I saddled my good old horse, Roper, and put my blankets and little camping outfit on my pack animal. I did not know in which direction I was going to start out in my attempt to get away from my old cowboy life.

Just as I was going out through the big gates, I met a man, to whom I have already referred, named Charles W. Alexander, better known in Wyoming as Wild Horse Charlie, a name given him because he had at one time been engaged in capturing mustangs. Charlie had succeeded in catching plenty of wild horses in western Colorado and Kansas. It was not an extremely profitable occupation from a financial point of view, because these wild horses were small and only fit for saddle animals or light drivers, and Indian ponies and saddle horses from Texas were very cheap in those days.

I had first met Alexander on my trip north to Fort Laramie in 1876. He was at that time employed as a government teamster. He now recognized me and asked what I was doing for a living. I told him I was foot-loose and as free as the wind and asked him what he was doing. He told me that he had a little hunting outfit and was killing game for the market in Cheyenne. I confessed that I was looking for a chance to do some hunting and trapping. He said he had heard a great deal about me from his friend Little Bat, at Fort Laramie, and that he should be glad to have me "throw in" with him as a partner, as he did not like hunting alone. He had a team and a light wagon, a tent, and a good camping outfit. His animals were both good hunting horses. I knew that my two horses were good in any kind of camp life in which thoroughly trained horses would be needed. He also had a splendid Remington rifle. (I had only the Winchester carbine which I had brought up over the long trail from Texas, a gun not fitted for long-range shooting.) There was more money to be made by hunting and trapping than by catching wild horses; therefore, Charlie had turned to hunting for the market, and was doing very well at it when fate or Providence brought us together at the old Black Hills Corral in Cheyenne.

We became partners that day and started out after some antelope for the Cheyenne market. We went down into Little Crow Creek, about thirty-five miles southeast of Cheyenne. There were plenty of antelope in that section. The first day we hunted I did so well with my little carbine that Charlie said, "If you can keep up this gait, all I will have to do is take the meat and hides in to Cheyenne and sell them." I think I kept up my gait, for Charlie was busily occupied hauling game to market most of the time. We soon had made money enough so that I was able to buy a very fine Sharps 40–90 target rifle, for which I paid $125.00. We loaded all of our cartridge shells and moulded and patched our bullets. The prices we received for the antelope and deer meat ranged from five to eight cents a pound. The hides, when dry, brought us from sixteen to twenty-five cents a pound.[1]

[1] As far back as the white man has any knowledge, the tanned hides of deer and antelope have been used by the Indians of the United States to make wearing apparel. The first white men who came into contact with the Indians soon discovered the value of buckskin—the name applied by them to all tanned deer or antelope skins. Buckskin not only made good tough wear-resisting clothing, but it was also soft and pliable and of good protective color for the pioneer who hunted game and disputed with the savages their right to do so. And there were times when it was more available to the pioneer than cloth of any kind. White hunters and scouts for the United States regular army often became overheated when they had to make a hard run or crawl in trying to secure game or approach an enemy. Then, perhaps, they had to drop down and lie motionless for a time. They found at such times that they did not chill so readily when wearing buckskin clothing as when dressed in other garb of wool or cotton make.

One disadvantage under which the frontiersman labored in wearing buckskin in all sorts of weather conditions was that buckskin, when once allowed to become rain-soaked, was uncomfortable to wear until it became dry again. If taken off and dried by the heat of a campfire or the sun, it would have to be watched and dried very slowly, with considerable rubbing and handling; otherwise it would shrink greatly and become very hard.

The Indians tanned the deer hides by rubbing the brains and fat of the deer into them and rinsing them out in water repeatedly. It was a long and tedious process to make a really fine piece of buckskin. The Indians made two kinds. One was white, the other smoke-tanned. The last-named was thoroughly and repeatedly smoked during the tanning process, over an arch of

After hunting with Charlie a few weeks, I went into Cheyenne one day with him on a load of meat and hides. As I was going into the gun store of P. Bergersen, I met the old trail comrade with whom I had parted in Cheyenne just recently. He said he had secured work and was doing well. He expressed pleasure on hearing that I was also doing well at my favorite occupation. He told me he had met a very dear boyhood chum of his own in Cheyenne that day, whom he wanted me to know. I went with him down to the Union Pacific Railroad Hotel, then managed by Colonel Jones. Here I was introduced to a Mr. Harry Yale, the friend of my old comrade. Mr. Yale was the steward of the hotel. We had a pleasant little visit, and I told him all about my project of earning a livelihood as a game hunter. He seemed to take great interest in what I told him. No doubt Mr. Wilson, my trail comrade, had said some nice things to him about me, for that same evening he came down to the Black Hills Corral, where Charlie and I were camped, to look me up.

Yale surprised me by stating that the Railroad Hotel and the eating houses of the Union Pacific Railroad in Wyoming used large quantities of game, and that he should be glad to aid me in disposing of all the game I could kill. I was delighted to hear this, for to me it meant a great deal. No more meat would have to be peddled out to butcher shops and private houses. I did my best to express my thanks to him for his kind offer and introduced him to Charlie Alexander, my partner. The dealings

---

willow sticks with a little fire undernearth, the fire being made of materials which would produce a heavy smoke and but little heat.

In portraying pioneer characters on the stage and in moving pictures, actors have worn buckskin clothing—a correct thing for them to do. But I never could take pleasure in looking over certain specimens of mankind whom I have often seen loafing about in public places or holding down chairs in dime museums, togged out in buckskin suits, moccasins, and sombreros, wearing on their faces the nearest thing they could contrive to a do-or-die expression. I never saw a frontiersman who had, among men who knew him, a high rating as a man of ability and brains, who ever cared to make a display of himself in towns and cities by wearing anything which he knew would make him conspicuous.

which we had with Mr. Yale in the months that followed were most satisfactory to everyone concerned. Moreover, Colonel Jones of the Railroad Hotel, Cheyenne, became so interested in Charlie and me that he not only purchased game of us for the use of the hotel of which he had direct charge, but also shipped it to other eating houses up and down the line of the Union Pacific Railroad. The Colonel was a most genial host, and he had many friends and acquaintances among the travelers who were fed at his far-famed eating station. Among the gentlemen whom he met at Cheyenne were many who desired him to secure choice game for them for club dinners or other occasions. All such requests the Colonel turned over to me to fill, he himself attending to having the game shipped to various cities, from New York to San Francisco.

Charlie and I now had something to do. We took great pains to have the game which we furnished dressed out and kept in the most cleanly manner possible until delivered—something that many hunters were often careless about. We also took great care in stretching, drying, and baling our hides for the market. The hide buyers of the great hide and fur house of Oberne, Hosick & Company, of Chicago, which at one time had branch houses all over the West, complimented us on the condition of the hides and furs which we sold them. In consequence, our bales of deer and antelope hides were not opened and inspected before paid for, for fear that damaged hides or a few pounds of dirt, gravel, or bones would be found inside. When we hunted too far away from Cheyenne to haul the meat to that city, we kept close enough to the Union Pacific Railroad so that we could ship game regularly to our market. We killed many antelope, black- and white-tailed deer, elk, and mountain sheep during the time of our hunting in Wyoming and Colorado.

When we found that we could not supply the amount of game required, Charlie and I took in another partner by the name of Billy Martin. He was a good hunter. Both Charlie and

Billy were very temperate men in every way. Neither had the drink or tobacco habit—something most unusual among hunters and trappers of that day.

When we hunted too far from the Union Pacific to handle our meat fresh, we built smokehouses and dried it. Our smokehouses were rather primitive in the manner of construction and material used, but the results obtained would compare very favorably with, or perhaps excel, those obtained by the great packing houses of recent years. Getting the empty whiskey barrels and salt to our camp (two most important necessities in pickling the meat preparatory to smoking it) was often a hard task, there being few wagon roads which we could use in getting to the railroad. When killing big game in the mountains of Wyoming, such as elk, buffalo, deer, or mountain sheep, we took all game killed into camp on pack mules or horses.

As it was necessary to cut the heavy animals into quarters in order to lift and lash them on to our pack animals, we invariably, before quartering them, cut out and kept intact long strips of loin meat, which were the choicest and most valuable part of all the meat we dried. In camp we took all the meat from the bones of the animals, cutting it as little as possible, opening the partings between the muscles and leaving each group of muscles as near their proper form as possible. The meat was then placed in the barrels and brine poured over it until covered. It remained in this brine for nine or ten days; then it was taken out and hung up, each piece by itself, in the smokehouse. We dug a long trench down a slope from our smokehouses, connecting these with the fireplace at the lower end of the trench. This trench would be covered with rocks and dirt, making a flue to conduct the smoke. Sometimes the trenches were as much as thirty feet in length, so that the smoke, when it reached the meat, would not be hot enough to injure it. As we could not remain in camp to attend to the fire, we put a large amount of the most slowly burning material available into the fireplaces or pits before leaving camp or turning in for an all-night sleep.

All the meat which we dried was carefully sacked, then hauled to the railroad and shipped, most of it being sent to Cheyenne, then forwarded to eastern cities by Colonel Jones on orders from his numerous acquaintances. Meat thus prepared brought a good price.

We certainly led a busy life, but it brought its rewards. We always had a camp appetite, and at night, when our camp work was done and we had reloaded our rifle shells for the following day's shooting, we were undeniably ready for a portion of nature's sweet restorer. Early rising in a hunter's camp must be the rule if success is desired. No alarm clock was needed in our camp. We awakened bright and early, refreshed by sleep and the pure mountain air. Never since those old hunting days have I been able so completely to relax and rest out in a few hours. I have been tempted by mahogany four-posters after a busy day, finished off with an after-theater supper; I have been surrounded with all the luxuries found in some of the most palatial homes of the United States—sleeping rooms in which ingenuity has been taxed for everything conducive to rest and comfort, even to a line of electric buttons on the bedpost to enable the occupant of the bed to call instantly the police, the fire department, the chambermaid, or, if a brandy-and-soda were desired, the "clerk of the buffet." When sleep has to be courted by those who live the demanding, swiftly moving life in our great cities, my recipe for insomnia is, start for the mountains, find a place as far removed from the busy haunts of man as possible, and curl up close to a little campfire.

During my experience as a hunter I made and saved a little over $10,000. Game was plentiful all over Wyoming, and it was impossible for me, during my hunting period, to foresee the day when the big game of the United States would become so nearly exterminated as it is.

I was brought up to believe that a Nimrod or mighty hunter

is as much to be respected as anybody—at least, among those who have the bread-and-butter problem to deal with in connection with securing the necessities of life. When, now, I hear the old-time hunters spoken of as game butchers or game hogs, I cannot help resenting the accusation. I take pride in knowing that I never was a hide hunter—that I never took pleasure in killing game that I could not use. And I derive some consolation from knowing that the game which I killed never had been anybody's pets. The wild animals had never depended upon mankind to furnish them with food or put their trust in creatures who, for either pleasure or profit, would deprive them of their lives. Nor was the extermination of big game in the West an unmixed evil. The passing of the buffalo meant a great deal to the civilization of our western ranges. It had more to do with starting the Indians of the Plains on the white man's road which they now are obliged to travel, than all the forces brought to bear upon them by the United States Army.

Part of hunting camp in Shirley Basin, Wyoming, September, 1880. Game just killed hangs at the right.

Front porch of the WS Ranch bunkhouse about 1884, showing three visiting English gentlemen, six of the cowboys, and, at the left, Ned the grizzly bear cub.

The mountain wagon, a favorite type of vehicle in the West before the day of the automobile. An outfit that belonged to the author. Photographed 1890.

Trophies of a hunt in the Big Horn Mountains of Wyoming Territory. Taken in camp in 1879, with a party of English sportsmen. Left to right: Charles Burke, old-time hunter, Hudson Bay Company and American Fur Company trapper; Mark Firth, English sportsman; George, the cook; M. F. S. Stevens and a Mr. Straker, English sportsmen; James H. Cook, guide in charge; Mr. Holbrook, English sportsman. Lying in foreground, Harold C. Wilson, English sportsman.

James H. Cook in buckskin hunting suit, 1886.

Billy Martin, hunting partner of the author.

10

Nature's Noblemen

IN THE FALL OF 1879, Billy Martin, Charlie, and I were hunting in the Shirley Basin country in Wyoming. Billy made a trip on the railroad down to Cheyenne. When he returned to camp he brought a number of young English sportsmen with him. Colonel Jones had sent them to our camp in order to give them a good opportunity to get some big-game shooting, and also to give us a chance to make a little extra money. These gentlemen proved to be as fine a lot as it was ever my privilege to meet. They were ardent young sportsmen—Oxford men, athletic, full of life, and with all the education necessary to make anyone fully enjoy living close to Mother Nature. They remained in our camp about a month and returned to England fully loaded with both trophies of the chase and, I think, the feeling that they had had a most enjoyable time in the American Rockies.

During the time I had been in Wyoming and Colorado, I had met on numerous occasions Professors E. D. Cope and O. C. Marsh, in their day two of the greatest naturalists of the world. (I had met Professor Marsh, one of the several paleontologists whom it was my good fortune to know, at the Red Cloud Agency during my trip of 1874, already referred to.) I was able, in one way and another, to render them a little assistance in their research work, both in Wyoming and, later on, in New Mexico. I also met and rendered a few favors to Professor Hayden and Professor King, scientists who did a great amount of work in Wyoming. My two partners were greatly interested in all things pertaining to natural history. We were all close observers of everything, animate or inanimate, pertaining to any section of the country in which we ever ranged. The evidence of anything connected with prehistoric animal or plant life was especially interesting to me. Conversations with Professors Marsh and Cope, and talks which I had heard them give, aroused in me a desire to know more about such things; and I was always on the lookout for any fossil material which I might find exposed, in order that I might direct to it men who made a special study of such material.

Meanwhile, Colonel Jones took more and more interest in me—an interest which he often expressed by sending to our camp interesting visitors who either needed rest and a change or wanted to enjoy big-game hunting with reliable guides. One of these men was Dr. Charles P. Murray of New York City, whose stay we enjoyed very much. (Some years later he visited me in New Mexico.) About others I shall have something to say in the course of my narrative.

My partner Charlie went to visit a brother who lived in the oil regions of Pennsylvania. While there he had an experience which was luckier for him than for me: he fell in love, and soon after married the girl of his choice. Thus I lost the companionship of one of the best boys I ever knew.

Later on, two parties of sportsmen happening at the same time to want Billy Martin and me to take them out for a big-game hunt, Billy went with one party and I with the other. I missed my old companions very much in many ways. Besides their other accomplishments, both were good camp cooks. They preferred cooking to other camp duties, such as the care of our horses, pegging out hides for drying, baling them, and the like, all of which were comparatively laborious.

When I parted company with Billy at that time, I little thought that our next meeting would be over forty years later at my ranch home in Nebraska, which meeting came about in a most odd, though pleasing, manner. For some years past I have been in the habit of spending my winters in southern California, to escape the rigors of the Nebraska climate. During the winter of 1919 I became acquainted with a newspaper and magazine writer of Los Angeles named E. A. Brininstool, and we were soon very good friends, he being greatly interested in all matters pertaining to the old Indian and frontier days. (He was engaged at the time in writing a history of the old Bozeman trail.) I gave Mr. Brininstool some of my personal experiences and recollections of Chief Red Cloud, to be used in his book. After my return to the ranch that spring, I received a letter from Mr. Brininstool, stating that he was acquainted in Los Angeles with an old-time market hunter named Martin, who said that he used to hunt big game out in the Big Horn Mountains of Wyoming with a partner named Cook, with Cheyenne as headquarters. At that time I had not mentioned any of my hunting experiences to Mr. Brininstool, and he was not aware that I had ever had a hunting partner; but the fact that Martin had hunted in Wyoming with a man by my name struck Mr. Brininstool as a peculiar circumstance, and he at once wrote me asking if I had ever known a big-game hunter named Billy Martin. It was indeed my old hunting pal. I wrote him to pack his belongings and come to my ranch at once. He did so and today is comfortably settled on two hundred acres of land adjoining my ranch. Needless to say, I am glad to have him with me, and it is very pleasant to recount together the old days when, in partnership, we hunted the buffalo, elk, antelope, deer, and bear in a section devoted now to agricultural pursuits, oil development, and grazing.

After the departure of Charlie Alexander and Billy Martin, I was left to go it alone, but I found enough to do to keep me busy. Guiding sportsmen from various parts of the world, and also men interested in research work in several branches of science, grew to be such a business with me that, when I finally left Wyoming to go to New Mexico to live, I had a hunting outfit consisting of one hundred head of saddle, work, and pack horses, wagons, complete pack outfits, a cook, a steward, camp tenders, tentage, and camp equipment of all sorts—probably as complete an outfit as could be found anywhere in the world at that time. Among the noted sportsmen who came to hunt with me were Sir Eustace Downey and Sir Guy Downey, men who had hunted big game in many parts of the world. There were also, among many others, such distinguished men as Lord Brassey, Gordon Cummins, Lord Fairbairn, Rev. Foakes Jackson, Paul du Chaillu, the noted African explorer, Harold C. Wilson, Montague F. S. Stevens, and Mark Firth. I furnished everything complete for making these trips, and sometimes received as much as £150 a month for each sportsman taken out. On one occasion I took a party of eighteen noted English sportsmen out on a hunt for big game in northwestern Wyoming. No expense was spared to have everything that would tend to make the trip something to be looked back upon with pleasure, and hardships were avoided as completely as possible.

The benefit which I derived from hunting trips with such people and, whenever possible, from men of science, did not come to me in the form of money. Nearly all of the men with whom I associated in camp could well be called nature's noblemen—scholars of high attainments. Many had had every educational advantage which the world had to offer and were further favored by having inherited wealth which enabled them to pursue the life or study most interesting to themselves, a knowledge of which they could pass along to others less fortunate.

When I had climbed almost over Fool's Hill, after groping in ignorance for quite a period of my earlier years, the thought dawned upon me that if ever I attained any fruit from the tree of knowledge—even from its lowest branches—I should have to take advantage of every opportunity offered me of association with those who possessed attainments and talents far superior to mine. A desire to do this was of the greatest possible value to me, for it brought much sunshine and pleasure into my life, and the choicest of heaven's blessings in the way of many dear friends among men whose lives have been of the greatest value to mankind.

Late in the fall of 1880, I guided a party of Englishmen on a hunting trip into the Big Horn Mountains of Wyoming. We found plenty of game—elk, buffalo, deer, and mountain sheep being there in abundance. Bear also were unusually plentiful, and we had some great sport hunting them.

One morning I started out with two of the party on a bear hunt. It was their first hunt, and they had never seen a bear in its wild state. As still-hunting bear usually requires the utmost skill, I had little hope of success; especially as the heavy hob-nailed shoes worn by the Englishmen made so much noise against the rocks that I was sure we should not be able to get within gunshot of a bear. When we reached the place where I knew there was good bear ground, I instructed the men to move, in line with me, very slowly and carefully through the thick timber, to keep within sight of me, and also, if they saw any animal, to beckon me to them.

When we had moved along cautiously in this manner for perhaps a quarter of a mile, one of the Englishmen motioned to me to come to him. When I reached his side he said that he had seen what he thought was a hog enter a little thicket about a hundred yards distant. Knowing that there was not a hog within a hundred miles of us, I was sure he had seen a bear. Looking the ground over carefully, I could see where we could get to a low, rocky point of land that overlooked the thicket into which the strange animal had gone. Backing slowly away until out of sight, we slipped around to the point. Reaching there, I peered over into the thicket. In a few minutes I saw a bear within fifty yards of me. He was digging into the ground after some food, and, as I observed that he was not alarmed, I watched him several minutes.

Suddenly I thought I saw something move in a clump of brush a short distance from the bear. Changing my position a few inches, and watching the place, I caught sight of a very large silvertip grizzly lying down. Just as I made this discovery, to my astonishment three more bears put in an appearance. They slouched up to the bear which was digging into the ground, and he snarled at the newcomers as if warning them not to disturb him in his efforts to secure food. I motioned for my companions to slip up beside me, and they soon had a view of the bears.

The Englishmen were armed with double-barreled express rifles of heavy bore. I whispered to them that I would shoot the big bear which was lying down, and that, the moment I fired, they were to open up on any of the others that were in good positions for shooting. I shot the big fellow, and at the report of my rifle he tried to rise, screaming with pain and rage. The one of the bears which was nearest my victim immediately sprang upon the wounded animal and began to bite him. The Englishmen began shooting at once, but the bears, instead of trying to escape, sprang at each other like demons, fighting and growling savagely. In less than a minute those four bears were merged into one struggling heap, into which we poured shot after shot. The big fellow which I had shot first was out of the battle entirely.

Presently the smallest animal broke away from the others and ran about fifty yards, as fast as he could streak it. Climbing up on a fallen log, he rose on his hind legs and stood looking back at the battle, which was still raging with unabated fury. He offered a beautiful mark; I shot him through the heart, and he dropped off the log with a yell.

One after another, the remaining bears went down under our rain of bullets, each hit not less than ten or twelve times. It was an exciting scene. My English friends were greatly elated, and I myself had witnessed a sight such as I never would have dreamed could be. Very seldom are five bears found together by a hunter, and their reason for flying at each other in such a savage manner, paying no attention whatever either to the reports of our rifles or to ourselves, was inexplicable.

When we packed the hides of those five silvertip grizzlies back to camp that evening, we certainly had something to talk about. My two English friends, Messrs. Graham and Maynard, if still living, probably remember with pleasure that exciting bear hunt with me.

After the party of English sportsmen whom I had been guiding had returned to England, I made a trip to Cheyenne. One of the first friends whom I called on was Colonel Jones of the Railroad Hotel. He had used tons of game which I had killed and shipped to him, and had also sold for me tons of elk meat and other game to parties in Omaha, Chicago, and New York City. At that time the only railway line across the continent ran through Cheyenne, and many of the most distinguished travelers stopped off there for a day or two in order to break the monotony of the long journey from the East to California. This included many sportsmen who were anxious to hunt big game in Wyoming, as well as noted scientists, both geologists and naturalists. Health-seekers, too, were numerous. The Railroad Hotel was the most popular hostelry in Cheyenne in those days. All the celebrities stopped there. Those desirous of having a big-game hunt would inquire of Colonel Jones where to find a reliable guide, and he invariably referred all such persons to me. If I were too busy with others at the time, I always tried to find good, reliable men who were available. Many parties came to grief by going to Cheyenne and employing strangers to take them out hunting.

When I talked with Colonel Jones on this trip, he said he had a guest who wished to go out for a little trip into the mountains. He cared nothing about hunting but wanted to regain his health by living out of doors for a time. Colonel Jones said he was a very distinguished man, and gave his name as Mr. Roebling. His father had built the Brooklyn Bridge. It appeared that the father had lost his life, and the son completely ruined his health, by working down in the caissons, directing the laborers when they were laying the foundations for the abutments of the bridge. At the bottom of the East River the air in the caissons was so foul that the strongest and hardiest workmen could work only in fifteen-minute shifts. I was introduced to Mr. Roebling and found him a very pleasant gentleman. I took him out into the mountains and stayed with him about a month, after which we returned again to Cheyenne. I enjoyed being out with him very much, save for the fear that he would die in one of the awful cramping spasms which seized him at times.

In Cheyenne, Colonel Jones introduced me to J. M. Ward, better known as "Monte" Ward, one of the greatest baseball players of that day. He, too, wanted to go out on a hunt for big game. It was now very late in the year to go into the mountains, but Ward was anxious to make the trip. My old friend Bergersen, the leading gunsmith and gun dealer in Cheyenne was also anxious to go on a hunt. I therefore took them up to Carbon Station on the Union Pacific Railroad, from which point we went out to Elk Mountain, that being about the nearest point to the railroad where good hunting could be expected.

Before we started, Mr. L.——, the express agent at Cheyenne, came to me and said, "I will furnish the transportation for your camp outfit and your party to Carbon and return, if you will ship me down a nice saddle of mountain sheep for my Christmas dinner. I expect a party of friends to dine with me, and want to give them a real treat."

I told L—— that it was very late in the season for mountain sheep in the section where we were going, and that probably the snow had driven them all out of the mountains, but that I would gladly do my best to find and kill one for him.

"That's enough!" he exclaimed. "I am sure of my meat." He therefore shipped our guns, bedding, snowshoes, and other effects, to Carbon, also securing round-trip transportation for us. When we reached Elk Mountain, and I endeavored to fulfill my promise, I found that the sheep had all left that part of the mountains, and that, as I had expected, it would scarcely be possible to ship L—— his desired mutton. There was nothing left to shoot but antelope and deer. I felt exceedingly sorry for my friend the express agent.

One day I happened to kill one of the fattest antelope I ever had seen. It was a barren doe—the choicest of all antelope meat. I dressed it nicely, being careful to remove all antelope hair from the meat. I then sawed the legs off short, so that the size of the leg bone would not serve as a giveaway, after which I sacked it very carefully and shipped it to him.

We stayed out on that hunt for several days and had loads of fun. Ward had never killed any game, but on this trip he shot several antelope. We had each taken a pair of Norwegian snowshoes along. Bergersen was an expert on them, but poor Ward and I had a hard time learning to manage them. One day Ward and I had worked our way nearly to the top of Elk Mountain on our snowshoes. We were both pretty well played out from our exertions. On our way we had killed an antelope. Bergersen had gone out in a different direction. It was nearly night, and time for us to start for the old cabin at the foot of the mountain where we were camped. The cabin could be plainly seen, and it was at the end of a straightaway slide from the point where we were, down a cañon nearly filled with soft snow. Neither of us had confidence in his ability to handle snowshoes sufficiently well to make a success of a slide from the top of the mountain down to the cabin. Ward said he would not try it for the world. I told him that I was going to try the slide act, and that if he would go ahead down the ridge, I would soon pass him. He said he had had all the snowshoeing he wanted for one day and would walk down the ridge on the side of the cañon where the snow had blown off. Ward thereupon started.

After resting a few minutes, I lashed our saddle of antelope to my back. I had my rifle and steering pole to carry in my hands. I summoned my courage, turned the points of my snowshoes toward the cabin, and, putting the pole under my arm, shoved off. The next second I was rushing down that cañon at a terrific speed. Just about the time I was scheduled to pass Ward, I struck a place where there was a streak of crust on the snow. My shoes crossed in front of me, and I sailed into the air like an arrow from a bow. I landed on my head in the snow, many feet down the hill. I had tied the snowshoes to my feet, and that saved me, for I went my full length down into the soft snow where it was yards deep, and my shoes fortunately prevented my going deeper. I had to climb up my own legs, so to speak, to get out of my awkward position, and I was nearly smothered and blinded before I succeeded, the soft snow filling my mouth, nose, ears, and eyes. My rifle was down in the snow, too.

As soon as I could recover my breath and look around, the first thing that met my gaze was Ward. He was rolling over and over on the ridge, shouting with laughter at the sight he had just witnessed. That was enough for me. I was determined to finish that slide or break my neck in the attempt. After finding my rifle by pawing around in the snow, I climbed out and made another start. But this time I sat down on the snowshoes, so to speak, and kept them well together. I slid clear to the cabin, and it was the fastest ride I ever had in my life. Ward returned as soon as possible.

When we packed up and started for Cheyenne, I dreaded meeting the express agent, as I had not heard from him regarding the "mountain sheep" I had shipped him. As we stepped from the train he was the first person I saw. He came running up and gave us all a good handshake. I could not look him in the face, but Bergersen innocently inquired how he liked the sheep.

"Well, boys," was his hearty response, "that was just great! My friends all said that was the finest meat they ever tasted in all their lives." He then said that people could talk to *him* about elk meat, antelope, or deer, but in his estimation mountain sheep was the best meat on earth, and not to be mentioned in the same breath with any other kind of wild game. "I have lived here a long time," he added, "and eaten all kinds of game until I can tell by the taste just what kind of meat it is, but believe me, nothing can compare with that mountain sheep you sent me, and I shall always remember it."

This was so rich, and was announced in such a convincing and sincere manner, that he was not informed of the trick we had perpetrated on him. Nor did we request him to change his opinion regarding the qualities of mountain-sheep meat.

Late one fall, when I was hunting in the mountains south of the Shirley Basin, Wyoming, there came a very heavy fall of snow, covering the ground to a depth of about eighteen inches. The game in the mountains seemed instinctively able to tell when, to prevent being trapped by deep snows, it was time to leave the high ranges and seek a lower level where the snowfall had not been so heavy. We could see signs everywhere about us that the game were moving to the lower feeding grounds. We therefore prepared to break camp and follow.

A few days prior to this heavy snowfall, we had killed three or four elk high up in the mountains. We had dressed them out, quartered them, hung the meat up in trees, and left it until we could return with pack horses and carry it to camp. Not wishing to leave the meat, Billy Martin and I took some pack horses and a man whom we had hired, and started through the deep snow up into the mountains. We had much trouble breaking a trail to the spot where we had left the meat. When we reached the place, we were somewhat surprised to discover that an immense bear had been having a feast on the elk meat. We had hung the hindquarters on stubs of limbs of big pine trees, and the bear had stood on his hind legs and, reaching as high as possible, had stripped off the fat and kidneys and shredded a good deal of the best of our meat. What he did not eat, he had playfully or maliciously left lying about. Thinking that the season had arrived when bears would all be in their dens taking their winter sleep, we had had no thought of a bear hunt when we started out after the elk meat. But here was the chance of getting the largest bear which we had ever seen sign of in the Shirley Basin country. Martin and I talked the matter over, finally concluding that, as there was some of the elk meat which the bear had not spoiled, we had better send the man back to camp with it while we tried to kill the pesky varment that had tampered with our meat cache. We carried some of the elk meat along with us, in case the chase should prove to be a long one.

It was not a difficult trail to follow: the big fellow had left a plain record through the deep soft snow. We had, of course, no thought of finding the bear anywhere in the vicinity of the spot where he had eaten his last meal. After we had followed the trail about two hundred yards, it made a sharp turn, doubling back almost to the starting point, then led off in another direction. We cut across this bend in the trail and followed cautiously along for perhaps another hundred yards. Finally I saw where the bear had climbed over a big pine log. Mounting the log, I was startled to note that the trail had come to an end! Within six feet of me grew a cluster of young pines. Looking closely down into them, I could see a big bunch of hair. Old Bruin was taking a nap! Probably the feast of which he had so recently partaken made him sleep more soundly than usual.

That bear's awakening was a rude one. My partner Billy was behind me but a step or two as I mounted the log over which the bear's trail led. The instant I saw that things would soon happen, I made sign to Billy to look out for squalls. Then I took aim for the center of that big ball of hair and pulled the trigger of my 40–90 Sharps rifle, immediately jumping back off the log.

The next instant I both saw and heard something. The great head and a large portion of the front end of a huge grizzly loomed up in very plain sight from the opposite side of that log. I was aware that a bear could, on occasions, utter fearsome screams, but that old fellow, as he rose up out of his bed in the pines to see what had dared sting, smoke, and so rudely disturb his slumbers, gave vent to the most awful sounds I had ever heard. At that short range he looked very tall and very wide to me, and the expression on his face was far from pleasant.

Things were now happening rapidly. No sooner had the bear exposed his head and body, with his forelegs all set for smashing an enemy, than Billy sent a bullet through his heart. This was too much lead, and down went Bruin. The man with the pack animals heard the shots and came back to us. We took our bear to camp. When we dressed him, we found that our bullets had both passed through him, not half an inch apart. Billy had shot to kill. I, however, could not see what part of the bear I was shooting at. As I now look back to that affair, I can see where I might have really started a roughhouse with that bear.

We shipped the hide and carcass to Cheyenne. One of our customers, Mr. Dan Ullman, who conducted a meat market there at that time, sold both meat and hide for us. The latter brought us $50.00, as it was an exceptionally large and fine specimen, classified as silvertip grizzly. It was on exhibition in Cheyenne at the Ullman market for some time.

When we were drying and smoking meat in our camps, a great number of bones accumulated at the place where we attended to this feature of our hunting business. Small amounts of meat naturally clung to the bones, and there was always some meat so shattered by our bullets as to be undesirable for food. Many varieties of meat-eating animals were thus attracted to our bone-piles. Sometimes, after returning to camp late in the day, getting supper, and attending to our stock, we could not go to arrange the fires at our smokehouses where the meat was cured until well along in the evening. Knowing that some of the larger carnivores, such as the puma (mountain lion) and bear, when driven by hunger, might be encountered in the darkness, even a short distance from camp, we usually went prepared to protect ourselves when visiting the smokehouses at night. We had numerous scares about these bone-piles, especially on dark nights. Even the sound of a badger, scuttling hurriedly away from his dinner into the timber and rocks, would cause us to start and grasp our weapons. We had to trust to luck to carry us to victory in the event of a battle in the darkness with some ill-tempered bear or puma which might resent being disturbed at its evening meal.

One dark night I went from our camp to the smokehouse, a distance of about a hundred yards. It was located in a little cañon which was well hidden by a dense growth of brush. An old elk trail, which could be followed by the sense of touch when the eyesight failed, led from our camp direct to the smokehouse. For some reason we had no lantern in camp that night. Knowing that I should have to attend to the fire, I took along, in order to kindle it, a little bunch of coarse, dry grass which, stuffed into an old flour sack, I had been using for a pillow. Kneeling down in front of the pit, I struck a match and set fire to a handful of the dry grass, in order to give me light enough to throw some fuel into the fire pit. A sudden flare lighted the immediate surroundings for a moment, and as the flame leaped up, something else did likewise and bounded past me very closely into the darkness. I must have been prepared, for I took a snap shot at the animal as, with a growl, it disappeared.

My first flare of light died out very suddenly, and darkness again reigned. I could hear quite familiar sounds coming from a short distance away, indicating that some sort of beast was very much wrought up. I was blinded by the light from the fire; nevertheless, I wanted more light—and right away, too! Holding my butcher knife in one hand for protection, I groped about for some more of the dry grass, struck a match, and started a fresh blaze, adding some of the fuel which was lying about.

Three English sportsmen were with me in camp that night. Hearing my shot, they started to come to my aid but were unable to follow the trail in the darkness, and they had considerable trouble and somewhat damaged their skins and clothing before they reached me. I told them of my quick snap shot at some animal which had passed me from the bone-pile, and called their attention to the sounds which could yet be heard but a short distance away. They wanted to make some torches and get after the beast right away, but I persuaded them to wait until morning. I figured that we should have a good-sized creature of the cat family to deal with, and a wounded one at that.

The next morning we marched up the cañon in open formation, and just a few feet away from the smokehouse found a dead puma. He was a big fellow, but very thin in flesh, and showed signs of having recently been in some battle royal in which he had been bruised and cut up considerably. My shot had struck him well back in the flank but had ranged forward and torn to pieces the lobe of one lung. I kept his old hide for some time in my camp. Later I gave it to a friend to adorn the wall of his cabin home.

Even elk hunting, during the days when great bands of elk could be found in many of the mountain ranges of Wyoming, had its occasional elements of danger. A wounded bull elk might turn on the hunter and do him great injury, especially if the animal's horns were grown and in fighting condition. Any buck of the deer families, when wounded, may become a most desperate warrior. I never took many chances when dealing with wounded animals, but on one or two occasions I had rather exciting experiences with them.

One day when I was hunting elk with Billy Martin, we shot down six from a band found in the pine timber on a mountain south of old Fort Caspar. One old bull with an exceptionally large set of horns had dropped so suddenly in his tracks that we thought a bullet had broken his neck. Going to the spot where he lay, we leaned our rifles against a tree some twenty feet away and made preparations to dress the game. After using my whetstone a few moments, I picked up one of the forelegs of the big bull to add a few finishing touches to the edge of my knife by stropping it on his hoof—a trick I had learned from the Mexicans in the jungles of Texas.

Hardly had I started in to strop my knife on his hoof when the elk drew a deep breath and started to spring to his feet. He had only been creased by the bullet, which had passed through the top of his neck. He had been badly stunned from the shock, but his recovery, when it came, was equally sudden and thorough.

I hung to the bull's foreleg, holding it up so that he could not get his forefeet under him. In some manner he was successful in giving me a kick on the elbow, which caused me to lose my hold, and I fell across his neck. Grabbing hold of the horn farthest from the ground, I managed to scramble over and get my feet on his other horn, hoping thus to be able to hold his head to the ground. This was my first and only experience at bulldogging an elk.

While I was having my troubles at the front, Billy had rushed in in an endeavor to get a hold on the flank of the bull, trusting that he might thus be able to keep him down until I could take advantage of a lull in the proceedings and draw my knife across the animal's throat. The kick on my elbow had sent my knife to a distance far beyond my reach, but Billy had not noticed that detail. By some manner of means, the bull got his hind legs into action, and Billy, according to his own story, was kicked to a distance of about fifteen feet, landing on his back close to the guns. Scrambling to his feet, he grabbed his rifle and, taking advantage of a moment when he could shoot without danger of hitting me, put a stop to that bull's struggles.

I was not sorry when that scrimmage came to an end. I had a bloody nose and a black eye to care for, the results of a few whacks about the head and face from the prongs of the elk's horns. My clothes were pretty well stripped off, also some skin. A moving picture of that tussle would be worth having right now. I should be interested in learning whether the elk or I myself wore the more frightened expression while the trouble was at its height.

Of the much that has been said and written regarding the dangers of hunting big game, more was true before the year 1870 than has been true since. With a flintlock rifle, which might only flash in the pan at an instant when most needed, or which, when once fired, did not make even a good cudgel, as was the case with all muzzle-loading rifles, conditions were far different from those of present-day hunting. In these days of high-power automatic rapid-fire guns of every description, no animal on earth has a chance for its life when once within range of such weapons. The steel-jacketed bullets now used will not flatten on the skull of some beast, as the soft lead bullets did in days past, when fired from a rifle having a slow twist (rifling) and using black powder. A modern steel missile traveling at the rate of about three thousand feet a second, followed, if necessary, by a shower of the same sort, reduces hunting dangers to the minimum, at least in so far as dangers come from the game.

Other dangers to which big-game hunters are subjected, such as sudden changes of climate, dangers by sea, and the like, will possibly remain as they now are for some time to come; but I feel that, no matter how large or how fierce any beast in the world may be, man can at this time very quickly destroy it. And, should aircraft be employed in so dubiously noble an endeavor, how quickly could the big game of the world be placed on the extinct list! Old hunters of great experience, such as Dr. William T. Hornaday, director of the Zoölogical Park in New York City, realize such conditions more than many others do. The work of such men in attempting to secure legislation which will prevent the total annihilation of the big game of the world is to me most commendable, and I trust that it will meet with the assistance necessary to secure success.

While I was hunting big game for the market or conducting parties of foreign sportsmen on hunting expeditions in the territory of Wyoming, it was necessary to keep good hunting country continually located. Game would shift its range at times, because forest fires had destroyed the grazing there, or because Indians, by hunting too closely in one section of country, would cause the game to disappear for a time. Before taking any party of sportsmen out for a hunt, I would ascertain to a certainty that game could be obtained in the section where they desired to hunt, or where I thought the shooting was likely to be good.

In the fall of 1881, I received a cablegram from some noted Englishmen whom I had previously guided, asking if I would outfit and guide them on another hunt in the Rockies. I replied that I would, and set a date when I would be ready to meet them with my outfit at Cheyenne. But first, hearing various rumors regarding the scarcity of game in parts of northern Wyoming, I made a scouting trip into the Big Horn Basin country to see if they were true. I took a pack outfit along and two companions. One of these was Arthur Sparhawk, an expert *cargador* or mule-packer. The other man, a Mr. Martin, was a friend of Sparhawk. He was a newspaperman, at that time acting as correspondent of the Boston *Transcript*, and was making a little visit in the West. We traveled by the way of old Fort Reno, thence up Powder River, crossed the mountains, and scouted about in the No Wood and Ten Sleep Creek country. We found grass plentiful, and, after making certain that my English sporting friends would find plenty of shooting, we started back for Cheyenne.

While we were traveling along the old Bozeman trail one hot day in the afternoon, a bunch of ten or a dozen buffalo came straggling into sight from behind a rugged butte, directly in front of us and not over a hundred yards away. I happened, at that moment, to be riding one of the best and fastest horses I ever owned. He was a thoroughly trained hunting horse, and the instant he caught sight of the buffalo was ready for action and eager to help me. For some unaccountable reason—for I had always derived pleasure from the thought that I never killed game when I could not make use of it—I let my good horse, Bunt, have his head, and away he headed for the game. In a few seconds I was within range of the buffalo, and I had shot down six of them before my blood had cooled to the point where I could think normally about what I was doing. We had no use whatever for the buffalo meat or the hides: we had plenty of good fat antelope meat on our pack horses, and buffalo hides were valueless to us on that scouting trip. When I returned to my friends, who had halted to watch me, I remarked that I had certainly just performed one fool stunt, and I think they agreed with me at the time.

We again started along the trail, and had gone but a couple of miles when we met a train consisting of about fifteen emigrant wagons bound for the northwest country. They were from Arkansas and Missouri, and were driving some good horses and mules. They also had the usual complement of dogs —which, seemingly greatly interested in our pack outfit, were the first to greet our appearance.

As we approached the leading wagon, the entire train came to a halt. Several men climbed down from the wagons to talk to us. One very venerable man with long, silver-white hair and beard, appeared to be the leader of the party. He asked us the usual run of questions—"Where are you from?" and "Where are you bound for?" which queries we answered truthfully and fully. The old man then told us where their party was from and whither bound.

I observed that one man in the train seemed to be overcome with sorrow, as if he had recently passed through some great trial or affliction. Tears and moans which he could not restrain came from him at intervals, although he appeared to be a very rugged type of man. The aged leader of the party explained to us that during the previous night a child had been born to the wife of this man, and the mother had died. They had laid the poor woman to rest by the side of the road that morning.

We were also informed that the entire party was suffering greatly for water. Little children in many of the wagons were crying for a drink. The whole train was also in want of meat; for they had seen but little game since leaving the Platte River, and had been unable to secure any at all, despite the fact that they had been told that they would find, all along the road, game which could easily be secured.

I told them that, if they would follow me, I would lead them to a good camping spot about two miles distant, where they would find plenty of water for themselves and their stock, as well as the best of grazing for their wearied animals. I also said that I had just shot down some buffalo a short distance back on the trail, and that if, when they reached the camping spot, they would unload one of their wagons and accompany me, I would fill the wagon with meat enough to last them to their journey's end, and also show them how to jerk or cure meat so that it would not spoil.

We could easily see that the emigrants were rather suspicious of us, and doubtless they had good reason for so feeling, for we were certainly armed to the teeth and considerably travel-stained. Possibly their thought was that we might be after their horses. The men of the party drew aside and held a council. They finally decided that, as they greatly outnumbered us and were themselves well armed, they would take a chance and ac-company us to the camping spot which I had described. We thereupon placed ourselves at the head of the train, and I led them to a fine spring of water—a place I well knew. Here one of the wagons was unloaded, and half a dozen men of their party started with me for the spot where I had killed the buf-falo. I left Mr. Sparhawk and his friend Martin in camp, close by the emigrant train.

The men who accompanied me were surprised and delighted when I took them to the scene of the buffalo slaughter. The bodies were still warm, and the men could see for themselves that I had told them the truth. Their wagon was loaded so full of meat that the driver had to walk, and we started back for the camp. Upon our arrival the entire assemblage turned out to see the buffalo meat, and when suppertime arrived they had a feast of broiled steaks. Although it may have been a simple meal, I am certain that it was thoroughly enjoyed by the hungry emigrants.

Whatever suspicions may have been directed toward us now vanished, and we were invited to remain in their camp for the night. If they had been entertaining thoughts that we were horse thieves, they may have concluded that, as they kept a night guard, they could watch our movements better if we remained in their camp than if we camped elsewhere. Anyway, we made our sleep with them under the guns of their guards, who went on duty the moment they had had their supper.

The smaller children were put to bed with full tummies rather early that night. Before the older members of the party turned into their blankets, the venerable leader called us together, saying that he had something to tell us. When we were all assembled he told us that he considered their meeting with us a direct act of Divine Providence, and that it must have been an act of God which caused the killing of the buffalo which had so bountifully supplied them with food. Perhaps it was. Who knows? At any rate, I am glad that on that one occasion, when that little bunch of buffalo came in sight, I acted on impulse working in conjunction with my Winchester rifle. The aged leader of the train then offered up a prayer which was surely from his heart, thanking the Creator for his kindness to them in their hour of need.

The following morning I instructed our new-found friends in the art of jerking meat. None of their party had ever before seen a wild buffalo or tasted buffalo meat. When we bade them good-bye, not only were their stomachs full, but their hearts as well; and I know that the "God bless you's" which were uttered on that occasion were sincere and genuine.

PART III
THE APACHE WAR: NEW MEXICO

*James H. Cook during the Geronimo campaign in 1885,
on his favorite war horse, Old Curley.*

*A view in Socorro County, New Mexico, showing the kind of
country in which the Apaches had their strongholds.*

11

Geronimo

IN THE FALL OF 1882, after a most enjoyable big-game hunt
in the Big Horn Mountains with a number of English gentlemen whom I had guided on previous annual hunting trips in the
Rocky Mountains, I went to southwestern New Mexico with
these same gentlemen. They were about to engage in cattle
ranching, and I assisted them in purchasing and managing some
large ranch properties in that country, making my headquarters in Keller Valley, on the San Francisco River, about eighty
miles north and west of Silver City, on a ranch purchased by
one of my English hunting friends, Mr. Harold C. Wilson of
Cheltenham, England. I was general manager of this ranch from
the time of its purchase until 1887. I used a "WS" brand on all
the cattle and horses purchased or raised by Mr. Wilson, and
this ranch was soon known among the cattlemen of New Mexico as the WS Ranch. My other English sportsmen friends purchased large ranch properties within a radius of fifty miles of
the WS, and I assisted them whenever needed in the management of their ranches while I remained in New Mexico.

The WS Ranch was at that time some distance from a railroad, Deming being the nearest railway point. A stage ran to
Silver City each day, drawn by six horses. At the time of which
I write, one of Wells, Fargo & Company's most noted shotgun
messengers, Dan Tucker, helped guard the passengers and
treasure carried by the stages. Tucker had some thrilling experiences with stage robbers in the Southwest. He had the reputation of being one of the bravest of the many gun-fighters of
the southwest borderlands. Guarding treasure entrusted to the
care of Wells, Fargo & Company was a pretty hazardous occupation in that bandit-infested country at that time. New

Mexico contained its full quota of bad men, both white and black, and redskins at times caused the ranchmen, freighters, miners, and mail carriers to go heavily armed and ready for war at any moment.

It was an interesting country to me for several reasons. Evidences of a prehistoric race of people abounded on all sides. There was also proof of prehistoric life in the shape of petrified bones of extinct animals deposited in the sedimentary rocks, and tracks of flying reptiles or prehistoric birds may be seen there to this day. These ancient tracks stand up on the lava rocks like the raised type used by the blind. They were evidently made while the lava rock was still soft, the pressure of the feet having doubtless made the material firmer than the surrounding material. The undisturbed lava rock has settled more than that where the pressure was applied, and left the tracks standing out plainly on the surface of the rock.

For an unknown length of time before the coming of the whites, this section of the country had been the home of the Apache tribes of Indians. The Apaches have the reputation of having been the most warlike and merciless savages with whom the people of the United States ever had to contend in their winning of the West. Some of the instances of their savagery, such as the murder and butchery of Judge McComas and his wife and the abduction and murder of their little son Charlie, are matters of recorded history. Of the many travelers on the old southern trails to California—prospectors and others—who have been wiped out by Apaches during the territorial days of New Mexico and Arizona, but few written records have, I think, been kept.

At the time of my advent into that country, some evidence could still be obtained of a few persons, at least, who had met death at the hands of Apaches. Visible proof could be seen in the form of parts of the skeletons, or often whole skeletons, of white men, bearing the marks of bullets, knives, and arrows, skulls crushed by blows from stones, and other such evidences.

Metal buttons and buckles, and even parts of clothing, stored near by by the pack rats, often added their mute testimony to these deeds of bloodshed and human suffering. One unfortunate fellow, whose bones I found down in a cañon in the Mogollon Mountains, had tried to scratch a few words on the side of a cliff near by with his knife, the rusted blade of which I discovered. The writing was so weathered away that I could not decipher it. A thigh bone badly smashed by a bullet, and a partially rusted iron arrow point lying among the bones, as if it had been imbedded in his body, told a little story of the thrilling scene which had been enacted there.

The country about the ranches which we established had been, just previously to our coming, the stronghold of the old Apache chiefs, Mangus Colorado, Cochise, and Victorio. After the killing of Victorio, a short time before our arrival, there was a lull in the Indian troubles, until the summer of 1885. Then came the Geronimo outbreak.

Up to the time of the establishment of the WS Ranch, the cattlemen of southwestern New Mexico had no roundup system in handling their herds. Every ranchman looked after his own stock, each by his own method. Soon after my arrival, I helped organize a stockmen's association, with a system of roundups similar to that employed on the northern cattle ranges. I superintended the western division of these roundups for the first two years of their existence in Socorro and Grant counties. This work on the range made me familiar with the country lying between the Mogollon Range of mountains and the Arizona and Old Mexico boundary lines. This knowledge proved valuable to me, and perhaps to others, when one of the worst Indian campaigns in the history of the Southwest came on.

Two of my friends had purchased a ranch near the San Francisco River, about thirty miles north of my headquarters, and had named it the SU Ranch. An English friend of theirs had been visiting with them during the summer of 1885, and on numerous occasions this gentleman had ridden down to visit with me at the WS. One day he came down to see me and also to say good-bye, for he planned to start for his English home in the near future. The day before he left the WS we were out hunting quail nearly all day, little dreaming of what was to happen within the next few hours. The following morning about nine o'clock, he bade me farewell and started for the SU Ranch. About half an hour later, a man riding at full speed dashed up to the ranch house and shouted that Indians had been chasing him. Judging from the number he had seen, he thought all the Indians at San Carlos and Camp Apache must have broken off their reservations. He was so frightened and excited that he could scarcely talk, but at last made out to inform me that he and some companions had camped near Blue Creek, about ten miles west of the WS Ranch, that morning, and that a large party of Indians had attacked their camp and killed his companions. He was just bringing in the saddle and pack horses to camp when the Indians jumped them, and, being mounted, he had escaped. I told him to ride to Alma, a little mining settlement about a mile and a half distant, and warn the people living there.

My brother and all the cowboys employed at the ranch were that day branding calves out on the range. Charlie Moore, an old employee whose duty was to look after the bands of saddle and stock horses on the range, was the only person at the men's house. A housekeeper and a Mexican boy about sixteen years of age, with myself, were all then living at the main ranch house. As soon as the rider who had brought the warning had started for Alma, I hurried into the house and notified the housekeeper and the boy. We went to the storeroom and got a lot of empty gunny sacks. Hastily filling them with sand from the garden, we piled them in the deep windows of the adobe house, leaving only loopholes from which to fire. We then opened several cases of cartridges and placed them near the arms they fitted. (We always kept a good supply of arms and ammunition at the ranch.) Charlie Moore soon came in. When he heard the Indian news, he said that he had been out toward Blue Creek that morning but had seen no Indian sign, and it was his verdict that the bearer of the news must have been either drunk or crazy. I told him that we would go out and get in as many of the saddle horses as possible, anyway, and guard them until we knew the truth.

We rode out at once and brought in as many of the saddle animals as we could get handily into a corral near the bunkhouse. Soon after we had started out, a party of five men from Alma came to the ranch after me. They wanted me to go with them out on the range to ascertain if any Indians were in the neighborhood. Not finding me, they had started on, as the people in the Alma and Cooney mining camps were greatly alarmed by the fresh tidings of an Apache outbreak, both these places having been besieged by Apaches before. This party of men, when but a few miles from the ranch, was fired upon by a party of Indians lying in ambush, and two of them instantly killed. The names of the murdered men were Calvin Orwig and Nat Luse. The rest of the party escaped by running back through the brush and rocks.

Just as Charlie Moore and I corralled the saddle horses, an animal which had been ridden by one of the party from Alma came running to the corral with the bridle and saddle on. When we caught him we saw that both horse and saddle were covered with blood. We knew well enough then that someone had been shot, and we made up our minds that Indians were in the country.

I had two teams of driving horses in a small pasture near the house, and I sent Moore to get them. I rode up on a little hill near the house, where I could see the animals in the pasture and also get a shot at anyone who attempted to prevent Moore from securing them. He had ridden but a short distance into the pasture when I saw a string of Indians, about twenty-five in number, part mounted, the rest on foot, moving directly toward the horses. Moore, who could not see the Indians, was riding directly toward them. I tried to stop him by shouting, but he apparently did not hear me; and I immediately opened fire on the Indians with a 40–90 Sharps rifle at a range of about one thousand yards. This checked them, and they ran to cover in the rocks and brush. The horses in the pasture, when the Indians returned my fire, stampeded and came running to their stable. Moore located the Indians by their firing and, getting onto high ground where he could see them, helped me send a few leaden compliments to speed the parting guests. They made a good run back into the mountains. In doing so they had to cross some fairly open ground, but the range, with such rapidly moving targets, was too great for us. I could not see that our bullets injured any of them.

Night was coming on, and Charlie and I returned to the house. We stood guard all night, he at the corrals and I at the main ranch house. I took my pistols and two double-barreled shotguns loaded with buckshot, and stayed outside within the shadow of the buildings, there being some moonlight. Just as day was breaking, the housekeeper called me to come in and get some coffee. At the time I was standing by the side of an adobe storehouse about fifteen feet from the kitchen door. I went in, drank a cup of coffee, and returned to my station. To my surprise I observed the tracks of two Indians within a few feet of the spot. One savage had worn moccasins; the other had been barefoot. I was certainly startled, but I soon saw, by their tracks in the soft earth of the garden, that they had left the place. I signaled Charlie to come to me, and when he arrived we followed the tracks a short distance. We concluded that, as the Indians were not trying to conceal their tracks, we might be able to overtake and get a shot at them.

It was now daylight, and we followed the trail of these Indians to the top of a hill a short distance from the ranch. At this point we discovered that they had been joined by several other Indians. With my field glasses I took a look over the trails that led into the Mogollon Mountains. Looking over on what was called the Deep Creek trail, I could see a line of objects moving along. They were too far away to be seen plainly, but as no range stock had ever traveled over that trail, I was sure the objects were Indians.

We returned to the ranch. After getting some breakfast, Charlie and I rode out to the top of a high hill about a mile west of the ranch, where we could overlook our horse range. Leaving our animals hidden in a clump of cedar trees, we climbed to a place in the rocks where we could get a good view of the surrounding country with our powerful field glasses. I soon detected some objects moving along on the Eagle Creek trail. This trail led within a hundred yards of the point where we were hidden. The moving objects were coming toward us, and as they came nearer I could make out about a dozen Indians on foot and a white man mounted on a mule following them. He wore a suit of brown overall stuff. The ground along the trail at the place where it passed us was quite free of brush and rocks.

Charlie said, "Let's let them come right up close to us and kill the whole outfit before they can get to cover."

I told him to wait until I started shooting. By this time they were within a hundred yards of us. Letting them come still closer, I called out, "Halt! Don't try to run!"

The man on the mule pulled up instantly, and the Indians, after a word from him, stood still.

"Who are you?" I demanded.

"I'm Lieutenant Gatewood, and these men are Indian scouts," he replied.

I thereupon rose up in plain view and told the Lieutenant to come nearer, but to let the Indians stay where they were. He did so, approaching to within thirty yards of us. He then asked who I was. When I told him my name, he asked if I were Jim Cook, the hunter and guide of whom he had so often heard Captain Emmett Crawford speak. I told him that I probably was, as Captain Crawford was one of my friends.

Gatewood then told me that he had been stationed at Camp

Apache in command of a company of Indian scouts; that Geronimo and his band had broken away from their reservation, where they had been held as prisoners; and that he had got together a few of his men and started in pursuit. He said he was being closely followed by a pack train and two troops of the Fourth U. S. Cavalry, commanded by Captain Allen Smith and Lieutenant Parker. Looking back along the Eagle Creek trail, I could now see the troops coming. Gatewood had left the trail of the Indians a short distance back, and he and the troops were rushing for the nearest point on the San Francisco River, to give the command a chance to get food and water. They had traveled about seventy miles over very rough mountain trails, hardly stopping for food or rest, and both men and horses were very tired. Many of their animals had lost their shoes and, traveling over the hard volcanic rocks, had so worn their hoofs that they limped painfully. I told Gatewood where I thought he could strike the main trail of the Indians over at Deep Creek, thus making a big cutoff.

When Captain Smith and his command came up, we all went back to the ranch, where they had breakfast and about an hour's rest. During this chase Captain Smith had buried a number of bodies which he had found dead along the trail—bodies of persons whom the Indians had killed.

While the troops were getting breakfast, a man from Alma arrived and told me that the Indians had killed two of the men who had gone out the day before with the scouting party. He wanted to know if I would go and help find the bodies and bring them in. He told me the direction which the party had taken, and, as it was near where the troops would travel if they went to Deep Creek to strike the Indian trail, I asked Captain Smith if he would help me search for the bodies. He replied that he would, and we soon started. We located the bodies without any trouble: they were lying within a few feet of the trail in which they had been traveling.

I then accompanied the troops to the place on the Deep Creek trail where I had observed the moving objects. It proved to be the trail which had been followed by the main body of Indians. I turned back from this point, went to the ranch, got some men from Alma, and went out and packed the bodies of Orwig and Luse on two horses; and the men from Alma took them home for burial.

Charlie Moore and I then rode to Devil's Park, a spot in the mountains so named by gold prospectors because of its hidden situation. The main trail of the Indians led in that direction. A man named Stallworth and his family were living there in a little log cabin home. We wanted to ascertain whether the Indians had molested them. When, from a point near where the cabin was located, we heard some rapid firing, we knew that an attack on the Stallworths was being made. Leaving our horses concealed in a thicket, we hurried to the aid of our neighbors and friends. Two of Geronimo's warriors ceased shooting into that cabin very suddenly when we opened fire upon them. The rest of the attacking band, twelve or fifteen in number, made a hasty departure to the rough shelter of timber and gulches close at hand, firing a few shots back at us as they ran. Doubtless they did not know the number in the party which had come to the rescue, or the incident might have ended differently. I believe that the two Indians who did not run away when their companions started so hurriedly into the Mogollon Mountains were the first to lose their lives at the hands of white men after starting on their murderous trip from Camp Apache. Whether our bullets injured any of the others we never knew, for we did not follow them. The Apaches at that time were, as a rule, very poor shots with firearms. Most of the white persons killed by them were fired upon at short range, from cover. In the art of concealment and ambuscade they were as expert, I think, as any savages on the American continent.

When the firing was over, I called to Mr. Stallworth, and he came out of the cabin with his family. Mrs. Stallworth had been wounded, and we first cared for her, after which we listened to their story. Just a short time before our arrival, Mrs. Stallworth had been out upon the doorstep of the cabin, giving the children their morning lessons. Looking up from her work, she had seen an Indian with a gun, stealthily making his way from behind one tree to another within a short distance of the house. She instantly grabbed her children and hurried them into the house. Just as she closed and barred the door, a bullet crashed through the planks and tore its way through her arm. Mr. Stallworth was in the house repairing a saddle when the attack started. He had a rifle and was a good shot but had allowed his supply of ammunition to run low, and had but two or three cartridges upon which he could depend. These he did not want to use until forced to. He told me that he had taken one cartridge which had missed fire and tried it from a loophole on an Indian at very short range; but again it failed to explode.

Mrs. Stallworth, in giving her version of the attack, said, "I kept telling Stallworth to shoot, but he refused to shoot for quite a while. At last he did pull the trigger, but the gun merely snapped. We have plenty of cartridges but no ammunition." She meant by this that they had plenty of empty cartridge shells, but no powder and ball for them.

Sending Charlie Moore to Alma to get people to move this family to a place of safety, I remained with the Stallworths until help arrived. We felt that a second attack by the Indians might be made at any moment. As it was seldom that the bodies of Indians slain in battle were left without an effort by their brother warriors to secure them, we expected that a move of this sort might be made. However, when Mr. Stallworth returned to his home several days later, after having taken his family to Alma, he discovered that his hogs and the coyotes and buzzards had left but little for him to dispose of by way of Indian remains.

"Peaches," Apache scout with the U.S. Army during the Victorio and Geronimo campaigns in New Mexico and Arizona.

General view of the WS Ranch, Keller Valley, on the San Francisco River, western Socorro County, New Mexico, 1882: bunkhouse and corrals at left, main ranch house at right.

*Salice Cañon, on the WS Ranch, Socorro County, New Mexico,
where the author's English friend, Mr. Lyon, was killed by Apache
Indians at the beginning of the Geronimo outbreak in 1885.*

*A noonday gathering in the Mogollon Mountains, New Mexico,
during the Geronimo campaign of 1885–86. Left to right: Mr. Upcher, an English gentleman; Dr. Maddox, surgeon of the Eighth
U.S. Cavalry (killed in action); Colonel DeRosey C. Cabell; Major
General S. S. Sumner; Major A. G. Hammond; J. F. Cook and the
author, James H. Cook, civilian guides and scouts; Mr. H. L. Mc-
Laughlin, civilian visitor; and General S. W. Fountain.*

12

Victims of the Rebellion

SHORTLY AFTER THE ARRIVAL of the relief party at the Stallworth home, I went over to the trail made by the main body of Geronimo's people. Following it a short distance, I met Lieutenant Gatewood and some of his Apache scouts. He was leading the troops back over the trail which they had just made. A short distance from the place where I met Gatewood, a rear guard of the Indians, cleverly concealed on the top of a bluff which could not be scaled by the troops, fired into them as they halted for a ten-minute rest to adjust their saddles. When the firing began, Captain Smith was rinsing his bandana handkerchief in a little creek. An Indian bullet cut several holes in the bandana but missed his hands. While the rear guard was engaged in firing into the command, one Indian scout was shot through the arm and two horses were killed.

After this attack upon the command the Indians fled, their trail leading in the direction of Fort Bayard and Silver City. These places were about seventy or eighty miles distant in a direct line. The Indian trail led, however, into the roughest part of the Mogollon Range, and the Gila River cañon—which could not be crossed by mounted men for many miles, either above or below, although Indians on foot could cross it by scaling the precipices—lay between the command and Fort Bayard. The Apaches, when pursued by mounted troops, headed for the most rugged and inaccessible parts of the mountains. If they themselves were mounted, upon reaching a place where horses could not go, they killed their mounts and then scattered like quail, meeting again at some prearranged spot in the country which they so well knew.

Captain Smith's command, being out of necessary supplies

for both horses and men, was forced to turn back. He was anxious to get a message to Fort Bayard, in the hope that the troops there would be able to intercept the Indians. As there was no one in his command who knew the trails to Fort Bayard, and his horses were nearly all unfit for such an undertaking, I volunteered to carry the message. In order to make time, it was necessary to travel about one hundred and ten miles with the message, following roads and trails which led over comparatively open country. I left the command about five or six o'clock in the afternoon, and the following morning at sunrise I was at Fort Bayard. That morning, between the time of my arrival at the fort and nine o'clock, the Indians killed a number of persons within three miles of both Fort Bayard and Silver City. Sixteen in all, I believe, was the number murdered by the Apaches between Devil's Park and Fort Bayard upon that occasion, several of them being women and children. One or two of the children were tortured to death by being hung up on spikes outside their houses.

In a very short time after my arrival at Fort Bayard that morning, the Sixth Cavalry troopers were out looking for Indians. This expedition caused the main body of Geronimo's people to scatter and escape for a time into Old Mexico. Major General W. H. Carter, United States Army, was at that time a lieutenant at Fort Bayard.

Upon delivering Captain Smith's and Lieutenant Gatewood's messages to Colonel Morrow, who commanded Fort Bayard, and securing answers to them, I hurried back to the ranch, arriving there before midnight of the same day. On this trip I had the use of all the mail horses from the Mormon settlement on the San Francisco River to Silver City; from Silver City to the fort I used a livery horse. The nights were cloudy and all objects indistinct. I certainly thought I saw a lot of Indians on that trip. Every soapweed and dead stump looked bad to me. On my return trip I passed Captain Smith's command. They were encamped on Dry Creek, about fifteen miles from the

WS Ranch, on their way to Fort Bayard. I stopped at the camp only long enough to deliver the messages which Colonel Morrow had sent them.

Upon my arrival at the ranch, I found that my outfit of cowboys had returned. The Indians had passed within two miles of them. Working down Blue Creek, the boys had struck Indian signs in the shape of moccasin tracks and horses lanced to death. They found next the bodies of three prospectors. One of these men had been caught away from camp unarmed and had been murdered with rocks, his skull being crushed.

Some of my English friends from the SU Ranch, who were awaiting my return from Fort Bayard, now informed me that Mr. Lyon had not arrived at their ranch. They had come to the conclusion that he must have been killed. At four o'clock the following morning, a small party, made up from among my friends and some ranch hands, went out to look for Lyon. We found his body about fifty feet from the trail in which he had been riding. His horse and saddle were gone. From the sign, I could see that he had been riding along reading a letter from home. The Apaches had seen him and lain in ambush, letting him come within fifteen feet of them. The shot that killed him had struck the center of his body and torn a great hole, knocking him from his horse. The Indians did not stop to mutilate his remains but merely took his gun and cartridge belt. After they had gone, Lyon had apparently recovered sufficiently to get up and stagger about fifty feet. He had rolled up his shirt to a point above the wound, then fallen again and expired. After two days of exposure to the hot sun, the body was in an awful condition, and it was a revolting task to get it to the ranch for burial.

Some troops from Fort Bayard were soon stationed at Alma, and not long afterward two troops of the Eighth Cavalry came to the WS Ranch and made their headquarters there until the end of the campaign, which lasted about sixteen months. The officers with the troops were Major S. S. Sumner, Lieutenants

S. W. Fountain, A. G. Hammond, DeR. C. Cabell, and C. W. Farber, and Drs. T. J. C. Maddox and Francis J. Ives. I went with them as scout on numerous occasions when small bands of Indians, which were constantly committing depredations, came within reach.

It was on one of these trips that I found Major S. S. Sumner to possess qualities such as are seldom met, either in or out of the army. He had a most kind and unselfish nature, and he never complained of the hardships, of which he took full share at all times. He was as brave, skillful, and kindhearted an officer as it has ever been my good fortune to meet during my experience in the West in the days when soldiers and Indians played prominent parts therein.

On the occasion to which I refer, he and his command were ordered to a point about fifty miles from the WS Ranch, in the mountains along the Gila River, to pick up an Indian trail which a company of militia had lost in following it. I accompanied him, and we reached the place as quickly as possible, found the trail, and followed it until night. Just at dusk a courier arrived in camp and informed us that Indians had killed a freighter that morning near the White House Ranch, on the road between Alma and Silver City. As the trail which we were following was several days old, and as it was finally determined that the savages whom we were following and those who had killed the freighter were one and the same band, Major Sumner decided to go and try to pick up the fresh trail where the murder had been committed. It was over twenty miles distant, but we moved there before daylight, and the command was hidden from view by camping down in a little gulch near the White House Ranch. As the Indians kept a lookout for troops, great caution was at all times required.

After a short rest I went out with a white man whom Major Sumner had employed a few days previously as a guide. This man was supposed to have a pretty thorough knowledge of the Mogollon Range, having prospected for mineral and hunted game there for years. We went to the spot where the freighter had been ambushed and killed. He proved to be an acquaintance of mine named Sauborin, who owned a general store in the Cooney mining camp. As the parties who generally hauled his supplies did not care to undertake it during the Indian uprising, Sauborin had taken his own team and was on his way back from Silver City with a load of such goods as he most needed. The Apaches had seen him coming and lain in ambush for him. At a distance of but a few feet they had riddled him with bullets. The team ran away with the load, followed by some of the mounted savages, and about a mile from the road they were caught. The Indians destroyed everything about the wagon which they could not carry away.

We took the trail of the Indians from this point and followed it to a point in the mountains about ten miles distant. The trail was not so difficult to follow as some others which I have traced over the barren rocks of the Mogollons. Among other goods found in Sauborin's wagon was a lot of candies. The Indians carried a quantity of this away with them. The candies which did not suit their taste, such as those known as "heart mottoes," they discarded. I picked up a number of these hearts. Some of them bore such mottoes as "I Love You," "Kiss Me," and "You Are My Honey." A box of fancy toilet soap, delicately perfumed, doubtless mistaken for candy, had been carried along until the bearer tasted it. He had attempted to bite off a huge chunk from one of the cakes, which bore a row of deep toothprints on each side. A deep dent in this particular cake of soap, which had been hurled with considerable force against a sharp rock, told of the disgust with which it had been discarded.

We then returned to camp, and as soon as it was dark the command moved to the place where we had left the Indian trail in the mountains. Here we lay down for a rest until daylight, no fires being built and as little noise being made as possible. The country was so rough that I could not ride my horse, and he was put into the pack train. The cavalry horses had to be led.

When we left Duck Creek, by the White House Ranch, we knew that the trail was leading into a country where there was no water for many miles. The canteens were all ordered filled, and everyone was cautioned to use as little water as possible. Having no canteen, I expected to make a dry trip. We followed the trail all that day. The weather was very warm. The trail led us into the mountains, where we encountered a lot of hard climbing. When night came on, and we could no longer see to follow the trail, we again lay down. Horses and men were now suffering for water. We had a little hard bread and bacon to eat.

Soon after lying down to rest, one of the men of C Troop began to complain in a loud voice because he was not allowed to make a cup of coffee. He was disturbing everybody, and his voice could be heard a long distance in those quiet mountains. Major Sumner at last asked for the name of the disturber. When informed, he said to one of his officers, "Tell that man he is making as much noise as if he was drawing a general's pay, and that I would like to have him keep as quiet as possible for a few hours." The man had sense enough to appreciate this quiet rebuke, and subsided.

The next morning at daylight I went, with the ranchman guide and a small detachment of soldiers, to see if we could locate the camp of the Indians; for we could tell from the sign that we were close to them. We located their camp before we had gone three miles, but the Indians must have heard our thirsty animals whinnering and braying during the night and become alarmed, for they had killed their horses and hastily covered with earth and rocks their fires, on which the meat was half-roasted. The soldiers returned to the command. The ranchman guide and I each attempted to take the trail of an Indian and follow it to a point where it was likely that the savages would all come together again and make a trail which the troops could swiftly follow. It was understood that the troops would move up to the deserted Indian camp and there wait for us.

I had not followed the trail more than half a mile when I heard a shot in the direction taken by the ranchman guide. I concluded that the Indians had seen him coming, lain in ambush, and shot him down. I was fearfully tired and thirsty by this time, and, as the trail seemed to lead straight for the Gila Cañon, which no horse could cross for a distance of forty miles, I started back to the command. But on the way I decided, after all, to go to the spot where I had heard the shot fired and see if I could find the guide. I had to cross some deep cañons. At last I struck his track going back to the command. I followed it to the deserted Indian camp, at which the troops had already arrived. Here I saw the guide. I asked him what he had fired at, and he told me that a big buck deer had jumped up close to him and he had shot at it before he thought what he was doing. His service with the command ended that day.

While I was telling this man what I thought of him, Major Sumner came up to me and said, "Jim, will you have a drink?" I replied, "No, Major, I had a drink last week." But, as he placed his canteen in my hand, I discovered by its weight that it was full. My tongue was thick, and I certainly was thirsty. I told the Major that, to prove my appreciation of his unselfishness, I would take a wee drop. In his quiet way, he replied, "Jim, in this line of life men sometimes get hurt and need water badly." As the water in his canteen was probably all that was in the whole command, and as he was having to walk and lead his own horse the same as everyone else, that act of unselfishness was stamped deeply on my mind. He certainly had himself under control, as one must where others are to be controlled. Doubtless the other officers and Dr. Maddox had shared the water from their canteens with some of the weaker ones among the troopers. There is always a certain percentage of men who will not or cannot stand hardships about which others think but little. I could pay but scant attention to what was going on back in the command. We were campaigning on some of the roughest ground in New Mexico, and in such places a scout will generally have his full share of both duties and hardships.

Our next move was to get water as soon as possible. Mogollon Creek, twenty miles away, being the nearest, we started for it. Before we reached the creek, the sky clouded over and we were struck by a cloudburst which thoroughly drenched us all. When we arrived at the creek, I saw some WS cattle, and it was not long before we were eating fresh beef. As the storm had washed away all Indian tracks, we returned to the ranch.

Along toward the end of the campaign, we received word that Geronimo's band of Indians were all across the border in Old Mexico. Having been under a strain for some time, I decided to take a few days' rest. I went to visit friends at Camp Carlin and Fort D. A. Russell, Wyoming, but had scarcely arrived there when a message came telling me that C Troop of the Eighth Cavalry had been ambushed while on their way from their camp at the WS Ranch to Silver City for supplies, and that Dr. Maddox as well as a number of others had been killed, and several wounded. Lieutenant Fountain was in command of the troop. He had some Navajo Indian scouts who, like most of the Indian scouts used during that and previous campaigns in the Southwest, seemed in some way to keep in close touch with the hostiles who were being pursued. Whenever danger seemed imminent, they would either balk outright or have to stop to "make medicine" until the time of danger had passed. On this occasion, these scouts were slow in breaking camp and getting ready to take their positions in front of the command. Lieutenant Fountain, after starting the troop and wagons on the road, went back to the Indians to hurry them up. Before he could return to his men, the Indians fired into them at close range.

Dr. Maddox was the first man hit. The bullet that struck him, although it made a mortal wound, did not knock him from his horse. He quietly dismounted and, turning to a trooper near him said, "Babcock, save yourself. I shall be dead in a minute." Just then a bullet struck him in the head, and he fell dead. Dr.

Maddox was a man beloved by all who knew him. He was a giant among men in many ways. Among those shot was a trooper named Wishart, one of the strongest men in the Eighth Cavalry. His back was broken by the ball. He lived for a little time after the Indians had been put to flight, then died in Lieutenant Fountain's arms.

Department headquarters had evidently been misinformed as to the whereabouts of the Indians.

Several sad and unusual incidents occurred during the Indian attack of which I write. A man named George Herr and his wife were living in the settlement of Alma when the news of the Indian uprising reached that place. All except Mr. Herr and his wife hastened to transform a large adobe store building, situated about in the center of the settlement, into a fort, into which they all went for protection. But Mr. Herr piled a lot of sacks filled with sand into the windows of his little adobe home and said that he and his wife would take their chances there. The first night of the scare he placed a large revolver under his pillow. In the morning, as he was getting out of bed, the revolver dropped to the floor, striking on the hammer and exploding the cartridge. The bullet struck Mr. Herr in the head, killing him instantly. He was one of the best-known and most respected men in that community. A carpenter by trade, he had assisted in the building of the WS Ranch.

Another incident of those times, which left vivid impressions on my mind, was the narrow escape from death of one of the cowboys who was working at the old White House Ranch on Duck Creek. This fellow was out on the range looking for some horses. Going up the side of a rather steep foothill, he rode into a bunch of Apaches who had cleverly prepared an ambush for him. A number of the Indians opened fire on him at short range, but missed both him and his horse. The firing frightened the animal. Belonging to the hair-trigger variety of broncos, it promptly tucked its head down between its legs and gave the Indians a splendid exhibition of a horse bucking down the side of a mountain, over all sorts of boulders and other obstacles such as shrubs and trees. The scene must have been interesting to the Indians, for they evidently forgot to shoot at the cowboy until both horse and rider were well out on the open country and making tracks for the home ranch. They fired an occasional shot at him as he fanned his bronco along with his quirt. After he had placed a distance of over half a mile between himself and the Indians, a bullet from one of their long-range guns struck him in the back of the neck, passing through his neck without either knocking him from his horse or doing him any serious injury. Just why that bullet did not break his neck or cut his jugular vein, I never could understand. He certainly had what was commonly called "good luck that shot."

The man who deserved the greatest credit for securing Geronimo and his band and bringing them where they could be placed on cars and taken to Florida as prisoners of war, was Lieutenant Gatewood. Had it not been for his heroic work, Geronimo would probably have been "out" for some time, and many more people would have lost their lives at the hands of his warriors. Gatewood knew Geronimo and spoke a certain amount of his language. Geronimo knew that Gatewood's tongue was not forked, and followed his advice. But Gatewood surely put his life in chancery when he went alone into Geronimo's camp down in Old Mexico and persuaded the last of the bloodthirsty old Apache war chiefs to surrender himself and his band of followers to a United States army officer, with no other promises made him than that he and his people would be protected from any harm that the white settlers of the country might try to do them. Geronimo's faith in Gatewood's words must have been strong, for he had ample time to change his mind about surrendering before he and his people arrived at Captain Lawton's camp north of the Mexican boundary line, where his capture or surrender was completed. If Geronimo could then have foreseen that he would never again see the land of his forefathers after boarding the cars which carried him so quickly to the far-off state of Florida as a prisoner of war, I think that wily old chief would have preferred death in the land of his birth.

Undoubtedly this Apache chief's name will be handed down in history to the many generations to follow; but I trust that the name of the brave Lieutenant who underwent so many hardships and, in effecting the capture of his wily and dangerous antagonist, ran a most desperate risk, will also be honorably mentioned in connection with the final acts of Geronimo's fighting days. Lieutenant Gatewood is now at rest, and words of praise for the heroic work which he so modestly performed cannot reach him; but when the history of the last of our Indian wars shall be written, I most sincerely hope that full credit will be given him for the service which he rendered during the Geronimo campaign.

Shortly after the close of the campaign I was married, and I took my bride to the WS Ranch from Cheyenne, Wyoming. Soon after our arrival there, we received a call from our neighbor Mr. Stallworth, whose ranch was in Devil's Park in the Mogollon Mountains, and who, but for our timely arrival when the Indians attacked his home, would probably have had a much more serious experience than he did have. He now came to pay my wife and me his respects, and he did so in a manner which impressed itself on my memory, for I knew that his words came straight from the heart. His greeting to me was, "Jimmie, I hope your honeymoon will last forever. I owe you more than I can ever pay, but I'm your friend—that's all." The rough-and-ready old mountaineer could say no more. His eyes were filled with tears as he bade me good-bye.

At the time of the establishment of the WS Ranch in New Mexico, nearly every ranch house in that part of the country had its little blockhouse, or fort, built near it. Generally a trench connected the house with the fort, which was usually built on some elevation. Part of the structure was below the level of the ground, above which it projected only about a foot. The part above ground was built of heavy rocks, leaving loopholes on all sides from which to fire. The roof was of rocks and earth, a foot or more in thickness.

Some hard fights took place in Keller Valley between the settlers and the Apache Indians. When I first went there I met a man who had taken an active part in most of the Indian troubles which had occurred in that part of the country since the arrival of the first white settlers. This man's name was Elliott. He had spent most of his life on the frontier. He was a good shot, and had pretty good control of his nerves when Apaches were trying to annihilate him or his neighbors.

One incident in connection with his life in the Mogollon Mountains was a little out of the ordinary. He was taking care of a ranch and some stock belonging to a settler named Bush, while Bush and his family were making a trip to Silver City for supplies. One morning while he was doing some chores about the place, he happened to catch sight of an Indian sneaking along through the brush and timber about a hundred yards distant. He did not have his gun with him, and instead of trying to get to the house by running, which would have drawn the fire of the Indians at once, he leisurely finished his work and went slowly to the house. Once inside, he grabbed his rifle and ran to a loophole in the wall, just in time to see seven Indians running across the little open ground surrounding the house. He opened fire upon them with his Winchester, killing six of them before they could reach cover, and wounding the seventh. A number of old razorback hogs that were about the place located and feasted upon the dead Indians. A day or two later a big grizzly bear got among the hogs, killing several of them and securing a good meal. When Elliott saw what the bear had done, he followed its track into the mountains and killed it. He took a good portion of the bear meat to the ranch, where it was eaten. Thus, indirectly, he and his ranch friends ate the Indian friends who had come to pay him a morning call.

13

Big Bat and Little Bat

OFTEN ONE HAS HEARD persons who lived during the days of
the Indian wars insist that the United States soldiers never really
wanted to catch the Indians—that they would always run out
of forage or food supplies just about the time they were over-
taking hostile Indians, and be forced to turn back. This, I think,
is a very wrong idea. During the days of Indian wars, promo-
tions came along slowly to any army officer, and a large pro-
portion of the officers were only too glad when an opportunity
for active service presented itself, so that they might have a
chance to distinguish themselves and to get away for a time
from the dull routine of garrison life.

Having no base of supplies to draw upon for his food,
weapons, or ammunition, the Indian has always been compelled
to make a running fight, taking as few chances as possible. This
was his only way of avoiding extermination when fighting
against well-equipped soldiers. The Indian methods of warfare
gave the Indians the advantage which the pursued always has
over the pursuer, especially in a rough country—the advantage
of ambuscade. Moreover, in trying to capture or destroy a war
party of Apaches, the soldier was badly handicapped. The
Apache country was extremely arid. The Indian knew about
the water holes in the mountains much better than anyone else
did, and he could live for weeks upon the moisture secured
from the cactus and from the roots of other plants—the Spanish
bayonet and other varieties of the century plant. And the
Apache could get along very well without horses. He used
them when convenient and seemed to take delight in stealing
them, even though, owing to the nature of the ground over
which he was traveling, he could use them for only a very short

time. When through with any animals which he might steal, he always killed them if he had time. The flesh of the horse made good food for the Apache, and a dead horse would never be ridden by white men who might desire to chase the thieves. I have known Apaches to kill their own horses when pursued, and then travel fifty or sixty miles a day on foot, over the roughest sort of ground. When a soldier started out in pursuit of Indians, he expected to ride only the animal upon which he was mounted when he left his post. This animal had been accustomed to rations of both hay and grain during the most of its life and, ridden day after day over a grassless, rocky, arid country, soon became badly jaded. A horse whose feet had always been shod would become footsore very quickly after losing a shoe. Whenever an Apache had use for a footsore horse, he killed an animal and cut a circular piece about eighteen inches in diameter from its hide; then he drilled holes around the edge of this and ran a rawhide drawstring through them; and then he placed the sore foot in the center of the piece and drew the string. This made a bag for the foot. Such rawhide covering would stand hard usage on the rocks for half a day, or perhaps longer, before it was worse than useless. The method most employed by the Apaches in dispatching horses which they could no longer use was to run a lance through the jugular vein.

Having seen cowboys, buffalo hunters, freighters, and militia (made up largely of men whose life-training had been clerical work or barbering), as well as United States troops, pursue bands of Indians which had committed some depredation, I formed the opinion that the regular soldiers were the ones who could successfully cope with such undertakings. The officers of regular troops would want to go. The enlisted men would have to go whether they wanted to or not. A group of men hastily made up under the excitement of the moment would rush out without any preparations for a stern chase—which is usually a long one—and with no organization that would hold them together for more than a day or two. Frontiersmen would, of course, stay longer than those who were not trained to hardships, such as going without food, water, or sleep for days at a time. Most such men, however, were a pretty independent lot, and each would have notions of his own as to the proper thing to be done to bring good results. Discipline did not appeal to them. There would generally be a scattering within a few days, even among such men.

The average trooper among the enlisted regulars, after a few weeks or months chasing Indians in southern New Mexico or Arizona, was ready to fight anything or anybody rather than endure longer the hardships and privations incidental to such work.

During the past few years an organization known as the Boy Scouts has been created and, I am told, has enrolled a great membership both in the United States and abroad. The word "scout" has become so popular that a man, instead of being called a "good mixer" or a "jolly good fellow," is now called a "good old scout." Let me tell you about another kind of scout— a kind which many persons who have spent their lives east of the Missouri River probably know little about. I refer to the United States army scouts. William F. Cody, "Buffalo Bill," has given the people of many lands a view, with his Wild West Show, of battles between the United States soldiers and the American Indians, in which the army scout plays a conspicuous part. But perhaps a few words regarding them and their work, with a little word picture or two which I shall attempt, will help bring out the character and value of these scouts during the times when the North American Indian was one of the factors which had to be dealt with in the settlement of our western country by white men.

Army scouts are men who are sent ahead of bodies of troops for the purpose of observing the motions of the enemy or discovering danger, such as an ambush, and giving notice to the commanding officer. In an uninhabited and almost unknown country, scouts must ascertain where water, grass, and fuel can be obtained for the command.

Few who served as enlisted men in the army had any training in woodcraft, for the ranks were largely recruited from the densely populated districts. Consequently, few knew much of frontier life or of campaigning against hostile Indians. Indian scouts have been considerably used by the United States Army in all the Indian wars of the western states and territories. Comparatively few white men have ever been employed in this capacity, because a special training, such as few white men possessed, was always required. The success or failure of many an expedition has depended entirely upon the sort of service rendered by its scouts. Did they prove incompetent or tricky, a command of troops following hostile Indians would be certain to encounter serious difficulties.

The services of many Indian and half-breed scouts whom I have personally known proved extremely valuable, and they were much more loyal than white people could well have expected, considering that they were being employed to lead soldiers against their own parents and relatives. Such Indian scouts would not be traitors to their own people, but they would generally be men who had been endowed with sense enough to see that there was absolutely no use in the Indians' fighting against the white soldiers. The latter were too numerous, and there could be but one ending—the Indian would be exterminated.

Woman's Dress was one of the last of the Sioux Indian scouts —an old warrior whom I knew intimately for forty years. At the time of his death, which occurred at Pine Ridge Reservation, South Dakota, he had army discharge papers showing that he had served *twenty-one enlistments*.[1] Not only do these papers show that he was a most excellent scout, but special marginal notes written on them by many army officers of high rank who had commanded troops led by Woman's Dress, state that

[1] Indian scouts were enlisted for periods of six months.

the services rendered by him had been of the greatest value. General George Crook and many other officers had often told this old scout that on account of his good service the Great Father at Washington would always be a good friend to him and his family. Woman's Dress's princely salary of one dollar a day and rations stopped with the expiration of his enlistments, and most of the officers whom he served have crossed the great divide. During the month of May, 1913, Woman's Dress, with his family, visited me in my home. At that time he complained to me most bitterly of the way he had been treated by the Great Father at Washington. Soldiers whom he had served as a scout and led into battle had killed some of his nearest relatives. When leading troops after old Dull Knife's band of Cheyennes, near Fort Robinson, Nebraska, Woman's Dress was shot through the arm. At the time of his visit to my home he was an old man, unfit for any work, and at times he suffered greatly for want of the actual necessities of life.

On January 9, 1921, this remarkable old Indian scout died at a very advanced age. On January 13, I received the following letter informing me of his death. It was written by Baptiste Pourier, himself one of the last of the old United States army scouts—a man with a reputation second to none in his particular field, and well known to every old army officer of the seventies. He was known far and wide simply as "Big Bat," to distinguish him from Baptiste Garnier, another remarkable frontiersman, known as "Little Bat." The two men were not related in any way.

Manderson, S. D., January 13, 1921

Mr. James Cook
Agate, Nebr.
Friend Jim:

How are you making it this winter? My health has been pretty good. Well, Jim, we lost our old friend, Woman's Dress. I seen him before he died. He was pretty weak then, but he thought of you and said he would like to have seen you before he died. I hope this letter reaches you in good health. Let me hear from you.

Your friend,
Baptiste Pourier.

The last of the white men who served the United States Army as scouts will soon have passed on. Few of them are living today. As one of the old boys who knew the life in the West of Yesterday, and as one who numbers among his friends many of the last of both Indian and white army scouts, I shall attempt a word picture of the white scouts who served the United States Army during the days when it was having trouble trying to make the red brothers of this continent forsake their ways and travel the white man's road—which, we trust, leads to happy hunting grounds both here and in that unfathomable eternity to which reds, whites, and blacks alike are bound.

These men should not, I think, be rated as belonging to a class who placed but little value upon human life. Some of them, I am quite sure, used language which at times was more expressive than elegant, but not all of them were bad men in any sense of the phrase. My experience taught me this:

A good army scout had to possess certain qualifications in order to be fitted for his work. He had to have a strong body and a good eye. He had to be absolutely honest. He had to be resourceful at all times. He had to know well the life of the frontier, both on the plains and in the mountains. Knowledge of the savages and of their customs, habits, and language was a requirement. The sixth sense which enabled a man to keep his bearings under all conditions of weather, both day and night, had to be largely developed. He had to be a keen observer of details. These qualifications, supplemented by good common sense and the gift of being able to shoot straight, were the necessary nucleus of a good scout's equipment.

Two of the best-known army scouts and interpreters in the

land of the Sioux during the past half-century were Baptiste Garnier, a half-blood Sioux Indian whose father was of French descent, and the Baptiste Pourier already referred to. Both lived at Fort Laramie during Little Bat's early manhood. Each had the same given name, shortened into "Bat" by the soldiers, the older man being called "Big Bat" and the younger "Little Bat." Big Bat now makes his home on the Pine Ridge Indian Reservation, South Dakota. He has seen many winters, but he can still get about fairly well. He will, on occasions, talk with his old friends about his experiences. He and his wife both come to visit me occasionally in my ranch home. At the breaking out of the Spanish-American War, Little Bat was employed at Fort Robinson, Nebraska, as post guide and interpreter. We were close friends from the year 1876 up to the day of his death, which occurred soon after the troops of the Ninth Cavalry were ordered to Cuba.

Little Bat was well thought of by both officers and men of whatever regiment he was associated with. Good-natured, even-tempered at all times, he was a fine specimen of physical manhood. He was considered by such men as General Crook and General Hatch, of the United States Army, as being one of the best big-game hunters in the Rocky Mountain region. When such well-known civilians as William K. Vanderbilt and Dr. Seward Webb wanted to hunt big game in the Rockies, they usually secured the services of Little Bat for their trips. During all the years in which Little Bat and I were such close friends, I never knew him to have a quarrel with anyone. He was murdered by a barkeeper at Crawford, Nebraska, named Jim Haguewood, who kept bar for a man named Dietrich. Haguewood had been having some family troubles and was drinking quite heavily at the time when he took the life of my friend.

Little Bat went into the saloon and drank a glass of beer with an acquaintance. He was unarmed and was wearing a heavy buffalo-skin overcoat. While he was chatting with this acquaintance, Haguewood, who had served them with beer, exclaimed in an insolent tone, "Who pays for these drinks?" Bat replied, "I will when I get ready." He was at that moment unbuttoning his overcoat to get the money from an inner pocket. Haguewood grabbed a revolver lying handy under the bar and shouted, "You are ready right now!" Bat saw the movement and knew that the fellow meant to shoot. He crouched a little in front of the bar, but Haguewood reached over and, with the muzzle of the gun almost against Bat's neck, fired, the bullet ranging down through the center of his body. Several civilians who were standing by saw the shooting. After receiving the fatal bullet, Bat staggered out into the street, evidently intending to get to his horse. He got across the street, but there he fell helpless. Someone notified his wife at Fort Robinson. Bat was carried into a room near by, where he died about two hours later in the arms of his wife. He seemed to be able to converse with her only in the Sioux tongue. He told her, when dying, that he thought Haguewood was his friend, and he could not see why a friend should shoot him. Little Bat, the hunter and scout, who had no hatred in his heart except for the Cheyenne Indian who had killed his father, certainly met an undeserved death.

At the time of the shooting his army friends were, for the most part, in Cuba. A Mr. Freeman who had resided at Fort Robinson since the post was established was about the only close friend, besides myself, whom Bat seemed to have in northwestern Nebraska when the trial of Haguewood was held. Haguewood was acquitted of the charge of murder, or manslaughter, which was preferred against him. To many persons about Crawford, Little Bat was seemingly "nothing but an Indian." He was killed by a "white" man.

The services rendered by Little Bat as scout and interpreter for the United States Army, even as late as the Wounded Knee affair, in South Dakota, during the winter of 1890–91, should, I think, entitle him to be honored by old army friends and by the many other Americans who admire men of the West who have done good work, and to receive a more fitting monument than now stands at the head of his grave in the cemetery at Fort Robinson. This simple little marker gives his name, the date of his death, and underneath is chiseled the one word, "Employee."

When there occurred that most unfortunate encounter known as the Battle of Wounded Knee, which was perhaps the last clash ever to take place between United States troops and American Indians, Little Bat was present. When the order was given to search the lodges of the Indians for firearms, he was sent to interpret for the soldiers detailed for that duty. He was to inform the women what the soldiers were to do, and to explain to them that they were not to be harmed. When Bat had done as ordered, and some of the lodges had been searched, the firing began at the point where the Indians were assembled. In a moment death reigned on all sides. The Hotchkiss guns, trained on the Indian lodges, opened fire, and the Indian women and children who but a few moments before had been told that they were in no danger, were killed and wounded by the score. Some of the soldiers who were with Little Bat among the lodges were killed. Bat had taken no firearms with him when he went to the lodges with the troopers, for he wanted to impress the Indians with his conviction that they were in no danger. His clothing was pierced with bullets as he tried to get to his own tent, where his weapons had been left. When he reached the place he found that the tent had been burned. A dead Indian who had been killed in the tent was lying across his gun, the stock of which was half burned away. Bat's saddle was also riddled with bullets. When I met Little Bat soon after the affair, he told me that the sights which he had witnessed during that killing of women and children would never be effaced from his memory.

He had a family—a wife, one son, and six daughters. His wife was a daughter of M. A. Mousseau, a French Canadian who was one of the very early traders and trappers in the Rocky Mountain country. Little Bat was a man possessed of more than ordinary intelligence. During his later years he spent much time in my home, where I had an opportunity of learning to know him well. Although he had no school training, he possessed certain qualities which made him distinctive. His honesty and fearlessness never were questioned. His skill as a hunter and his knowledge of the Indian language and of the customs of the Sioux made his services as an army scout most valuable during the Indian troubles of 1876 and later years. He was a most modest and unassuming type of rugged frontier manhood. His home and family and the simple life of the western pioneer were the things which he most desired.

Baptiste Garnier (Little Bat), government scout and interpreter about Forts Laramie and Robinson.

Baptiste Garnier (Little Bat), scout, bringing in an antelope to Fort Robinson.

Baptiste Pourier (Big Bat), old government scout and interpreter

James H. Cook and a party of Northern Cheyenne Indians who were visiting the Cook ranch in Sioux County, Nebraska, in 1888. Red Hawk, Little Hawk, and their families.

Photograph by A. Thomson, New York; courtesy National Park Service

Part of an immense Indian camp, arranged in a great circle, at Pine Ridge, South Dakota, about 1908.

14

The Sioux's Choice

ON NUMEROUS OCCASIONS my Oglala Sioux friends of the Pine
Ridge Reservation in South Dakota, when visiting me in my
ranch home, had expressed the desire that I might come to them
and be their white father or Indian agent. They complained
that most of the men sent to them as agents were persons who
did not understand Indians and their ways and had little or no
sympathy for them as brother men. I tried to explain to them
as best I could that the agents sent to them were, in some instances at least, not selected for their special fitness for the place,
or because of either their knowledge of the Indians or their un-
questioned honesty. When such men were in office, the Indians
were very sure to get the worst of it, for there were few Indians in the United States sufficiently educated to check up the
business affairs of the agency. A number of the men who have
held positions as Indian agents could and would close at least
one eye, and in some instances both eyes, when the welfare of
the Indian was at stake and when some of his white brothers,
interested in contracts which represented large dealings with
the red men, needed more feathers for their nests.

In the fall of 1890—just about the time the Messiah craze
started among the Sioux—a number of the old head men of the
Oglalas came from Pine Ridge Reservation on a hurried visit
to my home. They told me that their rations had been cut down
until they were suffering and dying for lack of food, and that
trouble was sure to come unless something was immediately
done in the matter of issuing more food to them. They further
told me that they wanted to send a delegation of their people
to Washington to ask the Great Father if he would not appoint
me as the white father at Pine Ridge Agency; for they felt that

I was a friend to the Indians and would be honest in my dealings with them. I told them that, should I be appointed at their request, I would devote a few years of my life to endeavoring to help them get started on the white man's road, but that the appointment as Indian agent coming in any other manner than as the sole desire of the Indians themselves, I would not for any consideration accept.

The chiefs returned to the agency, and at the earliest possible moment a delegation was sent to Washington and petitions for my appointment as agent at Pine Ridge were signed by a large number of the head men among the Sioux, in the presence of Judge Barker, county judge of Sioux County, Nebraska, the district in which I made my home. At the close of the Wounded Knee campaign, petitions for my appointment were circulated and signed by many of the most prominent citizens of the Black Hills country and of the county lying adjacent to the Pine Ridge Indian Reservation. These people seemed to feel that with a different sort of man at that agency there would be no repetition of the Indian troubles which had just ended so disastrously for both Indians and whites. As the Indians felt that no petition signed by them would ever leave their agency by the United States mail, I assured them that their petition would be placed with the Commissioner of Indian Affairs at Washington—and it was.

Fortunately for me, perhaps, a new policy of handling the Pine Ridge Agency was adopted at Washington, and an army officer was detailed to act as agent for the Oglalas at that time. The salary of an Indian agent was not so great that I could well afford to neglect my own business at that time to accept such a position. Yet, having given my word to the Indians that if through their efforts I were given the appointment I would accept the position, I should certainly have done so, no matter what it might have cost me financially.

Some of the documents regarding my suggested appointment as Pine Ridge Indian agent are appended herewith.

The Sioux's Choice

Petition Signed by Red Cloud and Sub-Chiefs

Pine Ridge Agency, March 10, 1891

Hon. Commissioner Morgan,

Washington, D. C.

Dear Sir:

I, Red Cloud, chief of the Ogallalla Sioux at this agency, and my sub-chiefs, write to you as follows: I and my people have been at agencies and on reservations for many years. We have had many agents—ten, I think, to this time. They were all eastern men. They were unacquainted with the Indians. They did not know our nature. They had not seen an Indian before they came here. The could not understand us because they did not know about our life in past years, and knew nothing of our traditions and history. They have never lived with us and so could not sympathize with us. We have had trouble with some of them—most of all, the last one. There has been trouble the past winter. Many soldiers have been here. Some of our people have been in Washington. They told you we wanted an agent here of our own choosing, and that we wanted a civilian. They told you we had chosen a man to be our agent. You told my people to come home and hold a council and agree on some man whom we all wanted for agent. My people have come home. We have held a council as you told us to do: We have agreed on a man for our agent. All my people—men, women, and children—have agreed on one man. That man is James H. Cook of Harrison, Nebraska. He is the choice of us all. We have known him for seventeen years. He is a Western man. He has been among us when we were wild. He knows our nature, our history, and what we want. He is our friend. He will deal justly with us, and help us to learn the ways of the white men. He will treat us as men. We want him and no one else. We want him because, as I told you, he is a Western man and knows our ways. All our other agents have been Eastern men who knew nothing of us or our past. We could not get along with them, because our ways were different. We want the agent appointed at once.

We want James H. Cook appointed now. My people want it. It will settle this trouble, and there will be peace. The sooner the appointment is made, the better. Spring is near. We want this matter settled before long, so we can plow our fields and raise our crops, and not be bothered with this matter. We ask you to give this your attention now, and not keep us waiting long. We are all agreed on this matter, and set our names to this letter.

Red Cloud	*No Water*
Jack Red Cloud	*Black Shield*
Big Road	*Far Thunder*
Spotted Elk	*Knife Chief*
Young-Man-Afraid	*Bear Head*
Little Wound	*Lone Bear*
He Dog	*Little Hawk*
Plenty Bear	*Yellow Bear*
Far Lightning	*American Horse*

Joseph A. Mousseau, Interpreter

OFFICE OF
COUNTY JUDGE OF SIOUX COUNTY
Harrison, Nebr., March 12, '91

Hon. Thos. J. Morgan
Commissioner Indian Affairs
Washington, D. C.
Dear Sir:

   Herein I transmit a letter from Red Cloud and the sub-chiefs at Pine Ridge agency, asking you to appoint Mr. James H. Cook as their agent at that place. The letter explains itself sufficiently so that comment is unnecessary. I was present when the enclosed letter was read and interpreted to Red Cloud and several assembled sub-chiefs. They said it was a correct statement of their wishes in the matter.

Mr. Cook is a resident of this county, and is highly esteemed by all who know him. The Indians estimate a man by his standing as a warrior. Mr. Cook comes up to their ideas of a man because they know him to be a man of unwavering courage, and better skilled in the use of arms than any of them. This commands their respect. His neighbors know him for those qualities also, but they also know him as a cultured gentleman of strict integrity and sense of honor. These last qualities count nothing with an Indian, for if a man lacks nerve, all else counts for nothing with them.

The settlers desire that something be done soon. They are settled all along the border of the reservation, exposed to Indian attacks if trouble comes, and they feel uneasy. The impression is prevalent everywhere I have been that there will be more trouble next spring, and that the Indians will break up into small bands and attack the settlers wherever found, as has been their custom at times in the past.

If an agent of their choice is appointed, the interpreters tell us trouble will be avoided. The people have had enough of Indian scares, and want no more. I write for them, for hardships are plenty enough without Indian wars on the frontier.

Hoping that this will receive your consideration at your earliest convenience, I am

> Very truly yours,
> *S. G. Barker*
> County Judge

UNITED STATES SENATE
WASHINGTON, D. C.

> February 13, 1891

Hon. John W. Noble,
Secretary of the Interior,
Washington, D. C.
Sir:

I beg to present herewith a number of letters from prominent officers and citizens of the state of Wyoming, recommending Mr. Jas. H. Cook for appointment as Indian Agent at Pine Ridge agency.

Mr. Cook has had much experience with the Indians of Arizona, New Mexico, and other southern points, as well as with the Indians in the northwest, particularly at Pine Ridge. I can fully endorse the good things said of him, and believe he would be a painstaking, conscientious, and satisfactory representative of the government in this capacity.

Mr. Cook is a resident of Nebraska, and I do not, therefore, request this appointment for or on account of Wyoming, but desire to add my recommendation to that of others as to the merits of this applicant.

Very respectfully,
Francis E. Warren

UNITED STATES SENATE
WASHINGTON, D. C.

January 21, 1891

Hon. John W. Noble
Secretary of the Interior
Washington, D. C.
My dear Sir:

I enclose numerous letters from prominent citizens of northwestern Nebraska, urging the appointment of Mr. James H. Cook of Harrison, Nebraska, as Indian agent at Pine Ridge. The letters enclosed will show that he is a man exceptionally well qualified and fitted for this position, and that the Indians have trust in him and earnestly desire his appointment. The state of Nebraska has a larger population interested in the condition of affairs at Pine Ridge and Rosebud than the state of South Dakota, where the reservation is located, and I earnestly hope that a man so well fitted for the work as Mr. Cook seems to be, may be selected.

Respectfully yours,
Chas. F. Manderson

THE BANK OF HARRISON

CHAS. E. VERITY, PRES.   CHAS. E. HOLMES, CASHIER

Harrison, Nebr., Jan. 17, 1891

Hon. C. F. Manderson
Washington, D. C.
Dear Sir:

We who reside in northwest Nebraska are greatly interested in the peaceable solution of the Indian problem. We desire the affairs of the agency to be conducted in a manner that will insure peace in the future, and give us the necessary confidence to remain where we are, without thinking that we are constantly endangering our lives. We think that this result can be obtained by the selection of James H. Cook as the agent for Pine Ridge. We are informed that at a recent council fully 3,000 of the Indians decided to ask for Cook's appointment to that position. For many years Cook has been a noted frontiersman, and has the confidence and friendship of Red Cloud and the great body of the Pine Ridge Sioux. We think that if he is appointed the trouble will be over. Personally, he is a man of unimpeachable integrity and has the respect of all who know him. His appointment would be a credit to the administration. We take pleasure in adding our endorsement to his recommendation, and hope if a change is made that his claims will receive careful consideration.

Very respectfully yours,
Chas. E. Verity, Pres.
Chas. E. Holmes, Cash.

EXECUTIVE DEPARTMENT
STATE OF WYOMING

Cheyenne, Wyo., February 6, 1891

Hon. Francis E. Warren
U. S. Senate
Washington, D. C.
Dear Sir:

I have much pleasure in recommending for appointment as

Indian agent at Pine Ridge agency, Mr. James H. Cook, should a change be contemplated at that point.

Mr. Cook is known to me as a man eminently fitted to discharge the duties of such office, having lived among the Indians all his life, thoroughly understanding their nature, ways, and language, and above all, a person commanding their confidence. I am convinced that his appointment would tend in a large degree to restore a feeling of good will between the Indians at that place and ourselves, the lack of which has caused so much trouble of late.

> Very respectfully,
> *Amos W. Barber*
> Acting Governor

To Hon. Secretary Noble:
The bearer, Mr. J. H. Cook of Nebraska, whom I have known for many years, is an honorable, upright Western man, a good Republican, and is well and favorably known by the Indians. He will explain his business, which I hope will be favorably received by you.

With many thanks for past favors, I am,

> Very truly, yours to command,
> **W. F. Cody**

COUNTY CLERK AND CLERK OF THE DISTRICT COURT
OF SIOUX COUNTY
Harrison, Nebr., Jan. 17, 1891

Hon. C. F. Manderson
Dear Sir: I wish you would call the attention of Congress to the fact that James H. Cook of this county is the person who would be satisfactory to your constituency in this county for the position of Indian agent at Pine Ridge, and have recommended him for that position. He is at present one of our most prominent and respected citizens, but was at one time an experienced government scout, and on account of the experience he

has had in dealing with Indians, and the fact of his having the confidence of Red Cloud and the leading chiefs among the Indians, and being trustworthy in every respect, his appointment would allay all fears of trouble. Hoping you will give this matter your immediate attention, I remain,

Yours, etc.,
Conrad Lindeman
County Clerk

One evening at the time when Uncle Sam was having his last war with his Indian wards, I was sitting in the tent of the army scouts at Pine Ridge Agency, chatting with my old friends and associates, Little Bat, Yankton Charlie, old Woman's Dress, and John Brouier, as to the probable outcome of the hostilities. An Oglala Sioux friend came to the tent and told me that he had been sent by the head men of the Oglalas, who had just held a council, to ask me to come that night to an old council lodge located about half a mile from the agency buildings, for they desired me to "help them" in their time of trouble. Darkness came on early, it being winter time. Some Indian friends and a half-breed Sioux friend named Joe Mousseau, who spoke both the Lacota and English tongues very fluently, went with me from the agency to the place appointed.

A surprise awaited me. In the center of that old log Omaha house (as it was commonly called by agency employees) a fire of small logs was burning, and a *chair* had been obtained from somewhere and placed near the fire for my use. Seated about in rows, encircling both the interior and exterior of the lodge for some distance, were seated many hundreds of Indians. When I had taken the proffered chair as calmly as possible, I looked over the assemblage. The old leaders of many bands of warriors sat in the first circle, with their blankets about them, but with their faces uncovered. Behind them nearly all the Indians wore their blankets over their heads, for the night was cold. I could see but a portion of their faces.

After I had been seated for perhaps a minute—although it seemed a much longer time—an aged Indian, whom I had never before met, arose slowly from his seat in the circle, where he had been smoking the pipe[1] with the other subchiefs. Gathering his blanket about him, he extended his hand and walked deliberately over to me. I arose and extended my hand to him. Evidently, as we held each other's hand in a firm grasp, he was trying to take my measure as a man among men. Then he spoke, very slowly, seeming gradually to arrive at a decision in my favor as one worthy of his friendship. As nearly as I can recall them, these are the words he spoke to me:

"My friend, I have never seen you before. I have heard my people talk about you for years. Now I see you, and my heart is good toward you, for it tells me that you are a friend to my people. I want to tell you about our troubles now. My people could not get enough to eat; the women and children could not live because they were hungry, and it made them sick. Some of my people pray and dance to the Great Spirit of the Indians to help us. Soldiers have now come to fight with us and kill us. Can you help us? This is all I have to say now."

---

[1] When the pipe is freshly cleaned, filled, and lighted, the stem is first pointed straight up, as an invitation to the Great Father of all Creation to come and partake of the first whiffs of its smoke. The stem is then pointed to the West, where the Great Spirit of Thunder presides, inviting it to join the gathering; then to the North, where lives the Big Spirit who sends the buffalo to the Indians, requesting its presence; next to the East, where the Spirit of the Elk lives; then to the South, in order that the Great Spirit of the Sun may also receive an invitation to be present; and finally straight downward, offering the Great Spirit Mother, the Earth, a smoke.

Before the pipestone of Minnesota was known by the Sioux or Dakota Indians, they used, according to all the information which I have been able to gather on the subject from the oldest of these people whom I have ever met, the leg bone of the deer or antelope as a pipe in all their ceremonial smokes. Just before the time when the first white men brought the tobacco plant to the attention of the Indians, the Plains tribes used to mix the dried buffalo chips with the inner bark of the red dogwood and use it when making a smoke to the Great Spirits. Some of the oldest Indians still preserve the precious buffalo chips of the years gone by and on special occasions enjoy an old-time smoke with their ancient bone pipes, loaded with dried bark and buffalo chips.

The name of this old fellow was Few Tails.

After he had once more seated himself, another old man, named Little Wound, whom I had known for years, came and shook my hand. He said he knew that I was his friend and the friend of all his people, and that if I had been their white father (agent) there would have been no trouble, for I would have let the Great Father at Washington know that his people were starving, and that now I would write and tell the Great White Father the cause of all the trouble, and ask him to take the soldiers away and give the Indians enough to eat, so that none of them would starve. He then shook my hand again and sat down. Old Little Wound was an intelligent Indian and a great warrior. He would be classified as a bad Indian by many white people. His view regarding the entire white race was that they were invaders of his native country, and he had certainly done his bit to save his country from those who had at last, by one means and another, wrested the most of it from the red man.

After Little Wound was seated, another old Indian warrior arose and came to me. I do not at this time recall his name. He said that he had heard his people talk about me, and that they had two names for me. One was Little Eagle and the other was Buckskin Shirt. He had never seen me before. Now that he had seen me he wanted to ask me a question. I told him my ears were open. He then asked me what I would have done had I been the agent at Pine Ridge when the Ghost Dancing started. Would I have been afraid and asked the Great Father to send soldiers to kill his people if they did not stop dancing? He said that before I answered that question he wanted to know how old I was. I told him. Then he stated, as the explanation of his question, that his old people had always said that a man under forty years of age would not always "talk straight" (tell the truth). Now that he knew I had long since reached the age at which I would speak truthfully, he would like to have me answer his first question. He then shook my hand and sat down, waiting for me to speak.

Arising from my seat, I addressed my hearers in approximately the following words: "My friends, many of you have heard the question I have just been asked to answer. Those of you who could not hear his words have been told the question to which he desires an answer, as his words have been passed back to you. To my mind his question meant: Are you afraid of the Indians when they pray to their Great Spirit Father to help and protect them from those who have taken their country and food from them?

"As I stand here alone, the only white man among you, knowing that there are many among you who are feeling very angry toward all white men, and that I should have no more chance to live, if their desire is to kill me, than a little mouse would have if surrounded by a bunch of cats, I feel that my being here at such a time should have answered that question.

"Very many of you know, as you have often visited me, that I have a very comfortable and safe home far from this place, where I should now be but for the wish to try to aid you in your troubles by my counsel, as so many of you have asked me to do. Many of you old men, when speaking to me, and in sending to me letters, which you have your children write, call me 'brother.' I want to be a good brother to you and help you in any way that I can. I hope this trouble will soon be over, and that you will soon have food enough so that you will not be hungry."

Judging from the roar of "How's" and "Ho's" which came from the throats of that little sea of Indians, my words pleased them. Many questions were then asked me. Among others was one asking why letters which they had written to the Commissioner of Indian Affairs at Washington, telling of their distress, were never answered. Did they never leave the post office at the agency—never reach Washington? In answer I could only tell them that they were wards, or prisoners of war, of the United States government, and that any white man not associated with the Indian Department at Washington would be given credit for trying to make trouble, and be treated accordingly, if he attempted to advise the Indians how to get the ear of the authorities at Washington except through the regular agent sent to them by the Indian Department. I told them that my advice to them had always been to have their children learn, just as quickly as possible, the white man's language and ways of doing all sorts of things. Then they would soon learn how to protect themselves, not only from incompetent interpreters, but from those of the white race whose only thought regarding Indians was to make money by dealings of any sort which they might have with the red man. Our talk lasted until midnight. What effect my words had had on their minds would be hard to figure out.

Occasionally I can look back into the picture gallery of my brain and see again the weather-beaten faces of those old Indians who addressed me on that occasion. The flare of light from the cottonwood fire brought out vividly their features and the expressions on their bronzed faces. All of those aged warriors have now passed on to the Happy Hunting Grounds. My friend Joseph Mousseau, who acted as interpreter on that occasion, still lives on Pine Ridge Reservation in South Dakota.

15
Red Cloud

IN THE EARLY MORNING of December 10, 1909, the spirit of Red Cloud (Mahpiya-luta), the last of the great Sioux chiefs who fought against the invasion of the lands of their forefathers by the whites, started on its long journey over the ghost road, to meet whatever fate the Great Judge of all people had in store for it.

More than thirty years before, I had often told Red Cloud that it would give me great pleasure if he would tell me the true story of his life and let me have it recorded from his own lips. He said that a number of white men had tried to get him to do this, but that he did not want to say anything for white men to write down in order to make money for themselves by selling his words. I told him that there were white men who would be glad to have him tell his life story with no thought of trying to make money out of it, but simply to leave to the world facts regarding himself and his people during his lifetime, so that such facts might be handed down to the generations to follow; that this would offset many stories about himself that were sure to be written by those who had known him only since he and his people had been on reservations as wards or prisoners of war. I further told him that every Indian agent who had been in charge of him and his people—Indian traders and agency employees, as well as white men who had married into his tribe—might all tell conflicting stories about his characteristics, actions, and rating among his people since they had known him, and repeat as facts incidents of his early life told to them, perhaps, by forked tongues.

Many years ago, when visiting me in my home, he announced that he was ready to tell my wife and me the story of his life.

Red Cloud

I told him that I should be glad to hear it, but that what I most wanted was to have his story recorded, and that to record it a first-class interpreter and a stenographer should be employed. I stated to the Chief that when this could be done I should feel satisfied. Anything which he might tell me or the members of my family, we should always be glad to hear, but these stories, repeated by us, would not read like his own words, just as they came from his lips. We planned that some time the story should be told and recorded. But the years slipped by, and the old Chief's memory was so clouded the greater part of the time during his last visits to my home that it was impossible for him to tell the story that would have added so much to our knowledge of the Indian life west of the Missouri River before the building of wagon roads and iron trails through the land of the Sioux.

During Red Cloud's life he and his people had to meet such conditions as never before had confronted his tribe, and it was a most trying ordeal through which they had to pass. None of the leaders of his people, during the years in which they had flourished before the coming of the white man, had ever had to face such problems as Red Cloud and his wise men met and had to solve. Consequently no precedents had been established that would cover the conditions, and before we criticize him by our own standards of right and wrong, let us consider his side of the story.

Word pictures of the old Chief and of his history have come to me since his death, mostly in the form of newspaper clippings sent me by friends who knew of my friendship with old Red Cloud and of the annual visits to my home which he made, with some of his old people, whenever possible during the past thirty years. These word pictures are much alike, and they bring out one point very clearly to my mind—that the authors wrote from a popular point of view held by numerous white men, that the only good Indian is a dead one. All Indians never looked alike to me, for I have found them like all others of the *genus homo* with whom I ever came in contact—made up of good, bad, and indifferent material.

The Plains Indians are the most advanced in perception and general intelligence, for the reason that, in order to live almost wholly by the chase in an open country, they had to bring all the senses into play. Many of the tribes were at war with each other, for it was one of their customs to make raids on each others' villages and carry off a few scalps, women, and horses. While out in quest of daily bread, the hunter had to keep an eye open at all times for any of his brother men who might desire to lift his scalp lock. The desert Indian, who could subsist on grasshoppers, crickets, and green bugs, the mountain Indian, who could live on roots and nuts, and the coast Indian, who could "catchum clam in low tide and eatum in high," were all far behind the Plains Indian in several particulars of mental development.

From my youth I have taken pleasure in the study of the wild people of the Plains, and in the years spent among them as cowboy, hunter, and guide I have enjoyed the friendship of many among the last of those whose footsteps will never again follow the trails and customs of their ancestors. In my attempt to write a sketch of my old Indian friend and his life, I make no claim to having either discovered him or brought his life into the limelight from the cradle to the grave. I can only tell about him as I knew him, and about the conditions of the time through which he lived, so far back as I have any knowledge. He has told me many stories of his life that I cannot at this time write about. I know that others have been at work trying to secure all the material possible relative to Red Cloud's life history, and I hope that they have secured much valuable information regarding the old Chief's eventful life.

Red Cloud was my friend for about thirty-five years, and I think I knew him as well, in many ways, as any white man ever did—perhaps better. His friendship for me was, I believe, as genuine as any Indian ever had for a white man. The fact that

I met him on the common ground of a hunter and dweller in the Plains country, and in a different manner from most white men, had much to do, I think, with the establishing of a friendship that grew with the passing years.

Red Cloud was, to me, a most interesting student of nature, and his knowledge of the flora and fauna of the land over which he and his people roamed was simply marvelous to me. Naturally, he could not look upon the coming of the white man and the passing of the buffalo and other game with anything but sorrow and hatred in his heart. The buffalo herds meant everything to the Sioux. From them he derived the greater part of his food supply, also the skins with which to cover his lodges and make soles for his moccasins in warm weather, and warm covers for himself during the very cold spells, as well as robes that took the place of blankets. The sinews of the backs of these Indian cattle were used to make bowstrings for the weapon upon which he had to depend for securing his food and protecting himself from his enemies. Even the dried chips of this great animal were used, both for fuel and, when mixed with the bark of the red willow (dogwood), in the stone pipe. The extermination of the buffalo meant starvation to the Plains Indians, for the science of agriculture had never appealed to them. Red Cloud and many others of his people knew that, unless the white people could be kept out of the buffalo country, they were doomed, so far as being a free and independent people was concerned. They would have a strange master to look to for existence.

The Chief did everything in his power to hold his bands together and to oppose the coming of the whites; but the blankets and knives, guns and ammunition, as well as the powerful spirit water which the early white traders had brought and exchanged with them for robes and furs, had a countereffect. Some of the first white men who came to trade with them later became a part of the tribe by marrying into it; and later still, when treaties were made or dealings effected with the government officials, these same men had to be depended upon as interpreters. They made friends with some of the Sioux subchiefs and gained great influence over them—so much that the great Sioux nation became divided against itself over the question of allowing the whites to make roads across their hunting grounds. At times much blood was shed by warring factions over this question.

From the very first until he was completely overwhelmed and his sway over his people broken, Red Cloud was consistently opposed to allowing the whites to mark wagon trails across the Plains. He was a clear-headed, far-seeing man, with much greater brain power than many have given him credit for. He was at least brave and faithful to his people, and one of whom it may truthfully be said, "Here was a man."

Many of their dealings with the government were, from the first, unsatisfactory to the Sioux. At times they were compelled to use incompetent or dishonest interpreters, and they also had a few rascally Indian agents to deal with. These factors were not such as to inspire faith in the whites and their teachings regarding the Great Spirit who, ruling over all the peoples on earth, had decreed that the red man must eventually follow the white man's road in all things. It was not the Indian's nature to about-face and try to keep step with those upon whom he looked as coming to drive him and his people from lands which they claimed by birthright. Without money or resources of any kind other than the game of the country, on which to subsist and from which to secure clothing and shelter, and with a comparatively small area of country over which he could evade pursuit by his powerful and relentless enemies, the Indian put up the best fight of which he was capable, and continued it so long as there seemed to him to be the least chance of deferring the rapidly approaching time when he and his people would have to forsake forever the ways in which they had been trained for centuries.

Crazy Horse was one of the subchiefs of the Sioux nation who refused positively to make friends with the palefaces under the terms offered his people. In 1876, he had a large following of warriors among the different bands of Sioux, and they seemed ready to die, if necessary, fighting for what they considered to be their rights. The attitude of Crazy Horse was well known at Red Cloud Agency by the government officials stationed there, and he was watched closely. Indications of trouble caused these officials to decide that it would be a wise move to arrest and confine him for a time.

Being warned in time, Crazy Horse, when the plan for his arrest was being carried out, escaped and went to the Spotted Tail Agency in Dakota. But he was there arrested by the Sioux who were friendly to the whites, and brought back to Red Cloud Agency. He was taken to the adjutant's office at Camp Robinson, which was located about a mile from the agency buildings. His attitude there was so bold and defiant that the guards were ordered to put him into the guardhouse. This was a very delicate undertaking, for about three hundred of his relatives and warriors had followed him right up to the garrison, and they were in an ugly mood. When the guards started with him, Crazy Horse did not realize that he was to be locked up; but when we reached the guardhouse with some of the Indians who were friendly to the whites, and found himself closely followed by the soldiers forming the guard, he realized at a single glance what was to be done. He suddenly drew a knife which he had concealed under his blanket, and started to fight his way out to the spot where his friends were. He cut one of the Indians across the wrist as the latter tried to detain him. When Crazy Horse reached the soldier guards, they closed in on him, and one of them thrust his bayonet through the Chief's body. He did not die instantly but lived several hours.

When the news spread among the Indians that their great

fighting Chief had been stabbed, there was some excitement among them; and, in my opinion, only the fact that the Sioux nation was at that time so badly divided against itself prevented the sacrifice of the soldiers and civilians then living about Fort Robinson and the Red Cloud Agency. The man who above all others could probably at that moment have taken advantage of the situation and, in the excitement, once more have secured supreme control of a host of warriors and led them in a death-struggle against the whites, was Chief Red Cloud. But this sagacious leader fully realized at that time that armed resistance was a thing of the past, so far as a termination successful for the Indian was concerned. In the absence of a leader, the factional spirit soon asserted itself once more among the many Indians then encamped about Fort Robinson; and the event passed into history without more loss of life.

A few relatives and friends disposed of the body of Crazy Horse in a spot known to but few persons living today. But his name will be handed down for ages to come by the race which he so cordially despised, as the name of one who fought a brave but hopeless fight against an irresistible force; and the footfall of the white man will probably never sound upon his grave, though Indian spirits, in the form of coyotes or big gray wolves, may sing serenades about his bones for years to come.[1]

Should a time ever arrive when those engaged in scientific research discover the origin of the natives of this continent, with some record of their prehistoric lives that will throw more light upon them, it will be interesting knowledge. I am inclined to think that the Indians of this continent are all descended from the people who made the first signs of mankind left here, in the form of stone implements, earth mounds, temples, and pyramids. I find that some words of the Sioux language are identical with some of those used by the bands or tribes of what are

---

[1] Very few of the many tribes of Indians living in the Middle West in early days ever killed the big wolves or the coyotes, their belief being that these creatures were departed Indian spirits returned to earth in these forms.

commonly called the Aztecs or Toltecs—people of prehistoric times.

In 1877, quite a number of the Northern Cheyenne Indians who had been especially hostile during the Indian trouble known as the '76 Campaign, or Sitting Bull War, were sent to Fort Reno, Indian Territory, as prisoners of war. They were considered by the War Department as a very dangerous element—one likely to stir up trouble for the whites among the Sioux nation, with whom they were intermarried. No braver warriors ever lived on the Plains of our western country within the knowledge of the white race. Whenever the army people had any one of the Chiefs Dull Knife, Wild Hog, or Little Chief to contend with, they well knew that they had a serious situation to face.

After this band of prisoners had remained in the Indian Territory a few months, they became very much dissatisfied. The climate did not seem to agree with them, and many of them died. During the summer of 1878 Little Chief went to Washington with the interpreter Ben Clark and begged the Great Father to let his people return to the land of the Dakotas. His petition was denied. Upon the return of Little Chief with this information, it was planned that at the first opportunity the entire band would make a break for liberty and either fight their way back to the Sioux country in the north or die trying.

The outbreak took place in the fall of 1878. It was a complete success, in the sense that the Cheyennes were able to reach the country to which they wished to return. They outfought and outgeneraled everything offered in the way of opposition by United States troops or civilians. They left a trail marked by the blood of soldiers and settlers, until this trail was lost for a time in the sand hills of western Nebraska. There they were discovered by a half-breed Sioux, who informed the commanding officer at Fort Robinson of their presence in the country. The half-breed stated that he had run across the Indian camp in the sand hills. The Indians, however, maintained that runners from Dull Knife's camp had come into Red Cloud Agency and there reported the approach of the run-aways and where they were encamped. They stated further that the person who gave this information to the officers at Fort Robinson had secured it from the Indians whom Dull Knife had trusted, and upon whom he and his people had counted for aid in making a last stand, if need were, against the whites. When the commanding officer at Fort Robinson learned the whereabouts of the Cheyennes, he sent two troops of cavalry out and captured them. They had made a long, desperate march, but they were burdened with their old people and children. Receiving no encouragement from the Sioux, to whom they had sent runners ahead appealing for aid, they had nothing to do but surrender.

The Indians balked on the way to Fort Robinson and decided to die rather than go into the fort as prisoners. Some field artillery being brought and trained upon them, they yielded and were taken to Fort Robinson and placed in one of the barracks, where a strong guard was placed over them. But when they were told that they were to go back to the Indian Territory, they insisted that they would die first. They were told that they would have to go, nevertheless, and the Department at Washington decreed that they must be returned to the Territory even if it became necessary to haul them there in wagons. The Indians stubbornly refused to yield. In an effort to induce them to change their minds (so I have been told by some of the Indians who were confined), their fuel supply was cut off, and, as it was very cold weather, they began to suffer. This treatment not having the desired effect, food was next denied them. This also failed to deter the Indians; then their water supply was shut off. By this time the prisoners were desperate and half-crazed. While this heroic treatment was being administered by Commandant Wessels (doubtless under orders from Washington), the guard had been strengthened and every possible precaution taken to prevent an escape.

Before they were placed in the barracks under guard, a few carbines and pistols belonging to the Indians had been taken apart and the pieces distributed and concealed beneath the clothing of the women. After confinement in the barracks these guns had been assembled. I understand there were about a dozen weapons among them. One bitterly cold night when everyone about the garrison was keyed to excitement over the situation, the confined prisoners fired upon the guard and made a most determined and desperate break for liberty.

The soldiers in the garrison turned out quickly and pursued the Indians, who were trying to gain the rough ground about two miles from the fort. Twenty-eight of them were shot down on the ground adjacent to the barracks. The Indians secured the arms of a few soldiers whom they had killed at their first fire. The Cheyennes who escaped that night were followed about two miles; then the pursuit was abandoned until the next day. The trail was then taken up and followed into the Hat Creek Basin, where a great number of the runaways were overtaken and slaughtered. In one large hole, or "blow-out," several Indians had taken refuge. These were all killed. The last one alive was an old man. After his companions had all been shot to death, this old warrior suddenly sprang up in view of a group of soldiers and dashed toward them with a knife in each hand. He was quickly riddled with bullets.

I had met Dull Knife, Wild Hog, and Little Chief, who, knowing Red Cloud's friendship for me, were also friendly. After those days of war and privation, Little Chief visited me in my home with a number of the survivors of the little band which had preferred death to imprisonment. (Not all of them were captured by the troops at Fort Robinson, for the reason that, after reaching Nebraska, the Cheyennes divided into two or three parties and many of them escaped the soldiers.)

The officers and men who were forced to guard and pursue this band of Indians endured their share of the sufferings and hardships incident to such warfare. A list of the killed, wounded, and frozen soldiers, taken from the hospital records kept at that time, would tell a mute story of what soldiering in the Indian country meant, even so late as 1878.

*Chief Red Cloud, from a United States government official photo-
graph taken about 1875.*

Professor O. C. Marsh, Yale University, and Chief Red Cloud holding the peace pipe, a ceremony and pose symbolizing the peaceful manner in which the Sioux permitted Marsh and his parties to collect fossils in Sioux territory. This is the only known photograph—taken in New Haven, Connecticut, about 1880—of Red Cloud wearing white men's clothing.

Chief Red Cloud and his wife, about 1899. This is said to be the only picture ever taken of his wife.

Photograph by Thomas Beans, Nebraska; courtesy National Park Service

Old Chief Red Cloud just before his death, on his way for his last visit to the author at Agate, Nebraska. At his right stand his son, Jack Red Cloud, and Jack's wife and daughter. In the background tower the Red Cloud Buttes, named after the old chief, at the foot of which was located the old Red Cloud Agency. This picture was

*taken on the Fort Robinson Military Reservation, near where
Camp Robinson, later Fort Robinson, was established in 1874. The
Black Hills Treaty, which ceded this whole region, including the
rich Black Hills area, from the Indians to the whites, was signed
by Red Cloud near this spot.*

*Sioux women bringing wood into camp at Agate, Nebraska, 1916.
They had carried these loads over one-third of a mile without resting, before this photograph was taken. Note beef "jerking" (drying) on lines strung between poles in the right background.*

*Red Hawk, subchief of the Northern Cheyenne Indians,
and James H. Cook.*

Combined fort, bunkhouse, and stable on the range of the WS and SU ranches in Socorro County, New Mexico, 1884. Left to right: two Mexican cowboys; Ed Erway, ranch foreman; M. F. S. Stevens, Englishman (top); Jim Gedes, cowboy (below); Mr. Jenkins and Mr. Upcher, Englishmen; George Warden and Jasper Thomason, cowboys.

Photograph by A. Thomson, New York

At Agate Springs Ranch, 1915. Little Crow is telling a tale of his younger days, when white men were scarce in the land of the Sioux.

War correspondents and others at Pine Ridge Indian Agency, South Dakota, during the Wounded Knee campaign, 1890–91. Left to Right: Buckskin Jack, Indian; W. F. Kelley; Alf Burkholder; C. G. Seymore; Gilbert E. Bailey (above); Major John Burke, associated with Colonel W. F. Cody's Wild West Shows (below); Edwin B. Clarke; J. A. McDonough; Dent H. Roberts; K. V. Zilliacus, of Helsinki, Finland (above); James A. Cooper (below); E. A. O'Brian; and James H. Cook.

General Nelson A. Miles and his staff at Pine Ridge Agency during the Wounded Knee campaign, January 1, 1891.

Little Chief, war chief of the Northern Cheyenne Indians, presenting the author with his gun at Pine Ridge Indian Agency, Pine Ridge, South Dakota, when the Indians were disarmed at the close of the Wounded Knee Campaign, January 15, 1891.

*James H. Cook and Good Lance, Oglala Sioux, holding the Pipe
of Peace; Two Lance, Oglala Sioux, standing by.*

Chief Short Bull, Oglala Sioux, with author, at Fort Robinson, Nebraska, for the unveiling ceremonies of the two monuments dedicated on September 5, 1934, one in honor of Chief Crazy Horse, Sioux leader, and the other in honor of Lieutenant Levi Robinson, for whom the fort was named. In the dedication ceremonies, the author represented the white race and Short Bull and two other chiefs, White Bull and James Red Cloud, selected by the Indian Tribal Council, represented the Sioux Nation. Short Bull and his brother, He Dog, both very old men in 1934, participated in the fight with General Custer's command in 1876. Short Bull gave the author an old-time buffalo robe at this meeting, in token of their old friendship.

16

The Ghost Dance War

MY FRIENDSHIP with Red Cloud began in the autumn of 1875, when I made a visit to the Red Cloud Agency with my old friend, Baptiste Garnier (Little Bat), a man whose record as a scout and hunter stands second to none in the section of country in which he spent his life, and in which his body now rests. His mother, by the way, was a full-blood Sioux and his father a Frenchman. Red Cloud made us welcome in his lodge when Little Bat said that I was his friend and that I was a hunter who knew the country from the Shell River (North Platte) to the ocean on the south, and something of the many tribes of people inhabiting it, as well as of its bird and animal life. Red Cloud sent one of his old men out among the lodges and had a number of his greatest subchiefs and warriors come to his lodge to meet and talk with me. Among those whom I met on that occasion, and who then became my friends and remained so as long as they lived, were Little Wound, Young-Man-Afraid-of-His-Horses, and American Horse.

The Red Cloud Agency was located at that time on White River, in the northwestern part of Nebraska, the agency buildings standing about two miles up the river from where the city of Crawford is now located. I was told of the treaty which at that time defined the Minitanka Wakpala (Niobrara River) as the southern boundary of the Sioux country. But not many years previously they had hunted as far south as the Wan-hi Wakpala (Arkansas River), whenever they were in strong enough force to fight the tribes which claimed that region as their hunting ground.

I told them that, although my skin was white, I had lived in very much the same way as themselves, and that I loved to travel over the plains and mountains and see on all sides the wonderful works of the Great Spirit. I spoke of the change which, I could then see, was fast coming over the entire western country, and said that but a few years more would pass before the last of the big buffalo herds would be wiped out forever, and many, many white people would sweep over and possess the lands then claimed by the Indians and wild creatures as their own.

It was on this occasion that I first learned of the bones of strange creatures which had once lived in the land of the Sioux —bones now turned to stone. I was shown some of the petrifactions. A piece of gigantic jawbone containing a molar three inches in diameter was shown to me. American Horse explained that it had belonged to a "thunder horse" which had lived a long time ago, and that the creature would sometimes come down upon the earth in a thunderstorm and chase the buffalo, striking and killing some of them with his great hoofs. Once when the Sioux people were near starvation, this big horse had driven a herd of buffalo into their camp in the midst of a violent thunderstorm, and the Sioux had killed a great many of them with their arrows and lances. This occurred "way back," when the Indians had no horses.

While I was the guest of Red Cloud on this occasion, Professor O. C. Marsh, of the Smithsonian Institution and Yale College, came over from Fort Laramie with a government escort. He wanted permission from the Sioux to hunt for fossils in their country. The Sioux, however, did not take kindly to this proposition, thinking that it was really gold and not "stone bones" that the white chief wanted to find. I heard a great deal of the Indian side regarding bone-hunting in the Sioux hunting grounds. I met Professor Marsh and talked with him. Then I went to Red Cloud's lodge and talked the matter over with him. I told him that Professor Marsh was a friend of the Great Father at Washington; that, if he were allowed to hunt for stone bones, I thought he would be a good friend to the Sioux people; and that I was sure he was not hunting for yellow lead (gold).

Red Cloud said that if Professor Marsh were a good man, he would help him and his people get rid of the agent who was then in charge of them, and whom they cordially disliked and openly accused of dishonesty. When this was brought to the attention of Professor Marsh, he took the matter in hand, and an investigation of affairs took place at Red Cloud Agency. Records of the U. S. Indian Department show that the result of this investigation was most pleasing to Red Cloud and his people, if not to some of their white brothers. Professor Marsh was given a Sioux name, Man-That-Picks-Up-Bones (Wiscasa Pahi Huhu) and was allowed to come with his field parties and prospect for fossils without molestation. The Professor and Red Cloud became such fast friends that the Chief was entertained by Professor Marsh at his home in New Haven, Connecticut, and there the two were photographed with clasped hands and the peace pipe between them.

At the time of my first visit to Red Cloud, there were estimated to be at least twelve thousand Indians about the agency, quite a number of whom did not belong to any agency, but were restless members of many bands, thoroughly aroused by the steady oncoming of the whites, and ready for desperate deeds of any kind.

Red Cloud had often told me about the part which he took in opposing the opening of the Bozeman trail and the establishment of military posts in the Sioux country. He had charge of the warriors who wiped out Lieutenant Colonel Fetterman and his little command near old Fort Phil Kearny. He well knew that it was then or never that the white man could be stayed from doing as he pleased in the valuable hunting grounds which the Chief had so long contested with the Crows. The brave soldiers and citizens who lost their lives on that occasion simply had no chance whatever. They were overwhelmed by vast numbers. The suffering and privation endured by handfuls of troops sent out by our government to establish military posts along the first western wagon roads to California and Montana were such that they cannot even be read without pain and horror.

My dear friend Major Tenedore Ten Eyck, now passed away, but in 1866 a captain at Fort Phil Kearny, was the man sent out with a relief party to bring in the bodies of his comrades whom Red Cloud's warriors had slain. Later, he often sent word to his old enemy, through me, that when he looked back to the conditions that existed at the time of the fight at Fort Phil Kearny, he could think with less enmity of those who had killed his companions-in-arms with such seeming ruthlessness. Major Ten Eyck wanted me to learn, if possible, the number of Indians killed and wounded by Fetterman's command before they gave up their lives. When I asked Red Cloud for this information, his reply was that but few Indians, eleven in all, he thought, were killed outright during the fight, but that a number were wounded, many of them so badly that they died later on in the camps which were quickly scattered all over the country. Red Cloud also told me that in this fight, his sub-chief, American Horse, killed Colonel Fetterman. American Horse has told me the same. These old Chiefs often talked with me about the details of this fight. Both told me that a number of the soldiers were so terrified, when they realized what a trap they had fallen into, that they seemed paralyzed and offered no resistance to the Indian warriors. The officers, however, did everything in their power, fighting gamely to the last.

In the 1876 campaign Red Cloud took little if any part. Many warriors from the Red Cloud Agency, however, were with the hostiles, and several old Indians who took part in the fight with Custer's command, and who have visited me in company with Red Cloud, have told me of the day when they wiped out the courageous General and so many soldiers. Their victory, as they well knew, was due only to their overwhelming numbers and to the fact that the cavalrymen were forced to fight on foot.

Red Cloud well knew at this time that war with the whites could result in nothing but suffering and death to many of his people; but he had lost control of many of the bands of Sioux, and they would not heed his pacific suggestions. Some of his subchiefs—for example, Crazy Horse—and many of the young men wanted war, and they had to have it. Red Cloud's popularity waned as others who were more belligerent led the young men on the war trails against the "long knives." Bad wounds and old age may have had a great deal to do with checking Red Cloud's warlike spirit at this time; but his judgment in laying down the hatchet at the time when he forsook the warpath was, I think, greater than that of his subchief Crazy Horse, who had to make his start for the ghost trail off the point of a bayonet thrust by an unduly excited soldier. When Crazy Horse was killed at Fort Robinson after having been summoned there for a talk with government officials, many of his people felt that it was a most treacherous and cowardly deed, and great efforts were required on the part of Red Cloud and other old men to restrain the warriors from attempting to avenge his death.

In 1878, when the band of Northern Cheyennes who had been held as prisoners of war at Fort Reno, Indian Territory, broke loose and fought their way back north as far as Red Cloud's country, their leaders (considered by both the white and the red men who knew them to be the bravest and shrewdest Indian war chieftains who ever lived on our western plains within the history of man) tried their best to persuade Red Cloud and his old subchiefs to join them in making a last stand, urging that it would be better to die the death of warriors than be obliged to live like dogs—to be fed such refuse as white men might see fit to give, and to be told where they might and might not go. Red Cloud, however, would not listen to their war talk, and he did everything he could to have the Sioux remain quiet and let the war trail grass over.

The next so-called Sioux uprising took place in the autumn

and winter of 1890–91. It was caused by the Messiah craze that came to them by way of runners from the Far West. Word had come from the Great Spirit of all Indians that the hated white man was to be wiped off the earth, and that former conditions, such as the return of the buffalo, would follow. They were to dance and pray until such conditions came to pass. The effect of these messages was like that of the arrival and efforts of a great revivalist of the shouting Methodist school, who could soon have great numbers of blind followers under the influence of what he styled "the power."

When the news of the coming of the Indian Messiah was brought to me by some old Indian friends from Pine Ridge Agency, South Dakota, I went with them to the home of Little Bat at Fort Robinson and talked over the situation with him and with the Indians. I could see no harm, I told them, in their dancing the Ghost Dance if they did not kill themselves while so doing, but I counseled them against doing any deeds of violence against the white people, for such deeds could lead only to serious trouble. I told them that if the Great Spirit were going to bring about any such changes, he would need no help in disposing of the whites; he could cause all of them—or such as he cared to remove—to die as suddenly as a flash of lightning.

When Agent Royer went out armed to order a ghost dance at Pine Ridge to cease, he was met by one Indian who was not afraid of a white man. The Indians who were present told me that this lone red man replied to Royer that white people danced when they wished to, and so did the Sioux. He asked the agent what he intended to do with the pistol which he was carrying, and whether he had ever killed an Indian. Then he bared his breast to the agent and said, "Here, kill me, for I am going to dance!" When this agent called upon United States troops at Fort Robinson for protection, Little Bat, the scout at that post, was asked what he thought of the situation. His reply was that, if the Indians were not disturbed in the dance and the new craze, they would soon wear themselves out and stop it. But this was not to be. One of the greatest and most expensive gatherings of United States troops since the Civil War was brought into the field, and a few more lives of both white and red men had to be sacrificed in order to settle the vexing Indian question.

I went to Pine Ridge Agency, Red Cloud's last stamping ground, at the first intimation of trouble over the ghost dancing, and remained there until General Miles and his command had our Sioux wards back on the reservation drawing rations, with only a small detachment of soldiers posted to look after the government property left by the troops at the close of the campaign. A number of war correspondents were at Pine Ridge Agency during a greater part of the trouble, and some of these gentlemen informed me that old Red Cloud was at the bottom of all the deviltry that was going on; that he was managing the hostiles who were out in the badlands, making his headquarters at the fine house which Uncle Sam had so kindly given him in order to make him comfortable in his old age. It so happened that I was with Red Cloud nearly every day at that time, and my associates every day and night were the headquarters Indian scouts, Little Bat, Woman's Dress, Yankton Charlie, Short Bull, and other Indian friends who knew about all that was going on, both at the agency and at the hostile camp. Neither these men nor I could ever discover that old Red Cloud had anything to do with either directing the hostiles or giving them aid and encouragement.

General Miles was kind to the old Chief and did not, I am sure, charge him with aiding the enemy. One day I went with Red Cloud to the General's headquarters, and the Chief told him that he was cold and hungry. He was soon supplied with both food and fuel. I think that General Miles and almost all the other army officers who have had to face the hardships of Indian campaigns, and who knew the Indian as well as most white men or better, have more respect and sympathy for the old-time wild Indian than those whose information about Indians came by hearsay. General Brooks was the first commanding officer at the Pine Ridge Agency previously to the coming of General Miles; and from remarks which I have heard that kindhearted officer make, I am sure he felt that there had been much ado about nothing at the outset, and that all trouble could have been averted had there been the right sort of official in charge of affairs at the agency when the ghost dancing began —one who knew more about Indians.

Red Cloud's father was a big chief, but the son had to fight hard and do great deeds of valor before he became the acknowledged head chief of the whole Sioux nation. This was what he had accomplished at the age of thirty years. He was a magnificent specimen of physical manhood and, when in his prime, as full of action as a tiger. As a young man he was a terror in war with other tribes. The old warriors who fought by his side have told me of his killing five Pawnees in one fight, using only his knife as a weapon after sending one arrow from his bow.

He received one wound which came near ending his career. An arrow was driven through the center of his body from front to back, so that the head of the shaft projected beyond the barbs. His medicine men pulled the arrow through, and for three days and nights he lay like a dead man, with hardly enough heart action to be felt.

His friendship for me saved not only my own life, but also the lives of several other cowboys who, with me, once took a bunch of Indian contract cattle into their country; so that I have occasion to be most grateful to him. Being used for a pincushion, with arrows for the pins, is not a pleasant or desirable proposition. I packed in my leg for a few miles one little dogwood switch which a Lipan Indian presented me, hot from the bow, down in the lower Rio Grande country, and I have never desired a similar experience.

When it became known that General Miles had given orders to Colonel Forsyth to intercept Big Foot's band of Sioux Indians, who had traveled from Standing Rock Reservation and were on their way to Pine Ridge Agency to surrender, a number of civilians at the agency prepared to be on hand in order to see Big Foot and his people give themselves up. Many of these civilians were press correspondents representing various daily newspapers throughout the United States. There was one European correspondent among them.

A Catholic priest, Father Craft, who had been stationed at Pine Ridge for some time, and who was well known to the Indians, also accompanied these sight-seers. I was acquainted with Father Craft, and I happened to meet him just as he was about to start off with the others. I remarked to him that he had better be careful, for it was not unlikely that lead might be drifting through the air should there be any kind of hitch in the surrender ceremonies. Father Craft replied that the Hovering Eagle—the name given him by the Sioux people—would be in no danger from the Indians; he felt that he was both a father and a brother to them. He said a "black robe" (priest) was always safe with Indians. I remarked to him that I had known Indian men to forget everything pertaining to the white man's religion when they were desperately angry or frightened. A white man garbed in black meant an enemy to them as much as one in the uniform of a major general of the army. He was apparently amused by my remark, for he smiled as he rolled a cigarette and took his departure for the scene of the surrender.

Two days later when I saw him, he was propped up on a cot at the agency—although he was still able to wrestle with a cigarette. The thought "I told you so" came into my mind, but he was prepared for me. He explained that the reason why an Indian who was dashing past him in an effort to escape from the soldiers who were firing at him, had paused long enough to drive a long butcher knife between his shoulder blades, was that "the poor fellow did not see that he was stabbing a black robe." I told him that it was no doubt a fact, but that the Indian could see a patch of white skin somewhere near the place he struck at. Father Craft must have had not only a sense of humor but also his full share of vitality. The wound which he received on that occasion would undoubtedly have killed some men. He was laid up but a short time, and if he stopped smoking cigarettes for two days because of that little cut, I have no record of it.

Among the war correspondents at Pine Ridge was one from Omaha. In this tale I shall call him "Cola." Mr. Cola had been at the agency waiting for hostilities to begin until he was beginning to become impatient for action. The hostiles stuck to their camp out in the badlands, doing little damage aside from eating an occasional beef which they did not buy and shooting the peace pipe out of the hand of an Indian brother who had been persuaded by General Miles to carry a peace message to them. Cola complained quite a bit to me about the inactivity, which was about the only thing going on. One day I told him he should be thankful that matters were no worse about the agency, and that any moment some little thing might happen which would try out the courage of us all. I asked him if he were prepared for a fight with the Indians. He said that he had no gun, and asked me if I thought he should have one. I answered that he might feel safer, in case he had to battle with a few hundred Indians, to have a good rifle—if he knew how to use a gun. He then asked what sort of weapon he ought to have and how he could get one quickly. I advised him to get a Winchester rifle using the regular army ammunition, for he could then get cartridges right there at the agency, and if he happened to get into a fight and use up his own shells, he could get some from the nearest soldier. I advised him to wire John Collins, a gun dealer in Omaha, for the rifle and a box or two of cartridges, which would probably be all he would require for any ordinary fight. In a short time the gun arrived. Cola showed it to me, and I advised him to make a note of the number of the gun, so that if he lost it he could claim it. I myself also took note of the number on the rifle.

When the war correspondents went out to Wounded Knee

to see the surrender of Big Foot, Cola could not get a horse. There were none to be hired, and he was "r'aring" to go to see the surrender. He was in a state of despair. At last I told him that he might take my horse and saddle, as I could get along without them for a few hours. Mr. Cola was not a rider, and he gave evidence of this fact very soon after starting. Some of the other correspondents had secured a team and a two-seated buggy for the trip. One of these gentlemen, Charles Allen, kindly gave Mr. Cola his seat in the buggy and took my saddle animal. Mr. Allen was a horseman as well as a correspondent.

Mr. Cola was in at the trouble, sure enough. Soon after the Battle of Wounded Knee he was hurrying to get back to the agency to send out his story of the fight. I met him, and he wanted me to help him get someone to carry a message to the nearest telegraph station, as General Miles had put a ban on the use of the government wires at the agency by newspapermen —with perhaps the exception of Mr. O'Brian, the Associated Press correspondent. Poor Mr. Cola was in a highly nervous condition. Under ordinary circumstances he stammered very badly, but now he was truly "beyond words." He wanted to tell me all about the fight and the part he had taken in it. He tried to talk and write and make maps on the ground with a stick, all at the same time, and the gist of his story was about as follows.

The Indian men of Big Foot's band had been told to bring out their arms and get in line, ready to surrender them to the soldiers. Cola was standing with some of the other newspapermen near Colonel Forsyth and Major Whitside, when suddenly an old Indian medicine man in the line leaned over and, picking up a handful of dirt, threw it into the air, making the sign "Back to the earth" and shouting "They are going to kill us!" A young Indian standing near the medicine man dropped his blanket off his shoulders and fired at the nearest soldier. Then the battle was on. Cola said that he ran to a line of picketed troop horses and threw himself on the ground near the end of the line. He made a map on the ground and showed me the positions of both the soldiers and Indians. He told me he emptied the magazine of his Winchester at the Indians. At this point I told him that, judging from his map, he was shooting point-blank into the faces of the troops. He said that he didn't give a damn, as they were all shooting at him. He said he refilled the magazine of his rifle and then ran to the other end of the line of picketed horses, where he again dropped flat on the ground and blazed away into the bunch of Indians and soldiers. Of course I believed all he told me. I assisted him in getting a half-breed courier to carry his message to the telegraph station at Rushville, Nebraska.

About two days after the fight at Wounded Knee, a friend named Louis Mousseau, who kept a store near the spot where the battle occurred, drove in to the agency. It seems that on the night previous to the battle several of the newspaper correspondents, including Cola, had slept in Mousseau's store. I went out to meet my friend and jokingly asked him if he had been very badly scared during the trouble. He answered, "No, but I got a good new Winchester rifle out of it. One of those newspapermen left it in my store, I guess." I asked where the gun was, and Mousseau replied that he had it in his wagon. He showed the weapon to me. I glanced at the number of the gun and saw that it was Mr. Cola's. Then I knew that he did not have a gun with him on the morning of the fight, and that really no Seventh Cavalryman or any Sioux Indians had been killed by Cola. I never knew whether Mousseau hunted up the rightful owner of that gun or not. I felt that a man who could handle the truth in such a reckless manner should never be trusted with a shooting iron of any sort.

My favorite saddle horse, which I had so foolishly loaned to Cola, had an opportunity to see the fighting on that occasion, for Mr. Allen rode him up close to the spot where the surrender was to have occurred. He had here dismounted, thrown the bridle reins on the ground, and left the horse to take care of

himself, knowing that most old cow horses are trained to stand
when the reins are so placed. After the battle Mr. Allen looked
for my horse. Not finding him where he had been left, Allen
concluded that the animal had been frightened by the heavy
firing and run away; but he happened to look toward the spot
where a machine gun had been in operation, and there was the
horse standing behind the gun. A bullet from some gun (not
from Cola's!) had cut a flesh wound about a foot long on his
shoulder, but the animal had stood his ground throughout the
fight.

During the years after the Wounded Knee campaign, as
the Indian trouble of 1890–91 was called, Red Cloud visited me
a number of times with his old people to the number of seventy,
his last visit occurring in 1908. On that last visit of ten days
with me, he told me many stories of his experiences while trying
to stop the white people from passing through his country, and
of his fights with the Pawnees, Crows, and other Indian tribes.
Each year when he came to my ranch, both he and his people
brought me such presents as they thought I would like—relics
of their old-time life. Some of these articles are very old and
date back to the time when a man with a white skin was as
scarce in the Sioux country as a white beaver.

To show that there was another side of Red Cloud's nature
than that of a "villainous murderer and horse thief," as has
been charged, I will relate an incident which occurred at my
home several years ago at a time when Red Cloud and some
of my old Indian friends were visiting me. It was early in September, and our eldest son was leaving home to attend school
in Lincoln, Nebraska. It was the first time in his life that he
had ever been separated from his parents and home. The Indians, who were encamped in their lodges about one hundred
yards from the ranch house, knew that our son was leaving us.
When the conveyance drove up which was to take him away,
the old Indian women lined up on each side of the walk leading from the door to the driveway; and as my son passed be-

tween them, each woman gave him a handshake, and then all began to chant the songs which they sing when they part from their own kinsmen. When the carriage passed the Indian camp, all the men came out, dressed in the best they owned, old Red Cloud taking the lead. The aged chieftain took my son in his arms and held him close, placing his cheek against the boy's and patting his back, and he said: "I am an old man. Your father is my friend. I and my people will give you his name and think of you with good hearts." All the men then came forward and embraced the boy, whose eyes by this time were dim with tears, as were those of a number of both the red and the white women who witnessed the scene.

Many persons have an idea that the Indian has no sense of humor, but some Indians whom I have known seemed to see the funny side of things fairly well. On one occasion about thirty years ago, a large party of Oglala Sioux came over to my ranch in Sioux County, Nebraska, from Pine Ridge Agency, South Dakota, for a visit. Among this party were some of the last of the prominent old men of the Sioux. Chief Red Cloud and several members of his family were there, as well as Little Wound, American Horse, No Water, Big Road, He Dog, and other famous old warriors. Two prominent medicine men of the tribe, Corn Cob and Black Elk, were also in attendance. I was away from the ranch when they arrived and made camp. Upon my return from a ride out on the range among my stock, I rode into their camp and met these old friends and their families who had driven so far to make me a visit.

Among the Indians who visited me on this occasion was an old Indian whom I had never seen before, named Wolf's Ears. He was one of the last of the men to come up and shake my hand when I greeted the party. As I was about to mount my horse and ride to the corral, this old man asked me to come to his tepee, stating that he had something to tell me. I followed him over, went in, and sat down. He produced a pipe from the "heart-bag," filled it with tobacco and the inner bark of the dogwood, and we "made a little smoke."

Then he solemnly told me in a low voice that a few years previously he had had a white-man friend living in the Black Hills country. Whenever he visited this man, his white friend always killed eight or ten cattle for him and for the few families who would always accompany him on such a visit, so they could have a fine feast and take plenty of meat back to the agency. I was glad to know that this Indian had had such a good friend, and I asked what had become of him.

"He is dead," responded Wolf's Ears sadly.

"But what killed him?" I inquired.

"I do not know," answered the old Indian.

"Well," I replied, with as straight a face as I could assume, "I will tell you what killed him. Giving eight or ten cattle to an Indian would kill any white man. I shall be sure not to do such a thing, now that you have told me what happened to your other friend."

Wolf's Ears saw the point, and it affected him enough so that he had a hearty laugh as I departed, saying, "Wa-ga-nisk-ta" (I am going now). I could hear the old Indian still laughing mightily after I had gone a hundred feet from his tepee.

When Red Cloud was born, nearly one hundred years ago, a large portion of the land now occupied by the Republic was a vast wilderness. When he became old enough to join the hunters and warriors, exploration by the whites had scarcely begun in the hunting grounds of the western Indians. His eyes had grown dim with age before the white man had completely subjugated the red tribes. His right to rule and to oppose the oncoming of the invading paleface, he never doubted. He died as he lived—an Indian who never pretended to be reconstructed. In his prime he was a factor to be dealt with when his country was needed by the white man.

The methods employed to bring about the conditions which

now exist and to place the Sioux in the position which they now occupy may not have been the best possible, but, whether the methods were right or wrong, the work is done. The younger people among the Sioux have so far taken to the white man's road that it is now as unpopular for one of them to appear wild and untamable as it was but a short time ago for any young man or woman to assume the white people's style of dress or haircut. Some had advanced so far toward civilization that they are almost ashamed of their old fathers and mothers and of their primitive habits and customs.

Until their side of the question has been examined and studied, I think that the old Indian people who knew the wild, free life of their fathers should not be judged too harshly by those who today occupy their former lodge sites. I feel sure that from this time on all our dealings with the people whom we at first forced, and are now leading, into our plane of life will be just and honorable, and that these people will soon be given at least the same rights and advantages as those extended to the ignorant, often vicious, masses which are constantly coming from other parts of the world, to take advantage of the opportunities and protection offered by this land of the free.

I take pleasure in knowing that today the danger of Indian uprisings has passed into history, and that, with the passing of the few helpless old Indians now left, savages on this continent will no longer have to be dealt with. The North American Indian has undeniably been one of the great factors with which we have had to deal in our winning of the West. But our government has never attempted to exterminate the Indians in wresting the country from them. It is the greed of some white men which has most impeded the conditions of peace which prevail today.

Education of the younger Indians is all that is needed to make good American citizens of our red brothers and sisters. Kindness and patience will, I feel sure, bring them into our plane

of thinking and living. Let us remember that the Indian, from
his own point of view, had the same right to live that his forefathers had in the land of their birth. It was only natural for
him to look at the invasion and conquest of his country by
the whites with the same feeling that we of today should experience at any attempted invasion of this country by a foreign
nation. Having been near death at the hands of the Indians,
and having seen some of my dear friends killed by them, I have
never, to the amazement of some persons, regarded the pro-
verbial dead Indian as the only good Indian. I can only say that,
had I been born an Indian, I might have made a bad one—from
the white man's point of view.

The people who established their homes in the western
country had very little reason to fear, at any time after the
middle eighties, that there would ever again be danger from
Indians to anyone living in the northwestern part of Nebraska.
Nevertheless, the unexpected occurred. During the winter of
1890–91 there came to pass, as I have already related, a genuine
Indian scare—the Ghost Dance War, as it is called by the Sioux.
It broke out on the reservation about sixty miles north of my
own ranch. Many persons left their ranches and went for safety
to the numerous little towns which had sprung up along the
line of railroad then being built into the country. The danger
was considered sufficiently great for the governor of Nebraska
to send companies of state militia to protect those towns.

In a publication of the Bureau of Ethnology of the Smithsonian Institution at Washington (*Fourteenth Annual Report,*
1892–93, part 2) this Indian scare is called "The Sioux Outbreak of 1890." The publication referred to is a very truthful
and complete report of the whole trouble caused by the Messiah
craze which swept over the Indian reservations of the entire
West and culminated in the killing of about three hundred
Indian men, women, and children, and thirty-one soldiers on
Wounded Knee Creek, Pine Ridge Indian Reservation, South

Dakota, December 29, of that year. That Indian outbreak was a most unfortunate affair for both the United States troops engaged therein and the Indians who lost their lives.

That such an event could take place without the Indians slaughtering in retaliation many white settlers about the region of the Black Hills country, can be accounted for by the fact that the Indians had at that time been so far civilized as to be divided against themselves on the subject of further war with the whites. Father was arrayed against son, brother against brother. The season of the year for a general outbreak of the Sioux people was also unfavorable. By the time of new green grass, they had had time to let their blood cool down to the point of realizing that nothing was to be gained by war.

Since 1891 the settlers of Nebraska have had little to fear from Indians. I trust that the curtain has been rung down forever on actual warfare with Indians in the West. Many sons and grandsons of the old Indians who had fought against allowing the whites to possess the last hunting grounds of the red men, went across the "big waters" during the late World War and fought side by side with the sons and grandsons of those same whites who had engaged in battle with their own fathers and grandfathers. Never again will the people living in sparsely settled regions of the West have to dread the Indian who knew not the ways of the whites, and who, when he took to the warpath, resorted to his own primitive and savage methods of battle.

The dangers actually infesting the lives of the folk who live in the West have probably increased about a thousandfold during the past fifty years. But they are of a wholly different sort —for example, the noiseless and sneaking automobile, which, without a cheery war whoop or even so much as a rattlesnake's warning, now kills, maims, and scalps hundreds of persons every year. I look back upon my experiences with wild people and wild animals in the West as having been a very safe life to follow, compared with that of us who are living today under "civilized" auspices.

The Ghost Dance War

Now that mankind is getting into its stride, I suppose people will never be quite satisfied until they can travel faster than the earth is now moving through space. Nevertheless, I trust that the pioneers of the old West—so long as there are any of them left—will be allowed the pleasure of telling each other how they used to knock over the running deer with a bullet at forty rods every pop, or ride broncs "straight up," raking off hair enough to fill a mattress every time one of them tried to hide its head between its hind feet. This indulgence is no more than fair. No doubt the rider of tomorrow will insist upon leaving some record for those who follow him—if only to tell them that he flew from New York City to San Francisco in ten hours and forty seconds, or hustled a speed bus over the highways of the continent at a two-mile-a-minute clip.

17

Troubles in New Mexico

DURING THE FIVE YEARS that I lived in southwestern New Mexico, I certainly had a fairly strenuous time. For one reason, outlaws of many varieties had strongholds in the mountains within two days' easy riding of the WS Ranch.

After my English friends had purchased the White House Ranch and the property had been turned over to us by its former owner, Jack Fleming, some eight or ten of the employees were paid off. A lively bunch, they must have craved more excitement than ordinary ranch life afforded them, for they got their heads together and, saddling up, rode down to the Southern Pacific Railroad and held up a passenger train. They managed to kill a trainman or two during this affair and secured a little loot, but they were not successful in making a getaway. They were all captured and taken to Silver City. Here they managed to break jail, and, after arming themselves from the guards' room, they marched to the livery stable, secured horses, and rode triumphantly out of town.

An alarm was immediately sent out; officers and citizens collected and started in pursuit of the daring robbers. The bandits did not try to escape by scattering, in an effort to throw their pursuers off the trail. Instead, they prepared an ambush for them. When the posse rode into it, the robbers opened fire, killing a man or two, but they had made the mistake of their lives. Old rangers such as Doc Best and Mr. Cantrell were on their trail. A battle ensued, in which all the robbers were killed with the exception of one man named Kit Joy. He managed to escape capture for a few hours, but at the end of that time he was a maimed prisoner. One of his legs had to be amputated where it had been shattered by a bullet.

Troubles in New Mexico

At the period of which I write, quite a number of men scattered over the southwestern country had a desire to become noted desperadoes. I aided in checking a number of these bandits—for a time, at least—in their foolish careers. A number of them with whom I talked after aiding in their capture, and whom I questioned regarding their motives for committing crime when there was so little to gain and so much to lose, told me that they could not explain to themselves why or where they got the idea that the life of an outlaw was a desirable career. A cold, wet, and starving hunted human being comes far from being a happy individual. Men like Billy the Kid, who made such a record in New Mexico during the days about which I write, caused a number of weak-headed young men to try to imitate him; and the reading of trashy novels, had, I think, much to do with starting young men on the wrong path. Billy the Kid had the reputation of being one of the most desperate criminals of the Southwest. Yet he was, to begin with, not a western product, but a New York City tough. Doubtless he had read some very yellow novels about the bandits of the West before he started on his career of crime in New Mexico.

During the year 1882, while acting as manager of H. C. Wilson's cattle ranch in southwestern New Mexico, I was out on the range one day with some of my cowboys. While going through a little brushy cañon, we came across a grizzly bear cub about three months old. After some scrambling among the live-oak trees and shrubs we succeeded in getting the cub out into open ground, and lassoed him. He was a little fighter, but we soon had him hog-tied and muzzled. I had one of the men carry the little beast on his horse to the headquarters ranch, where he was soon chained to a post. The cub soon became a great pet, but as he grew older we found that he was not exactly a plaything. Ned, as we called him, was always creating a disturbance somewhere.

One time one of the men was standing in the corral where

the bear was tied. He walked up to the animal for a close examination. Ned was lying down, seemingly asleep, but when the man turned his back, the bear suddenly jumped and caught the fellow through the calf of the leg. He had presence of mind enough not to attempt to tear loose, else the bear would certainly have ripped some of the muscles of his leg. Other men came to his aid, and with pitchforks the bear was made to release his hold.

Once he came near catching me. I heard the cook, down at the men's house, calling loudly. He was alone, the riders all being out on the range. I ran down, whereupon the cook yelled for me to look out—that Ned had broken his chain and was running amuck. The bear had located the swill barrel and partially upset it. He was busy fishing some choice bits from the bottom of the barrel as I appeared on the scene. I ran to the stable for a rope, thinking to slip up while the animal had his head in the barrel and tie it to the piece of chain which hung from his collar. Just as I succeeded in doing this, the bear backed suddenly out and, catching sight of me, evidently decided to add one more variety of meat to his bill of fare. He made for me in short order, and I turned to run. The woodpile was near, and, once on top of it, I thought I should be safe. Catching sight of an old axe handle on the ground, I stooped to pick it up. As I grasped it I saw that there was not time to escape; so I turned to face Ned. I struck at him with all my might, and luck was with me, for the heavy axe handle caught the bear squarely between the ears and stiffened him out in a hurry. I thought I had killed him. I called the cook to help me, and we dragged the animal to the post and secured him. We then stood back to watch him. Shortly he came to. He was very groggy on his legs for a time, but he recovered from the blow and, to judge by his actions, had more respect for me after that.

When Ned was about two years old, Professor Cope of Philadelphia was stopping with me while making a geological survey of that section of the country. One day he asked what I intended to do with the bear. I replied that I should probably continue to harbor him until he had killed somebody, and then I should have to shoot him. He asked if I would not like to present Ned to the Zoölogical Society of Philadelphia. I said I should be glad to do so if the Society wanted him. A few weeks after the Professor had returned home, I received a letter from the secretary of the Society, accepting my present and thanking me for the bear. The letter also stated that the Society had made arrangements with the express company to take Ned through to Philadelphia.

Our ranch was eighty miles from Silver City, the nearest railroad point and express office. How to get Ned to Silver City was the problem confronting me now. The road over the mountains was little more than an old Indian trail, which could be followed with wagons, provided the horses were strong and quiet and the driver was a man who understood his business. I finally concluded that the only way to convey the bear to the railroad in good shape was to crate him. I sent to the mining town of Cooney, in the Mogollon Mountains, and had a blacksmith and wagon-maker build a large, strong box, bound with iron, with a drop door in each end, and made just large enough to fit inside an ordinary wagon box. The box being finished and delivered, the next question was to get Ned inside.

To digress for a moment: When Ned was a little fellow, I went one day to the spot where he was tied. He was lying stretched out at full length, and I thought I should be safe in patting him on the head. He lay with his head on his paws, but his wicked little eyes were following my every move. Placing my hand on his head, I began stroking him. After a bit I grew more confident and put my other hand within his reach. Quickly he grabbed for it like a flash. One claw caught on the ring on my finger, and he jerked my hand toward him and tried to bite it. I pulled back with all my might, but the bear, now furious, rose to his hind legs. Hardly knowing what I was doing, I gave him a tremendous kick in the stomach that doubled him up in a hurry. He released his hold and became deathly sick. Ever afterward, when I came near and he happened to be in a playful mood, dancing around on his hind legs at the end of his chain, I got as close as possible to his circle and, watching my chance, made a move as if I were going to catch him by the top of the head; then suddenly I seized his lower jaw with my right hand and drew back my foot as if to kick him again. He seemed to grasp the situation, and as long as I retained my hold on his lower jaw and kept him standing he did not try to harm me. When I got him to the end of his chain and let go, he became very angry, racing around and tugging at the chain in his efforts to get at me.

When it came to getting Ned into the box, I wondered if my kick trick would not help us without getting the bear excited and angry by too much rough handling, as another method would. I had the box placed near him on the ground. We then passed a long lasso through both doorways, propping up the doors so that we could drop them quickly. Ned watched these operations closely. Having just eaten a hearty meal, he was in a very good humor.

I then had ten of the cowboys get hold of one end of the lasso. Taking the other end, I went near the bear's charmed circle. Ned, ready for a little fun, reared on his hind legs and began a little sun dance. I soon had my grip on his jaw with one hand, and with the other I tied the end of the lasso to his collar. Then, jumping back quickly, I ordered the men to heave away, meaning, as soon as the strain came on the rope, to unfasten the chain from the post, which, acting as an anchor, would have prevented Ned from going through the box before both doors could be dropped.

But no sooner had I shouted "Heave away!" than the men gave a pull such as old-time cowboys can give. Ned's collar snapped, and the boys fell in a heap. I yelled for everyone to look out and sprang for the nearest side of the corral. Ned was no longer a sun dancer but a full-grown warrior and right on the warpath. It was a lightning transformation scene. Every man in the corral had mounted to the top board in less time than it has taken me to tell it, and Ned was in full, undisputed possession of the ground.

Just about the time everyone was scrambling for a high roost, the cook, down at the men's house, hearing the shouting and laughter, came running out to watch the fun, followed by a little black bulldog, a ranch pet with a record as a fighter. The cook rushed into the corral, closing the gate behind him, the dog running ahead. The bear happened to be at the farther side of the corral when they entered, but, seeing this new enemy, he charged at once. The cook made a very hasty retreat and would surely have been caught and roughly handled had not the bulldog tried to fasten on to Bruin at once. The dog had but a few snags of teeth and could not secure a good grip, but his attack diverted the bear's attention long enough for the cook to make his escape.

We then drove the dog out of the corral and started in to lasso the bear. We had to stand on top of the fence to throw our ropes. Several times they encircled his neck, but each time the infuriated bear grabbed at the rope with his claws and threw it off. At last, as he passed near me, I threw my rope over his head, letting him jump through it with his head and shoulders, but drawing the noose tight about his flanks. With the help of the other boys, Ned was pulled up into the air, the rope being thrown over the top rail of the fence, and trussed up until only his front feet rested on the ground. The bear roared with rage and fought savagely, but we placed another rope around his neck, and several of the men jumped down into the corral and passed the ropes through the doors of the cage, in which we soon had the bear safe. The boards were wide enough apart so that we could pull the ropes out after working them loose from the bear's body.

The blacksmith had nailed a heavy tin can in one corner of the box, into which the express officials were to put water for the bear's comfort. This can was the only thing in the box upon which the aroused and infuriated animal could wreak vengeance, and he made short work of it. He tore it down, cutting his feet badly while so doing. This made him so furious that he bit himself savagely several times through the forelegs.

Having Ned safely in the box, we found it no small job to load His Bearship into the wagon, but it was soon accomplished. The man who was to drive to Silver City with the box came and hitched a team of big mules to the wagon, and everything was then ready for the start. But the moment the bear felt the wagon in motion, he let out a roar of fury. The mules stampeded at once, and away went the whole outfit, lickety-split! The faster the mules ran, the louder the bear yelled and roared. The driver, however, was cool and collected and knew his business. He headed the animals for the top of a long hill directly in front of the ranch house, and by the time the runaways reached the top, they were completely winded, and the bear had ceased to yell.

We had no further trouble getting Ned to the station and started on his long ride to Philadelphia. Shortly after the bear was received at Fairmount Park, I received the following letter from the Zoölogical Society.

ZOOLOGICAL SOCIETY (Fairmount Park)
PHILADELPHIA, PA.
January 31, 1884

James H. Cook, Esq.
Alma, New Mexico
Dear Sir:

In the absence of Mr. Brown, our general superintendent, it gives me pleasure to advise you of the safe arrival at our Garden of the young grizzly bear so kindly presented to this Society by yourself and Mr. H. C. Wilson, to whom the thanks of our society are given. The bear is in good condition, and I trust you will have the pleasure of seeing it soon in this city, as you desire, "fat and big." When you come to the garden do not purchase a ticket, but ask for Mr. Brown.

Yours respectfully,
John Maxwell
Sec. Zoo. Society

I never saw Ned after he was put aboard the cars at Silver City, but I heard from Professor Cope that he was doing nicely and growing into an immense fellow. The Zöological people had him for many years as one of the chief attractions at Fairmount Park.

One of the closest calls I ever had occurred while I was in New Mexico. It might have turned out badly for me, as well as for quite a number of people. My guardian angel surely must have been present on that occasion.

One evening in the fall of 1884, a rider came at a furious gait up to my ranch house door and hurriedly informed me that the Mexicans had gone on the warpath at a little settlement up the San Francisco River, about thirty miles away. He stated that they had killed one of Mr. Slaughter's cowboys and were going to try to wipe out all the Americans living near their settlement. This Mexican settlement was known as the San Francisco Plaza. It was divided into three sections, called the Upper, Middle, and Lower Plazas. The rider told me that he had been sent to warn Americans living along the San Francisco River of their danger and to get as many men as possible to go immediately and help guard the homes of the Americans living near the Mexican settlement.

I could not find out from the rider the cause of the trouble. He rushed away to carry the news to others. One of the ranches which I had helped some friends establish was located about two miles from the Upper Plaza. As they were the nearest neighbors of the Plaza people, I was, of course, ready to render them any possible aid. Getting as many of my ranch people together as could be spared, I rode at once to the ranch owned by my friends. When we arrived there, about midnight, we found quite a number of Americans gathered. They were from the ranches scattered about the country. They had received tidings similar to those brought me, and had come to render any possible aid. Before daylight quite a crowd had collected at the ranch.

As we received no further reports of what the Mexicans were doing, two men who were well known at the Upper Plaza rode down there. They soon brought back a report which not only explained conditions but also put them in an altogether different light from that of the news brought to my ranch by the runners who had solicited aid.

It appeared that on the previous day a cowboy named Mc-Carty, employed by Mr. Slaughter, a cattleman holding some stock a few miles from the Plaza, had ridden into the Upper Plaza. Securing a few drinks of liquor at a store kept by a man named Milligan, he had proceeded to shoot up the place. Riding back and forth in the street, he shot at everything, animate and inanimate, which met his gaze. While the drunken cowboy was thus engaged, a young Mexican named Elfego Baca rode into the Plaza. He was a special deputy sheriff from the county seat of Socorro County, and he was out on an electioneering trip, making speeches in the various Mexican settlements of the county. McCarty, the drunken cowboy, did not notice Baca's arrival, but Baca had noticed him. Meeting the justice of the peace and some of the other residents of the Plaza, Baca asked them why they allowed the cowboy to jeopardize their lives and property in such a manner. The reply was that, if they arrested or harmed McCarty, his friends would come and do a lot of harm to the settlement. Baca told them that when such things were tolerated it only made the cowboys bolder, and that it should be stopped at once. He insisted that they should not let the Americans living about them get the impression that the Mexicans were afraid of them. He further informed them that he was a peace officer, that it was his duty to stop Mc-Carty from endangering the lives of the citizens of the place, and that he would show McCarty that there was at least one Mexican in the country who was not afraid of an American cowboy.

Baca went out at once and arrested and disarmed McCarty with but little trouble, for he was really not a bad man—merely a little too playful at times. Taking his prisoner before the justice of the peace in the Plaza, Baca was informed by His Honor that he did not care to hear the case, as there would surely be an afterwards to it which would result badly for the Plaza. Baca replied that, in such a case, where the justice seemed intimidated, he considered it his own duty to take his prisoner to the county seat, where the case would be tried.

As it was too late for Baca to start at once for the town of Socorro, he decided to remain with the prisoner in the Mexican settlement overnight. He took McCarty down to the Middle Plaza, where there were more suitable accommodations for himself and his prisoner. By some means, word of McCarty's arrest had gone out from the Plaza. A number of Mr. Slaughter's cowboys, headed by Mr. Perham, their foreman, rode down at once to the place where Baca was holding McCarty and demanded his release. When Baca was informed that the prisoner would be taken from him right then and there, he told them that he would give them the time it would take to count three to get out of town. Baca counted "one, two, three" and opened fire on the Americans with his pistol. The Slaughter cowboys started to get out of harm's way very suddenly. By some chance, Mr. Perham's horse fell and killed its rider. One of the Americans, Allen by name, was shot by Baca through the knee. Baca held to his prisoner.

This was the state of affairs reported by our committee who had gone to the Plaza to investigate the situation. Word had gone out to all the Mexicans living within a day's ride that the Americans had taken to the warpath and were going to clean out the Mexicans at the Plaza.

We held a council and decided to select one or two of our number to go to the Plaza, see the justice of the peace and Mr. Baca, and try to arrange for the trial of McCarty at the Plaza; for the charge against him was not a desperately serious one, and we all realized that considerable trouble might easily be started. Our committee waited upon the justice and Mr. Baca, and they agreed to our suggestion. Baca stated that he would have the prisoner at the justice's office at a stated hour. The crowd which I was with, and which, the evidence later showed, was composed of eighty men, then rode to the Upper Plaza at the time appointed for the trial. Baca had McCarty at the justice's office. After taking his prisoner inside, he came out and greeted us, saying, "Good morning, gentlemen."

One man who rode close by me at the head of our party, taking advantage of the crowd of well-armed men about him, started making mean, abusive remarks about Baca. At the same moment one of the young men in our party in some manner fired his gun accidentally. This caused me to turn to see what had happened. When I looked toward the place where Baca had been standing, he was gone. He had backed around the corner of the justice's office and disappeared.

McCarty was tried, fined a few dollars, and liberated. I, for one, was ready to go home. But the Milligan whiskey had to work a little more harm before the incident was to end. Gathering my bunch of employees and friends, I proposed that we start for the ranch. This was agreed to, and we started. We had proceeded but a short distance when we heard shooting back at the Plaza. Knowing that many Mexicans had gathered in the hills about the Plaza, we were afraid they might have attacked the remaining Americans there. We thereupon rode hastily back, scattering as we went. One of my men, my trusted friend Charlie Moore, rode with me.

Upon reaching the Plaza we rode up rather close to one of the jacals, or Mexican huts. I could see no fighting going on; not a man was in sight. Moore started to swing down from his horse just as I saw smoke from a pistol shot floating from a window in the picket house which we had approached. Calling to Charlie to look out, I spurred my horse and made a rather sudden start away from the front of that window. As I was about to reach the shelter of another building, a bullet tore off a bunch of adobe and filled my eyes with dust and dirt. The shot was fired from the adobe which we had first approached.

Riding around behind the Milligan store, I found a number of Americans. They were gathered about a man who was down on the ground, and whom I soon found to be dying. His name was Herne. It appeared that, after McCarty was liberated, a few men, including Herne, had started out to find Baca. Baca had doubtless figured that something of the sort would happen, for he had barricaded himself into a picket house, which made a very good fort. After searching for Baca in other parts of the Plaza, the crowd went to this picket house. Finding the door barred, they started to force it open. A bullet was fired through it from the inside. It struck Herne, but it also revealed the hiding place of Baca. Excitement now ran high. Baca must be killed or captured. Just how either was to be effected was a question. Many plans were suggested. By this time everyone was convinced that Baca would sell his life as dearly as possible. He was at bay and thoroughly aroused. One party was dispatched to the Cooney mining camp after dynamite with which to blow up the house in which he was barricaded. A number of my English friends were with me at the Plaza, also my brother. I told them that I considered the Americans gathered at the Plaza neither more nor less than a mob. Baca, I was informed, was a county officer, and the law was on his side. I felt that, although he may have overdone his duty, the best thing possible for all concerned was not to kill him, but to secure him and get him to the county seat at Socorro.

An American deputy sheriff named Rose put in an appearance about this time, but he did not care to take a chance by showing himself to Baca in order to talk to him and persuade him to come out of his fort. Finally I thought I would try a scheme to capture Baca, for the Americans present had, in a manner, crowded me into the position of being one, at least, of their leaders. I told my brother and friends that I would go, without my rifle, out into the open space in the middle of the Plaza and call to the Mexicans who were now gathering in numbers about us on the hills that skirted the river valley. I would attempt to communicate with someone who was acquainted with Baca, and whose voice Baca would recognize and listen to—provided he were still alive. (The evidence showed that four thousand shots had been fired into the jacal in which Baca had been hiding since he had killed Herne.) I told the Mexicans that, if Baca were alive and would give himself up, I would be responsible to them for his life until he could be taken to the county seat. To my surprise, this offer was agreed to. A man came from the Mexican ranks and called out to Baca, telling him the terms of surrender. He further told Baca that I meant what I said; that I could not afford to lie, for I had property and lived near them and that many of the Mexican people knew me well.

Suddenly Baca sprang out of the jacal through a small window opening. He had a six-shooter in each hand and was clad only in his underclothes. As he came toward me, many of the Mexicans in the hills yelled for him to run to them. Luckily he did not attempt to do so, for many rifles in the hands of the best shots in New Mexico were trained upon him at the time.

Baca's Prince Albert coat and his other clothing were now secured for him. Several Americans present insisted that we hang him at once. I told them that they all knew how Baca had been induced to surrender, and that it would mean death to me if he were not given safe escort to Socorro. This talk did not satisfy many of them—I suppose my death would not have interfered with their happiness very much—so I talked to them in a different vein. I told them that we were a mob in the eyes of the law; that Baca had done things for which he could not escape being hanged; and that the laws of the land, not a mob, should attend to his case. For many reasons—the chief of which was that we were on the verge of starting a fine little race war, which might have lasted for some time and caused the death of many present—this proved to be the right move. Baca was escorted in safety to Socorro, although it was understood that he was not to surrender his gun. This was agreed to, and Mr. Rose, the deputy, took charge of him.

I left New Mexico a short time after the trouble at the San Francisco Plaza, and never knew the outcome of Baca's trial until within the last few years, when I learned that he was not hanged for the shooting of those men at the Plaza. On the contrary, he had become one of the most prominent attorneys in the state of New Mexico. Should Mr. Baca read about this incident, the part which I played in it, and my point of view about the affair, I think he will readily understand why I have reason to be very glad that no greater loss of life was caused by Cowboy McCarty's effort to work off a little surplus energy in an attempt to terrorize a peaceful Mexican settlement.

Out about forty-five miles northwest of Silver City, New Mexico, in the year 1882, there flourished a cattle ranch, already mentioned in this narrative, known as the White House Ranch. It was located on Duck Creek, a little tributary of the Gila River. This ranch was well known by most people who lived in southwestern New Mexico at that time. Its owner, Jack Fleming, was then one of Silver City's best-known citizens, and he had won the ranch a short time previously on a horse race. The ranch house was a large one, with adobe walls, white-washed both inside and out—whence its name. Its white walls could be seen for many miles. Shortly after my arrival in New Mexico, in 1882, I purchased this ranch for some friends of mine, Messrs. Graham and Maynard. Before it was turned over to its new owners, Mr. Fleming's foreman, who had charge of the place, gave a grand farewell ball, to which pretty much everybody within a radius of two hundred miles was invited. This ranch manager or foreman was known as "Buckshot" by everyone. If he had any other name I never heard it.

When the time for the dance arrived, there was a gathering large enough to have made a success of almost any undertaking. It was, I am sure, the largest affair of its kind ever pulled off in southwestern New Mexico up to that time. Saints and sinners of all degrees were present, and Buckshot was well prepared for their entertainment. Refreshments of every sort were provided in abundance. Nobody was supposed to go hungry or dry because of any dearth of choice foods or liquors. Nor was there to be a lack of music. The dance halls of all the mining towns in the territory could close, because of the absence of professors of music, while this greatest social event of the day was in progress. All the livery rigs and private conveyances of the country were used in transporting the crowd. Many merry-makers took along an extra case or two of liquid refreshment, for fear Buckshot would underestimate the amount required. A number started for the ball with this extra supply of wet goods, and, becoming very thirsty on their long drive, tapped the supply so frequently en route that all roads and trails leading to the White House became lost or mixed up, and they never did find the place. Some of them never got more than twenty miles from Silver City, and yet it took them three days to find their way back again, after the roads and trails got to "acting up."

I had received a very cordial invitation from the big chief, Buckshot, to attend that ball. Of course I accepted, but down deep in my heart I figured that I was going either to hire a substitute or break a leg before the day set for the ball. My carelessness in not keeping books on all my goings and comings at that time caused me to drive up to the White House Ranch a little after sundown on the night set for the dance, with a

Mr. Campbell of Silver City. We had been out on a ranch-purchasing trip up in Keller Valley, on the San Francisco River, and had forgotten all about the White House farewell dance. When we drove up to the ranch we found people enough there to have filled a pretty good sized circus tent, and more arriving every minute. Buckshot·saw us when we arrived and received us with open arms. We were in for it. Our team was taken from us and cared for in an old shed reserved for rigs belonging to special guests of the hour.

I told Campbell there would be good prospecting for lead anywhere within a mile of that ranch in the morning. He tried to comfort me by saying that we should not have to prospect for lead—our hides would be full of it before sunrise.

The ball opened promptly on time. I saw no gents in full evening dress on that occasion. Clothes did not make the man, and everybody came to have a real good time. Of course all the ladies who attended were pretty and beautifully gowned, and those whom I saw dance did their prettiest.

All went well until about ten o'clock. At that time I began to observe that some of the gents present were getting under some sort of influence which caused them to have a peculiar hitch in their gait and a glitter or stare in their eyes altogether different from a merry twinkle. I suggested to my friend Campbell that we retire. He asked, "Where to?" I told him I would find a bed-ground. I thereupon went out to our buckboard, took our roll of bedding, and carried it to a little depression near by. This depression had been made by some old bull's pawing, when he was proclaiming to the ranch herds that he was a great warrior and feared no foe. I had observed the lay of the land pretty closely when we first arrived at the ranch, and had not overlooked this depression. I made our bed, arranging our grips and one or two of our bed blankets in a manner which would make them most serviceable as breastworks if needed. After making everything snug, I went after Campbell. He was rather pleased with my arrangements for a night's rest but said that he was not altogether happy. What he would have liked best was to "put the Mogollon Range of mountains between himself and that ranch."

Soon after we had cuddled up in our little bull wallow, something in that ballroom popped. It was an old-fashioned Colt .45 caliber six-shooter. Then came a medley of sounds. Joy was evidently unconfined. One exclamation that came drifting to me on the evening air was, "If you do that again I will poke my gun down your throat and pull it off!" The music did not cease, and the floor manager must have stood his ground, for I could hear him calling off, "Honor your partners!" "All promenade!" "Grand right and left!" and so on. Moreover, I could tell from some of the sounds wafted to me that a certain bold dancer was being roughly handled by several of his friends. He was brought out the back door (after being disarmed) and chucked down into a combination root cellar and milk house situated a few yards from my bed. This cellar had a trap door in the roof and a short ladder leading to the floor. Number One was lowered into this cellar and a guard placed on the trap door, after which operation the ladder was hauled up to the heavy dirt roof.

Before the cold gray dawn of the following morning, that cellar was comfortably filled with gentlemen who had required the aid of their friends to place them where they would be doing the least possible amount of damage and giving others with more self-control their full rights in the pursuit of health and happiness.

The gentlemen who attended that ball toted guns, for at that time it was considered good form to do so. The Apache Indians at periods roamed over that part of the country, and if by chance they caught a white man unarmed, they had a custom of cracking his head open with rocks, in order, probably to see what the inside looked like. It was allowable on this occasion for anyone who felt so inclined to step outside the ranch house and fire as many shots as he chose at the starry firmament. But it interfered with the dance to fire pistols in the house—it put out the lights and made the musicians lose a lot of notes. Some poor fellows would forget which was up and which was down, when shooting at the stars. This kind of *hombre* made me lie very close to the ground when a few pellets of lead were sent in the direction of the Campbell & Cook wallow. Both the night and the ball wore on all right, but two men whom I know were also rather worn. About the time the morning star put in its appearance, I told my sleeping partner that I would slip over to the shed where our horses were, give them a little feed, and harness them; and as soon as the animals had eaten we would pull out and get our breakfast at a ranch about ten miles on the way toward Silver City.

Buckshot, in providing things for the ball, had not forgotten to have some hay hauled for his guests' horses. A load or two had been thrown into a little board pen about five feet high, near the back door of the shed where my horses were. When I got within a few feet of this pen, I pitched the fork up into the air so that it would land sticking into the hay. I was expecting to climb over the fence and throw some out for my horses, but when that pitchfork hit the hay, I saw the handle rise into the air very suddenly and a bunch of hay follow it! I also heard some sounds such as might come from a person who was either greatly scared or decidedly angry. I faded back into the shed—also through it, not pausing for breath until I was once more cuddled up in my downy wallow. In four seconds, more or less, I heard a man's voice from the direction of the shed door nearest me. He was saying bad words in a very fluent tongue. I crawled out of bed and asked him, in as sleepy a voice as I could muster, what was troubling him. He replied that some damn pelican of the desert had tried to paunch him with a pitchfork when he was asleep in the hay corral, and that if he could find the blankety-blank hyena who did it, he would sure fill his clothes full of buttonholes. He said the fork had been jabbed halfway through him. I was greatly interested in his case, but he soon had some of his friends about him, and I let them attend to his wounds while I fed my team some oats. They did not seem to need any hay that morning. Campbell wanted to make an early start for Silver City. When we were well out on the road, Campbell said, "Let's shake hands on having survived the night." So far as I know, no fatalities occurred, and the farewell dance at the White House was an unqualified success.

Courtesy Mrs. Grayson E. Meade

This photograph and those on the following five pages show the author's den, in 1922, and his collection of weapons and the Indian materials given to him by his Indian friends.

Dr. Elisha B. Graham, founder of the o–4 Ranch, 1878, and father-in-law of James H. Cook.

Courtesy Mrs. Grayson E. Meade

Katie (left) and Clara Graham, about 1883, at the time they used to go to the 0–4 Ranch on the Niobrara River with their parents, Dr. E. B. Graham and Mary E. Graham. At this time Dr. Graham operated the 0–4 Ranch, which later became the famous Agate Springs Ranch, built up and developed by James H. Cook, who married Katie Graham, on September 28, 1886.

Agate Springs Ranch, as it was in 1889, with Cheyenne Indians encamped in right background.

In the Agate Springs Fossil Quarries, Agate, Nebraska, where skeletons of many pair-horned rhinoceros and other prehistoric animals, partly exposed in the solid sandstone in which, entrapped when the sandstone was mud, they had lain embedded for thousands of years.

Photo by Mrs. Grayson E. Meade

Fossil Quarries area.

In the Agate Springs Fossil Quarries, from left to right: Professor Erwin Hinkley Barbour, State Geologist, University of Nebraska; Albert Thomson, in charge of field work for the American Museum of Natural History, New York; and Henry Fairfield Osborn, President of the American Museum of Natural History.

In the Agate Springs Fossil Quarries, Albert Thomson at work on the Big Bone Slab later mounted in the American Museum of Natural History. More than twenty rhinoceros skeletons were entombed in the rock of this slab.

This 6,000-pound block, from Agate Springs and later on exhibition at the American Museum of Natural History, contains twenty-one skulls of an extinct rhinoceros, skeletal materials to match, and a few bones of other prehistoric animals.

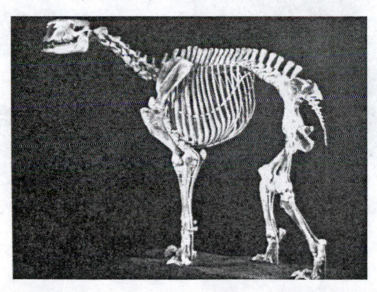

One of the strange prehistoric beasts from the Agate Springs Fossil Quarries: Moropus cooki, which stood about six feet high at the shoulders, a distant relative of both the horse and the rhinoceros families, but distinct from each.

Captain James H. Cook at his desk, 1922.

The Agate Springs Fossil Beds

IN 1879, WHILE ENGAGED in hunting big game for the market in what was then the territory of Wyoming, I met a physician, Dr. E. B. Graham, and his family. Some two years before this meeting, Dr. Graham had established a cattle ranch in northwestern Nebraska. This ranch was located about a hundred and fifty miles north and a little east of the city of Cheyenne, Wyoming, where Dr. Graham and his family made their home. The Doctor and Edgar Beecher Bronson, the well-known author (now deceased) and hunter of big game in Africa, were the first men to establish cattle ranches on the upper waters of the Niobrara River. Their ranches adjoined. Both of them lived in Cheyenne the greater part of each year, employing men to care for their ranches and herds of cattle throughout the season. During each summer season Dr. Graham took a vacation by driving with his family to his ranch.

Taking more than a passing interest in his younger daughter, I managed to happen in at the ranch more than once while he and his family were making their annual visit there. A horseback trip of three or four hundred miles meant little to me then so far as the ride itself was concerned, although I had to pass through an unsettled country, with no roads to follow or hotels to shelter and feed me and my good old horse. At the end of these journeys one of the greatest blessings ever given to man awaited me—a noble girl whose love for me was genuine and steadfast. My sweetheart and I used to take long rides on horseback over the great open range which surrounded her father's ranch. Hundreds of pronghorn antelope could be seen in those days by riding for a few miles in any direction from the ranch.

Riding one day along the picturesque buttes which skirt the beautiful valley of the Niobrara, we came to two high conical hills about three miles from the ranch house. From the tops of these hills there was an unobstructed view of the country for miles up and down the valley. Dismounting and leaving the reins of our bridles trailing on the ground—which meant to our well-trained ponies that they were to remain near the place where we had left them—we climbed the steep side of one of the hills. About halfway to the summit we noticed many fragments of bones scattered about on the ground. I at once concluded that at some period, perhaps years back, an Indian brave had been laid to his last long rest under one of the shelving rocks near the summit of the hill, and that, as was the custom among some tribes of Indians at one time, a number of his ponies had been killed near his body. Happening to notice a peculiar glitter on one of the bone fragments, I picked it up, and I then discovered that it was a beautifully petrified piece of the shaft of some creature's leg bone. The marrow cavity was filled with tiny calcite crystals, enough of which were exposed to cause the glitter which had attracted my attention. Upon our return to the ranch we carried with us what was doubtless the first fossil material ever secured from what are now known to men of science as the Agate Springs Fossil Quarries.

Later on I called the attention of scientists to our discovery. Many tons of petrified bones belonging to prehistoric animals which lived and died during the early Miocene period of the earth's history have, since those days, been collected by paleontologists from our national museum at Washington, D. C., the American Museum of Natural History of New York City, and the Carnegie Museum of Pittsburgh, as well as from Yale, Amherst, Princeton, and many other colleges and state universities and museums. Many hundreds of tons of these petrified bone records of the past were preserved in those two conical hills. Now that railroads, towns, and good motor roads have penetrated to the region of these oldest and most truthful records of the misty past, many persons from various parts of the world journey each season to see the place in which they have been preserved for unknown millions of years. Among the many who journey to read and study these records are some of our scholars in science and even theology.

Kate Graham and I were married in the autumn of 1886. The following year I purchased from my father-in-law his ranch and cattle interests in the Niobrara Valley. The old ranch had been known as the O-4 Ranch. I changed its name to "Agate Springs Ranch."

The days of the open range and of the roundup system of handling cattle came to a close in Nebraska soon after I established my home there. Home-seekers and builders came in and possessed the range, which for a period of about eight years had been occupied by cattlemen and their herds, and the time soon came when a cattleman had to own or lease all the land upon which his stock grazed. Windmills and wire fences, log, sod, and lumber cabins were soon in evidence over the most desirable parts of the old grazing grounds of the state. The flocks of antelope, also the white-tailed and mule-ear deer, were soon practically annihilated.

The fossil bones which I discovered in Nebraska, at the place on the Niobrara River where I later made my home, proved to be the clew which led, then, to a veritable house of records. In those twin hills, during the early Miocene period of the earth's history, the remains of vast numbers of the creatures which then inhabited that great flood plain region were deposited under hundreds of feet of sediment. Minerals in solution, in the form of calcite, silica, and manganese, were abundant in this sediment. As the organic matter in the skeletal parts of the animals were brought in with the sediment by the floods, and disintegrated molecule by molecule, these minerals in solution entered and, in time, transformed the bones into stone.

During the years 1891 and 1892, Professor Erwin H. Barbour, of the University of Nebraska, came with a party of students to my ranch. He was the first man of science to collect fossil material from and about those hills. The material which he collected was taken from the surface. He did at that time no excavating in the hills, in which was buried the great store of stone records which have since been opened and partly read.

Late in the summer of 1904, Mr. O. A. Peterson, collector for the Carnegie Institute of Pittsburgh, came by invitation to my ranch to prospect those hills for fossils. My son Harold and I took him to the spot. He had dug but a short time when he uncovered a deposit of petrified bones leading back into the stone of the hillside. The material secured during his first work there proved to be of such value that the Carnegie Institution excavated and secured a fine representation of the fossils which the hills contained. Mr. Peterson named these hills "The Agate Springs Fossil Quarry," after my ranch, which in turn is named from splendid springs which come out of agatized rock at the place.

The following season, 1905, Professor E. H. Barbour of the University of Nebraska again came out. This time he opened the quarry on one hill, which he named University Hill. The other, which the Carnegie Institution explored, he named Carnegie Hill.

Professor O. C. Marsh of Yale University, one of the most learned paleontologists of his day, had, with his assistant, Mr. H. Clifford, a government scout and interpreter of the Sioux language, collected fossils on the Niobrara River east of this point some time before the fossils were taken from the hills of Agate. Mr. Clifford was an intelligent frontiersman who had married an Indian woman and knew the land of the Sioux very well. But he had never happened to observe fossil bones near the hills at my home. Having accompanied Professor Marsh on fossil-hunting expeditions, he had become greatly interested in such work.

The Agate Springs Fossil Beds

Since the days when the first fossil material was taken from the quarries at Agate, many of the most distinguished men of science have visited the place. Representatives of several of the largest educational institutions and museums of the United States have made collections there. Men who are today rated as being the highest authorities in the world on the subjects of paleontology and comparative anatomy, visit the ranch and study and discuss the material found at Agate and its vicinity.

And many who have no knowledge whatever of fossils visit the ranch to satisfy their curiosity as to what the noise is all about. Some come, loaded on the subjects of Darwinism and evolution, who have perhaps secured their knowledge on such subjects from sources of little value. Pounding on the rock of truth with hammers of preconceived notions and prejudices is a hard and fruitless task, even when attempted by men who have accomplished great things in other provinces of study. One gentleman who visited my home introduced himself as a Mormon elder. He accounted for the great mass of petrified bones found there by saying that "Noah might have heaved a lot of dead animals off the ark when floating over their burial place." Another visitor at Agate—a circuit rider, who was making the rounds of the small settlements in northwestern Nebraska, preaching to the early settlers—informed us that those petrified bones were toys of the devil, placed there in the rocks by the devil himself to deceive people and upset the Bible story of the creation.

Unquestionable evidence shows that, back in Oligocene and early Miocene times, the country about Agate somewhat resembled the country at the mouth of the Amazon River today —a great flood plain. The animal life which inhabited the country in that age was sometimes entrapped on the higher grounds by sudden floods which caused all mammalian life to rush to the elevations for safety. Often creatures which, under ordinary conditions, would not live harmoniously together were forced together by the flood waters. Occasionally a herd of animals so entrapped was caught and drowned by a still higher rise of water, and their bodies were carried off and deposited in drifts made by eddies. The deposit of petrified bones at Agate represents such a drift. Sioux County, Nebraska, is most interesting to those who seek for knowledge of the origin and evolution of the plant and animal life of the world. Exposures of several of the geologic periods in the earth's history can there be found, and the stories of the life of those periods unearthed.

Doubtless one little petrified tooth discovered in this county by my son, Harold J. Cook, and described by some of our greatest men of science during the past twelve months, has attracted more attention in all parts of the world than any other one find from hereabout. Should further evidence prove beyond all question that this tooth belonged to our immediate ancestor of the human race, it would take the life-story of mankind back many thousands of years, into the Lower Pliocene age. This first anthropoid primate found in America has been named *Hesperopithicus haroldcookii*, in honor of its discoverer, by Professor Henry Fairfield Osborn, who first described it. I wonder what luck that primate would have had, in his day, trying to pronounce the name given him at this late hour?

The following institutions have collected material from the fossil deposits at Agate during the past twenty years: the University of Nebraska; the Carnegie Institution of Pittsburgh; the American Museum of Natural History, New York; the Field Museum of Natural History, Chicago; the Colorado Museum of Natural History, Denver; Yale University; Princeton University; the University of Chicago; the University of Michigan; and the University of Kansas. Representatives from several other institutions have also done collecting.

Many people come each summer to visit our ranch home, to see things which could not be seen on any other cattle ranch in the world. Clergymen of many denominations come to study the records in the rocks, also professional men in many departments of study. Such men are deeply interested, as a rule, in searching for the truthful answer to the question, Did, or did not, mankind evolve from a lower form of animal life into its present state of mental and physical development? and Does the Bible story of the creation of the world and of mankind, as usually interpreted by Bible teachers, ring more true than do the stories told in the records which have been kept in the rocks of the world since the time when living beings of any sort must surely, to make a success of living, have been veritable fire and gas eaters? These questions at the present time are being discussed in the pulpits of our country more than ever before. Evolution seems still to be, to many people, "one grand fish story."

Association, at various times during my life, with those who dig and scrape out of the rocks the tangible evidences on this subject has caused me to draw some conclusions. Of course, I might have to abandon them at any time, for each hour in the life of today seems to add in many fields to the accumulated knowledge of mankind. But one statement of which I feel tolerably sure is this: That the highly trained men who follow the study of biology and paleontology do not do so for the revenue which it brings them. Professor Marsh, Professor Cope, and many others have freely given of the best they had, as well as from their purses, in pursuing research work which has added greatly to the fund of human knowledge of the sources of life. The early fossil hunters surely had to endure hardships in the days when West meant West. I can well remember how most of my western friends regarded the early fossil hunters and naturalists who came to do collecting. They were usually spoken of as bone- or bug-hunting idiots. For anyone to go chasing about over the West hunting for petrified bones, or even bugs, was conclusive evidence of his lack of good horse sense, especially in sections of the West where the Indians were still wild enough to want to stick their arrows into anything wearing a white skin. For my part I can get far more real thrills now hunting for evidence of what has gone before in the way

239

of animal life or the works of prehistoric man, than I ever got out of hunting either game of any sort or armed savages who seemed possessed by the idea that the white invaders of their country should be recognized only as targets.

Fossil hunting in the United States is now attended with little danger or discomfort. Great changes have taken place in that respect since the science of paleontology was born. One hundred years back, mankind had no knowledge whatever of many things which we accept today without giving much thought as to "how come." Having been a western man, I could not but take intense interest in the changes that have come into my little world. The wild life of the West has been wiped out to an extent so near total extermination that the remnants have to be protected by federal and state game wardens. The American Indians of today who ever lived as their fathers before them, wild and free, are few and fast tottering into the long shadows of their sunset. Most of them are gentle enough now. They will eat almost anything which the white man cares to give them. Some of them may still be called wild or hostile; but the most they ever do is to plead with the Great White Father at Washington for the little portion of their former land which is left to them—a residue which they see gradually being taken possession of, in some portions of the West, by every means that white men of big and little interests can devise.

The frontiersmen of the type who used the flintlock and percussion-cap rifles, carrying bullets that ran from 60 to 120 to the pound, and whose headgear and clothing were made almost entirely of the skins of animals, have practically all journeyed ahead with the innumerable caravan. The ox team and stage drivers, also the cowboys of yesterday, are following closely after them. Were not the early pioneers of scientific research in the West also worthy of suitable monuments erected in their honor somewhere in or about the center of their activities? If so, is not the erection of such monuments a thing worth our doing at this time? Have we no people of wealth and culture who would take pleasure in doing something of this sort—something which would not only be a credit to the donors, but which would also give pleasure and comfort to the generations to come as the centuries pass?

Index

Geronimo outbreak: 140–60
Gold hunters in the West: 84, 147, 151
Graham, E. B.: 233, 235
Graham, J.: 121, 227
Grizzly bears: 119–21, 126–27, 160, 215–21

Haguewood, Jim: 167–68
Hammond, A. G.: 152
Hardin, John Wesley: 51
Harris, Allen: 38
Harris, Jack: 45–48
Hatch, John P.: 167
Hayden, F. V.: 115
Head, Dick: 76–77
Helbert, Bert: 72
Herf (Hurf?), Dr.: 64
Herne, ———: 225
Herr, George: 157
Hesperopithicus haroldcookii: 238
Holmes, Charles E., letter by: 177
Hornaday, William T.: 131

Indian point of view: 209–11
Indians as horse thieves: 6, 27, 39–43, 45, 46, 161–62
Ives, Francis J.: 152

Jack Red Cloud: 174
Jackson, F. J. Foakes: 118
Jaguar, in Texas: 23
Javalina: *see* musk hog
Jones, "Colonel": 110–16, 121–22
Joy, Kit: 214

Kansas, University of: 238
Keller Valley: 139, 160, 229

Index

Wounded Knee Campaign: 168–69, 172, 199–207, 211–12
WS Ranch: 139, 141–45, 150–52, 156–59, 214

Yale University: 196, 234, 236, 238
Yale, Harry: 110–11
Yankton Charlie: 179, 201
Young-Man-Afraid-of-His-Horses: 85, 174, 195

Zoölogical Society of Philadelphia: 217, 220–21; letter from,
220–21

UNIVERSITY OF OKLAHOMA PRESS : NORMAN